*Clown Princes
and
Court Jesters*

Other Books By Kalton C. Lahue

Continued Next Week

World of Laughter

Kops and Custards (with Terry Brewer)

Bound and Gagged

Collecting Classic Films

Clown Princes and Court Jesters

by KALTON C. LAHUE
and
SAMUEL GILL

SOUTH BRUNSWICK AND NEW YORK:
A. S. BARNES AND COMPANY

LONDON: THOMAS YOSELOFF LTD

A. S. Barnes and Co., Inc.
Cranbury, New Jersey 08512

Thomas Yoseloff Ltd
108 New Bond Street
London W1Y OQX, England

SBN 498 06949 4

Printed in the United States of America

To Bert Roach, George Rowe,
"Tiny" Sanford and all of the other
Clown Princes and Court Jesters
whose merry antics still bring
laughter wherever a thin beam of
light pierces the darkness.

Contents

Foreword

BY KENT D. EASTIN

Clown Princes and Court Jesters briefly tells the story of fifty men and women whose court was the Hollywood of those fabulous years from just before World War I to the close of the silent era. Some scampered on a thin silver beam of light in the big-city movie palaces—but all could be found at any time in the thousands of neighborhood theaters in the metropolitan areas, in the less pretentious houses in the small cities and towns, and on Friday and Saturday nights at countless places of exhibition in rural communities across the land.

Comedy had been in evidence in the film almost from the day the motion picture was invented in 1889, but was seen in different forms at different times. During the 1890s, almost everything filmed was produced for viewing on the coin-operated machines in the penny arcades—films that ran for a bit less than a minute and were seen on Edison's Kinetoscope or Biograph's Mutoscope. In the penny arcades, comedy subjects were overwhelmed by such factual titles as *Black Diamond Express, Governor Roosevelt and Staff* or *Sleigh Riding, Central Park*. And the comedy films that were included were usually single scenes with such titles as *Alfonse and Gaston Helping an Irishman, Boys Help Themselves to Foxy Grandpa's Cigars* or *Levi and Cohen, the Irish Comedians*. Movies at that time were not much more than a novelty and the performers in these little episodes of comedy were nameless to patrons of the arcades.

While famous personalities were pictured in the films for the penny arcades, they were either world leaders—mostly in the area of politics or the military—or names from the music halls, vaudeville or the midway; and these personalities from the entertainment world were invariably pictured in the specialty for which

9

they had gained fame; Annabelle in *Flag Dance*, Ella Lola in *Turkish Dance*, or *Miss Lillian Shaffer and Her Dancing Horse*.

With the coming of the new century and the appearance in 1903 of Edison's *The Great Train Robbery*, the movies began to tell stories, and store shows, where films were projected on a screen, started cropping up by the hundreds and thousands. Increased in length to a split-reel (running about eight minutes) or full reels (running about fifteen minutes), films began appearing in quantity from new companies such as Vitagraph, Lubin, Kalem, Essanay and Thanhouser, as well as the older Edison and Biograph. The trend during this period was away from the strictly factual film and into the area of short sketches, dramatic, and comedy subjects. Here too, the actors and actresses were not identified by names until approximately 1910. But as nickelodeons replaced store shows and production zoomed, many players became sufficiently well known as "Goldilocks" (Mary Pickford) or "The Biograph Girl" (Florence Lawrence) to develop importance in attracting patrons to the box-office, even though the public did not yet know their real names. The comedy of that era appeared under such titles as *Nervy Nat Kisses the Bride, A Leap-Year Proposal to an Old Maid* and *Reuben in the Subway*. Comedy output as such relied heavily on a picturization of vaudeville sketches.

But in 1910, a young man named Mack Sennett succeeded in pushing himself forward at Biograph and screen comedy began to break from its bondage to vaudeville and the stage. Sennett departed from these old restrictions with a new form of comedy and the screen was never again the same. Production companies finally began to identify their players by name, capitalizing upon the popularity of these personalities in attracting patrons to the theaters. It was here, in 1914, that the golden years of the silents began to dawn with the coming of the feature picture and continued for a decade and a half until the deluge of the talkies in the late twenties. This was the period of the movie palace and the mighty Wurlitzer. The "Clown Princes and Court Jesters" whose careers make up the text of this volume were almost totally the products of this period.

Sennett had left Biograph in 1912 to become Director-General of Keystone and the impact of his work was felt by every producing company in the field. Following Sennett's lead, comedy series started to appear with regularity from almost every one of the early studios. The great and near-greats of comedy began to emerge.

In the years from 1914 to 1929, tremendous numbers of feature pictures issued from American studios. Nearly a thousand a year played across the screen in the peak years of the period, and a comedy would be found on the bill with the feature presentations in almost every theater. No really satisfactory program could be presented without one. The demand for comedies during this period was almost limitless. While production each year totalled in the hundreds, probably in none of these years did comedy output run beyond half the number of features that were made. This meant that many comedies and many comedians had a far greater exposure than the features for which they were the "Added Attractions." In the largest cities, where a feature might ultimately play fifty or more different theaters, a single comedy might play twice that number. In the small cities, where a feature would have but a single booking, one comedy title might show up for a second and even a third engagement.

At varying times during these fifteen years, silent comedies were produced and distributed by almost all of the leading companies in the business. While feature exhibition was somewhat stratified, and became even more so with the coming of the theater chains, this tendency was less in evidence in the exhibition of comedies and other short subjects. One factor in this was a withdrawal from short subject distribution by such companies as Paramount, First National, Metro and Goldwyn in the early years of the twenties. Warner Brothers, who had produced comedies and a serial or two in the years following World War I, were exclusively feature producers until the coming of Vitaphone. United Artists hardly ever distributed anything shorter than an eight-reel feature. Fox, Universal and FBO all had modest short subject programs. But Educational Film Exchanges, Pathé and dozens of independent producers were releasing scores of different titles every year. Thus, the theater chains owned by Paramount, First National and Loew's all had to draw on short subjects produced outside their own studio organizations, which gave Educational and Pathé, particularly, a market of considerable size.

For the producers who had the right star and access to the right distribution, a real opportunity existed; movie audiences of the period expected comedies and they would have been disappointed had the program omitted one. But who were these comedians whose short films outbooked the features with which they appeared? As authors Kalton C. Lahue and Samuel Gill point out, the fifty comedians and comediennes covered by this work are only a sampling of the many and varied practitioners of the art of laughter.

In telling their stories, the authors have sketched a history of the silent comedy in a manner unlike anything previously attempted. In the capsule careers provided for each of these fifty funmakers, the public has available today more information about these comics than was generally available at the time they were at peak popularity. Depending upon your age, you will, at best, remember a number of the names and faces. And if you're one of those youngsters who really doesn't remember the silents, this coterie of funny people will be coming through to you for the first time.

How did it happen that only three Kings of Comedy topped the field? Could more members of this group also have become a King if at one or more spots along the road he had taken the other turn: if he had signed with a major company instead of an independent; if he had not been under contract to a producer for which "so-and-so" also starred; if he had been a better businessman himself; or if he led a more ordered life? All of this is pure speculation but from this group more than one might have also made it to the very top had the chain of circumstances been right.

Today, an interested individual has an increasing opportunity to view the work of many of the players from the silent era. This is particularly true in the field of short comedy, where literally hundreds of different films in which these fifty funsters played are available for purchase in 8mm. format at very economical prices—or on free loan from several hundred public libraries. Depending upon your enthusiasm and curiosity, the way is clear for you to make a personal assessment of the work of the "Clown Princes and Court Jesters."

Acknowledgments

The history of silent screen comedy, as of any subject, should be more than the compilation of facts accumulated
from the printed material of contemporary sources. While attempting to be historically accurate and factually precise, we have refused to ignore the incredible repository of information resting in
the minds of those persons living during the period of our research
and who were an integral part of the very era under investigation.
Through the patience and gracious cooperation of these people, a
fascinating period has gradually unfolded to two writers born well
after the era had already ended.

To these individuals who were the comics and comediennes,
directors, cameramen and writers of the silent screen comedies,
the authors wish to acknowledge their great appreciation: Babe
London, Eddie Baker, Billie (Rhodes) Collins. Neal Burns, Dorothy
Devore, Hazel (Chene) Asher, Dixie (Chene) Maire, Fred and
Berna Newmeyer, Andy Clyde, George Gray, Florence (Moore)
St. John, Rollie Totheroh, Grace (Haskins) Conklin, Minta Dur-
fee, Chester Conklin, John Francis and Faye Bunny, Daphne
(Pollard) Bunch, Norman Taurog, Billy West, Harold Lloyd, Anne
Cornwall, Dorothy (Davenport) Reid, Arthur Miller, Lucille B.
Smith, Dorothy Vernon, James Gruen, George "Spanky" McFarland,
Lillian Hamilton, Victor Heerman, George W. Stout.

The many critical appraisals in this book have been possible
only by the invaluable opportunity to view literally hundreds of
silent comedies from the private collections of many film enthusiasts,
and John and Dorothy Hampton's remarkable Silent Movie Theater
in Hollywood.

And for the loan of priceless photographs, the authors gratefully
acknowledge the kindness of the following individuals and institu-
tions: Mrs. Max Asher, Eddie Baker, Fred Newmeyer, Neal Burns,

Mrs. Frank Roland Conklin, Babe London, Mrs. G. Pat Collins, John F. Bunny, Dorothy Vernon, John Hampton of the Silent Movie Theater, Kent D. Eastin of Blackhawk Films and the Academy of Motion Picture Arts and Sciences.

Introduction

Although the story of silent screen comedy has been told before, invariably the viewpoint has been that of Chaplin, Keaton or Lloyd. Public acclaim and consensus has placed this trio at the very top of their profession, and by virtue of this ranking they have received the majority of attention over the years. But these were only three of the hundreds of celluloid shadows whose antics amused and delighted audiences in the first three decades of this century and even though these comics enjoyed a much longer span of popularity, the real story of the golden age of comedy is that of "The Clown Princes and Court Jesters."

The evolution of motion pictures after 1903 was extremely rapid and a great strain was placed on producers to satisfy the huge public demand for canned entertainment. This demand increased at a startling rate and created tremendous potential for instant fame and fortune. While stage personalities shunned the screen during its first decade of development, the second found them more than willing to exhibit their talents before the camera. The art of comedy became a firm fixture in the motion picture world almost from the beginning and its appeal to audiences was strong. The opportunities for comic performers were many, and accordingly a great variety of comedians and comediennes found their way to the screen—some had universal appeal, others met with only limited interest, but all had a contribution to make.

We have arbitrarily chosen fifty of these funmakers in hopes of representing all levels of the world of screen comedy, from the near-great to the obscure. In telling their stories, we have tried to present a more complete story of screen comedy than has been told before. Interest in the silent film has grown by leaps and bounds in the past decade, resulting in the location of many films which, only a few years ago, were though to be lost forever. It is now possible to evaluate the work of many screen personalities more fully than was done even during the height of their popularity, and although we have had access to many films not generally available to the public, wherever possible we have made reference to those comedies that can be viewed by interested readers.

While the reader may not be in complete agreement with our choice of fifty representative screen comics, we ask his forbearance. We are agreed that not every comedian or comedienne deserving of inclusion is represented within the following pages and will even concede that some we have chosen may not be so important as those omitted, but this is completely a value judgment and one only the authors could make.

With this in mind, let's turn back the pages of time and see how many of "The Clown Princes and Court Jesters" you remember.
Hollywood, California   K.C.L.
Sterling, Kansas   S.G.

Clown Princes
and
Court Jesters

"Fatty" Arbuckle

The stories in this book are filled with both happy times and a few sad moments, and the following pages deal with careers that read straight from Horatio Alger, and others that ended in dismal failure. But none was so tragic as that of Roscoe Arbuckle. From a position almost equal with Charlie Chaplin in 1921, "Fatty" Arbuckle fell overnight into an abyss so deep that he was never able to restore himself fully. His story was one of the first major scandals of the youthful movie world and although never convicted (in fact, the third jury to try the case exonerated him completely), Arbuckle was never allowed to forget. Today, his name is still associated with the sensational murder trial, overshadowing his contributions to screen comedy. Because the three Arbuckle trials were major copy for many months, his career contains a great deal of fiction beyond the usual publicity releases, injected by writers wishing to satisfy a sensation-hungry public. As a result, fact and fiction have become so intertwined that it is difficult to separate the two.

In 1895, the Arbuckle family moved to Long Beach, California, from Smith Center, Kansas. Growing up in Long Beach, Roscoe somehow found his way into show business after the turn of the century and toured the West Coast with Frank Bacon's stock company. In 1908, he married Araminta Durfee while both were members of the Elwood Musical Company. Legend has it that Fatty's first screen appearance was made during a brief stay with Selig during 1909, a fact seemingly borne out by the existence of a production still from a Selig film of that year.

But for all practical purposes, Arbuckle's screen career began in 1913 when he walked onto the Keystone lot asking for a job. Fred Mace had departed in April to start his own company and Sennett had need of a fat comic; it seemed axiomatic in those days that every comedy producer have a fat comedian on his payroll. Although Sennet conceded that Arbuckle was agile for his size, he was not too

19

Roscoe Arbuckle, whose stardom was destroyed almost overnight by the scandal revolving around the unfortunate death of Virginia Rappe.

impressed with Fatty, but under the constant prodding of Mabel Normand, Sennett agreed to hire the fat man on a day-to-day basis. Fatty's first Keystone role was a small part in *The Gangsters* and very shortly, he was co-featured with Ford Sterling in the rough-and-tumble comedies. Mabel Normand's keen eye for comedy had been vindicated. Within a few months, "The Fat Boy" and "Keystone Mabel" had become the most popular and profitable team ever to appear in the Keystones.

These early films served to produce a style that Arbuckle was to develop, perfect and use to good advantage during the rest of his short but prolific career. Although not physically attractive, Roscoe's bubbling personality and boyish appearance offset his sheer bulk and he put these assets to work in front of the camera. Knowingly directed at the audience, his broad, friendly grin seemed to say "It's all in fun," and succeeded in winning over the fans, who accepted Fatty as a nice young man in spite of his size and appearance.

Arbuckle worked long and hard at Keystone, making film after film at a rapid pace and playing as hard as he worked. But until he took a crew to New York City in 1916, Roscoe seemed unaware of the true dimensions of his popularity. Only then did he recognize that Keystone was not an end in itself, but just a step along the road. Writing, acting and directing his own pictures at Keystone, Arbuckle had learned all aspects of comedy and late 1916 brought his golden opportunity.

Paramount was gearing up to add comedies to its release schedule, and signing Arbuckle to a contract, Joseph Schenck established the Comique Film Company to produce two-reelers for the Paramount program. Scheduled to begin production in March 1917, Roscoe took leave of Keystone in January and began to gather the unit that would boost him to stardom. Al St. John and Alice Lake left Keystone to join Comique and a young vaudeville comic dropped by the studio one day and stayed to support the rotund comedian. In four short years, Buster Keaton would be acknowledged as one of the Kings of Comedy, while Arbuckle's career lay in ruins.

Fatty's Comique films continued the basic character he had evolved at Keystone, but were much slower in action and pacing. Characterization was more extensive, the plots were better defined, and Arbuckle showed much promise as an actor as well as a comic. His comedies were tremendously popular, as Paramount gleefully discovered. Accustomed to covering all its exchanges with seventy-five prints of a film, Paramount was now forced to issue two hundred or more of each Arbuckle comedy, just to keep pace with the exhibitors' demands.

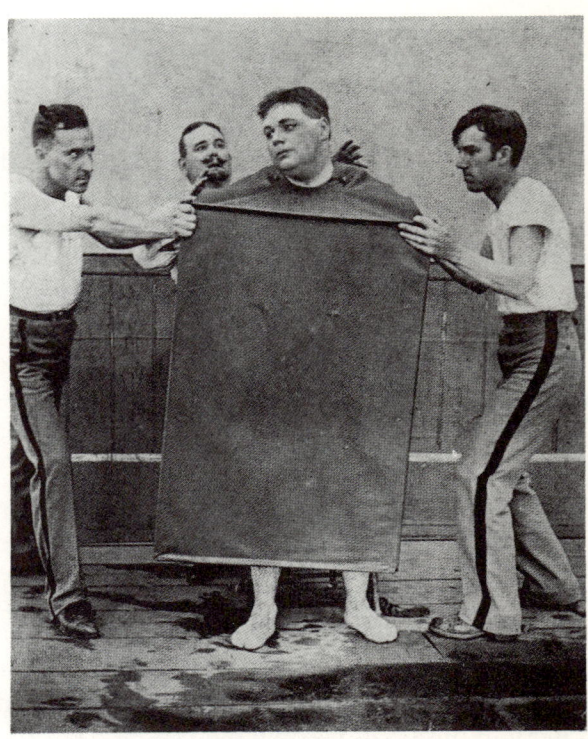

Roscoe made his first screen appearance in *The Sanitarium,* a Selig picture of 1909.

The two-reel shorts led Arbuckle into feature comedies, where his popularity continued to increase with each new film released. Basically adaptations of famous novels and plays, his stories were no longer written off-the-cuff. Fatty played the lead roles straight, with comedy added as a side effect to soften the edge of his portrayals. His acting ability came as a surprise to those who had thought of him as only an oversized comic. In less than a decade, Roscoe Arbuckle had risen from just another fat man to become one of the world's most beloved screen comedians. But trouble was just around the corner.

Toward the end of August 1921, the Arbuckle unit was putting the finishing touches on the last of three major features and Fatty was looking forward to his first vacation in months. Favoring San Francisco as the party town, Arbuckle left Los Angeles for the Labor Day weekend and a vacation which ended in disaster. There's no point in repeating the details which led to Arbuckle's trial; too many versions have already been printed and we can shed nothing new on

One of the most versatile of the Keystone comics, Fatty Arbuckle wrote, directed and starred in innumerable short comedies, such as *Fatty's Jonah Day* (1915).

Mabel Normand gives the competition (Minta Durfee) the cold shoulder as Fatty Arbuckle, Frank Hayes and Harry Gribbon look on in *Mabel, Fatty and the Law*.

Caught! By Edgar Kennedy, as Louise Fazenda looks on in *Fatty's Tin-type Tangle*.

Containing one of his best female impersonations, *The Butcher Boy* was one of Roscoe's Comique films which gave his career a boost far beyond his fame at Keystone. (Courtesy Jerome M. Kraemer)

Roscoe Arbuckle in 1918 with his co-star Alice Lake, and Buster Keaton.

Arbuckle's Paramount films elevated the round comic to a position closely behind the Kings of Comedy in 1919–20. Lila Lee's fast-rising career was boosted by her work with Roscoe.

the case. It's sufficient to note that the allegations of an orgy and the resulting death of Virginia Rappe, a starlet, destroyed his career, even though he was never convicted of the crimes he was supposed to have committed.

To be sure, Arbuckle's situation was of his own making. Not one who matured early and took life in its stride, Fatty's success had clashed with his immaturity. His was a life of excesses—too much food, too much drink and too many women. Four years before, one of his parties in Boston had cost the studio well over $100,000 to hush up. It was almost a dress rehearsal for the San Francisco event in 1921.

While Fatty's friends privately agreed he had nothing to worry about, noticeably few came forth to support him publicly. Militant womens' clubs across the nation took up the cudgel against this "monstrous criminal" and as a result, Paramount was forced to write off an anticipated million dollars on the completed but unreleased features. Roscoe made several attempts at a comeback, but each time he was driven from the screen by irate citizens (mostly women) who seemed to make it their business to remember Roscoe Arbuckle.

Under the pseudonym of William B. Goodrich, he directed *The Red Mill* with Marion Davies in 1927, but it was not until the early thirties that Roscoe was given an even break in the industry. From a low point of drunken despair in the mid-twenties, Arbuckle was now sober and the model of propriety. His fortune and two marriages gone, he had opened the Plantation Club in Culver City and married Addie McPhail. The night club went with the Depression, but Arbuckle was solvent again and Jack Warner signed him to make a series of comedy shorts for Warner Brothers.

Although Arbuckle did not live to enjoy the revival of his career, he died a happy man. Personal appearances, talk of a feature role for him and the adulation of children wherever he went in 1933 had restored Fatty's faith in himself and he looked forward to the future. Ironically, now that he had so much to live for, death came to the sad clown in his sleep, on June 29, 1933.

Destroyed before reaching the peak of his fame, it's impossible to say whether Arbuckle would have reached the exalted position held by Chaplin, Keaton and Lloyd, but he brought laughter into the lives of millions and asked only for their applause—a small price for his talent.

Max Asher

Max Asher's career began in the theater, but not on the stage. Like so many others who sought success in the entertainment world, Max had the desire long before an opportunity presented itself. The job of sweeping out a theater in his home town of Oakland, California, fanned the flame of his longing and gradually evolved into a chance to play bit roles and small parts. Concentrating on his comic abilities, young Asher soon created a vaudeville act, which transformed his talent in the art of magic from a parlor avocation to a paying proposition on the stages of various California vaudeville houses.

By 1912, the up-and-coming stage comedian had enough experience in show business to be a prime candidate for the newly emerging world of motion pictures. While Max's first taste of screen comedy came with a few months' work for Mack Sennett at the old Edendale studio on Allerandro Street, the home of the fabled Keystone Comedies, it was not long before his work came to the attention of Carl Laemmle, president of Universal and skilled talent raider of surrounding studios. Laemmle hired Asher away from Keystone and put him into the comedies of a growing Universal.

When Laemmle decided to begin the Joker Comedies in 1913, he released Max from the Powers Company (a member of the Universal family) and promoted him to head comic of the new series under the direction of Allen Curtis. Although rather crude in their conception and execution of screen comedy, the Jokers became one of the most popular of the early comedy series and Max enjoyed the returns of a success far greater than the stage could ever have afforded him.

As the settings for the Joker Comedies were of every conceivable type, Max Asher's makeup, costume and character had to be easily altered to fit any possible comedy situation, although the Dutch comedy character was his forte. The most popular of the Jokers were

Max Asher, as he appeared toward the close of a lengthy and successful career as a screen comedian in the late twenties.

those in which Max appeared in full Dutch comic regalia—polka dot shirts, striped vests, checkered coat and pants, a small tuft of hair pasted on his chin, high and broad painted eyebrows, abbreviated bowler hat, and the inevitable staple of Dutch comedy—the padded roll around his waist.

Although Max received fine support from the other Joker comics, his most devilish crony was Harry McCoy, whose funny little rectangular patches of hair stuck to either side of his wrinkled-up nose made him appear to be forever on the brink of a stupendous sneeze. McCoy and Asher made innumerable Joker Comedies in the roles of Mike (Max) and Jake (Harry). But when McCoy left in 1914 to join Keystone, the role of Jake was assumed by little Sylvion de Jardin (Bobby Vernon). His failure to catch on with the audiences brought about the end of two profitable screen characters—Mike and Jake disappeared from the screen.

The Joker Comedies gained additional momentum as Max worked with the increasing efficiency and mastery of a seasoned film comedian. Although there was little depth to the scripts, Asher never had to rehearse and it was not at all unusual in those days for the Joker troupe to turn out two completed comedies weekly. But his professional life was not without its share of troubles. As the Joker series had gradually acquired five lead comics (instead of the usual one, who would be supported by an assortment of young male and female leads and a few character players), it was not surprising that internal rivalries developed on set.[1] When Allen Curtis brushed off a complaint by Max, the dismayed comedian proceeded to walk off the lot and out of the Joker Comedies. The series continued but Max Asher never returned.

In October 1914, Max began work in Fred Balshofer's Sterling Comedies, but he was dissatisfied with the results and breathed a sigh of relief when Sterling was disbanded. He then returned to Powers to do a hilarious parody of the cliff-hanging serials entitled *Lady Baffles and Detective Duck,* which spoofed the melodramatic chapter plays that had already become clichés by 1915.

After his disagreement with Curtis and during the short stay with Sterling, Max began to feel that his formerly firm foothold on screen comedy was giving way. But the box-office success that met *Lady Baffles and Detective Duck* brought to the worried comedian a reaffirmation of his status and talents. Further proof came when Universal established the Max Asher Comedy series; but good times could not last forever, and when this group of comedies was completed Max briefly returned to the stage.

---

1 Billy Franey, Gale Henry, Louise Fazenda, Bobby Vernon and Max.

Although Max appeared at his best in Dutch comic makeup, the Joker Comedies required a versatility in costume and makeup that laid the foundation of an entirely new career for the comedian in the thirties.

Max has the drop on Lee Morris in *The Pearl of the Golden West*, a Powers Comedy released a month before he appeared in the first Joker Comedy, the long-running series that won him popular acclaim during 1913–14.

Max Asher and Harry McCoy plead for their lives in *Mike and Jack Among the Cannibals.*

Max was near the end of his career as a starring comic when he appeared in *Tit For Tat* with Harry Depp (noted for his female impersonations on screen) and Ruth Langston.

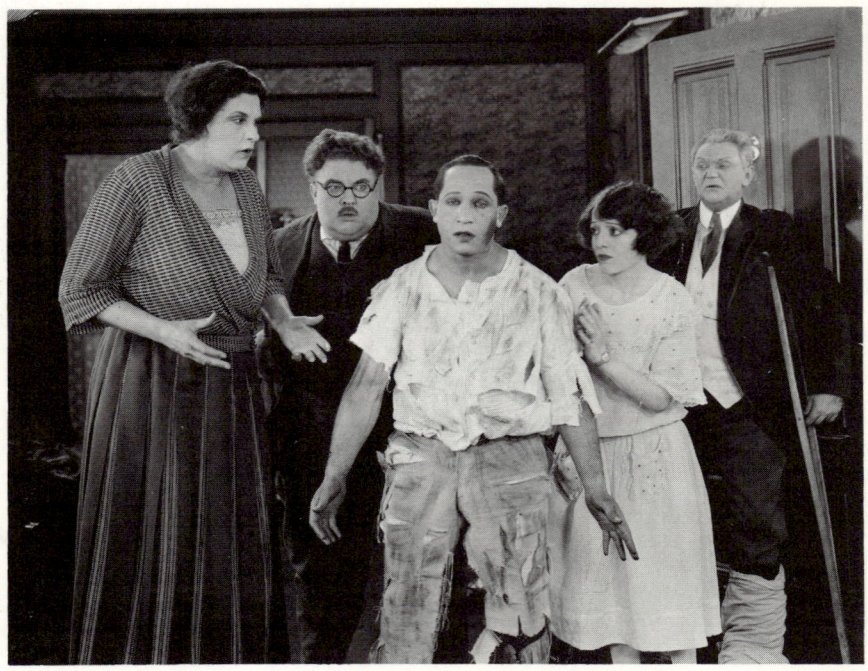

Max put his talent for makeup to good use in numerous comedies Joe Rock made for the independent market in the early twenties. Here he looks on as a battered Rock tells all to Blanche Payson, Frank "Fatty" Alexander and Billie Rhodes.

A great promoter of himself, Max Asher returned to movies as a character comic in the series of shorts made by the Vitagraph team of Earl Montgomery and Joe Rock. Recognizing Asher's versatility, Rock invited Max to join his independent production company formed when Montgomery and Rock broke up. The new venture was a success and Asher worked steadily in numerous comedies for the new company.

Throughout the twenties, Max appeared in the releases of an endless list of production companies but no longer as a lead comic. Long recognized for his value in character roles, portrayals such as Colonel Puckerlip in the Wallace Beery-Raymond Hatton feature comedy, *We're in the Navy Now* (1926), continued to reaffirm this distinction. But as the twenties passed into the thirties, the talkies replaced the silents and the art of the silent screen died. While the stage-trained Max Asher could have easily conquered the new medium, he chose not even to try.

After more than thirty years in show business, Max Asher had become a master of make-up and decided to accept the challenge now posed by the extreme need of the studios for qualified make-up artists. In one picture made in the twenties, Max had proven his versatility in this field by playing seven different roles, applying his own make-up for each character, a talent matched only by Jack Duffy and Andy Clyde. Among his more celebrated make-up efforts were those Max did on the inimitable W. C. Fields and many of the top stars who appeared in Cecil B. deMille's pictures.

To occupy the slack periods and for additional income—but above all else to fulfill a long-held desire—Max returned to his first love. He opened a magic store in Ocean Park with the well-known magician Hoffmann. Many pleasant hours away from work were spent in benefits, informal magic performances and charity work for a great variety of fraternal and professional organizations.

Shortly before his death in April 1957, Max Asher recalled his varied career with these words, "This world of moving pictures was really a silly and delightful scatterbrained world to live and work in. All that hard work seems now to be as funny as the comedies we made." This was not the tired voice of a disillusioned man but the ironic attitude of an individual who had realized early that the greatest and loudest laughs were the result only of the most serious and diligent effort a comedian could put forth. Max Asher had reached the enviable status of laughmaker.

Monte Banks

If you're old enough to have sat in the darkened confines of any movie theater on a Saturday afternoon in the early twenties, the chances are excellent that you will remember suave and dapper little Monte Banks, one of the most underrated laughmakers of the silent screen.

Coming to the screen from his native Italy, Monte played supporting comic roles at Triangle and Universal under his own name, Mario Bianchi. In 1918, he was cast in *The Geezer of Berlin,* Universal's two-reel parody of that year's popular anti-German propaganda epic, *The Beast of Berlin.* This short subject came off so well that Universal decided it should be a "Jewel" release, the company's brand name for its more exclusive product.

Although not the star, Mario stole almost every scene in which he appeared and proved his ability to carry a complete picture. But even with this example before them, Universal executives held out no promise of stardom for young Bianchi. Changing his name to Monte Banks, the little comedian sought further success in a series of Bulls Eye Comedies with Charlie Dorety.

But the real opportunity arrived in the person of the Warner brothers, who had struggled for years to establish themselves in motion pictures. Their toehold in the industry was the financial success of *My Four Years in Germany,* another anti-German film in 1918. Independently produced and marketed, this film was supposedly based on the memoirs of American ambassador James Gerard.

Casting about for some way to pyramid their profits into a permanent success, the Warners decided to reinvest their profits. Jack Warner felt that comedies could be most easily produced and sold. All they needed was a comedian whose financial wants were compatible with their desire to keep the budget as low as possible. Monte Banks leaped at the opportunity.

Caught in the act! By none other than Harry Depp in a female impersonation for *His Widow's Might*.

Now how did that happen? Only Monte Banks would complain about being handcuffed to Marianne de la Torre in *A Warm Reception*.

The Geezer of Berlin gave Monte his first taste of fame. Raymond Hanford made an imposing Kaiser in this burlesque of the popular 1918 war film, *The Beast of Berlin*. (Courtesy Don Overton)

Comedians went to fantastic lengths for publicity—here Monte wishes a Merry Christmas, 1926 to Pathé exhibitors of *Atta Boy*.

Banks had not wasted his time at Universal. In addition to developing a wistful comic character, Monte studied the techniques of direction. But he profited more from the early Welcome Comedies by working with Clyde Bruckman, one of comedy's best gag men, and Herman Raymaker, a former Keystone director. Together, the three men developed a brasher comic style that Monte would soon perfect and exploit successfully for years. In these comedies produced by the Warners, Monte projected to audiences as the eager young man whose human failings combined with the perversities of life to keep him in near-constant trouble.

A Bedroom Scandal was a typical example. The newlymarried Monte learned that he would meet his wife's parents for the first time that night. After a tremendous struggle with his collar button, Monte set out for work and gave every impression of a rising young executive as he strolled into the department store. Actually, he was merely a sales clerk with a sharp eye for his customers in the ladies department.

Try as he might, our hero was unable to conceal his intentions from the husbands present. After nearly being caught in the act of taking daring (for that time) measurements, he was forced to flee for his life with an enraged husband close behind. The usual chase took place, ending as Monte momentarily evaded his pursuer and plunged through the bedroom window of his own home, only to find the object of his most recent attention (and the cause of his present predicament) standing there.

To extricate himself from this situation, Monte attempted a complicated explanation to his wife, who had suddenly arrived on the scene. But the story came to an abrupt and happy halt when the attentive lady and her irate spouse were identified as Monte's in-laws, leaving the audience wondering just how well he would get along with a flirting mother-in-law and a jealous father-in-law.

Distribution difficulties hampered the success of this interesting series of Welcome Comedies, with Monte eventually leaving the Warners for Fox and then Grand-Asher, another independent. He spent several years with Grand-Asher, writing and directing his own two-reel comedies. During this time, the real Monte Banks characterization that we remember bloomed. The enthusiastic and impetuous young man was tempered with a certain bashfulness, which proved oerwhelming to his various leading ladies. An end-of-reel triumph composed of many small failures became his trademark.

Monte spent most of the twenties running up street. . . .

and down street—any place to escape irate husbands. From *A Bedroom Scandal.*

By 1923 and Grand-Asher's *South Bound Limited*, Monte had been chased by so many husbands that he thought twice about taking on four lovely ladies. (Courtesy Don Overton)

This is what usually got Monte in hot water. He doesn't know it, but the object of his flirtation is his new mother-in-law. (Courtesy Blackhawk Films)

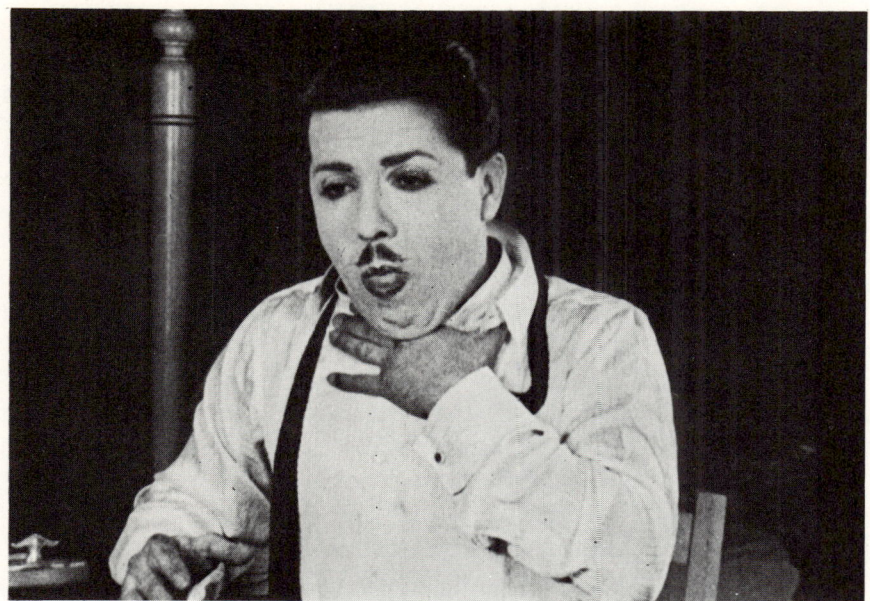

Wouldn't you know it? Our inept hero just swallowed his own collar button for breakfast!

Monte in a 1920 Reelcraft Comedy, *Don't Park Here*. By 1921, the rumpled costume will become the immaculate suit which characterized his comic character.

Like Harold Lloyd's, Monte's later comedies were strenuous exercises in knockabout comedy. However, his character was fundamentally different. Lloyd epitomized confidence, which saw him through to the end; Monte exhibited a large degree of uncertainty about his ability to conquer a situation but won out in spite of it.

Moving into production with his own company in 1924, Monte sought out his mentors from earlier years, Herman Raymaker and Clyde Bruckman, to make a number of thrill-packed, fun-filled features. One lengthy excerpt from his Pathé release of 1927, *Play Safe*, has become a classic example of his style. Reissued in recent years as *Chasing Choo Choos*, it still holds audiences on the edge of their seats with laughter.

Placed in a position where he had to rescue his sweetheart from a runaway train, Monte manfully made the attempt, but was himself saved several times by the girl. A combination of stunt comedy by Banks and tabletop photography of a miniature set was skillfully blended and paced into an unforgettable sequence, which was resurrected from the past by Robert Youngson in his *Days of Thrills and Laughter*, a feature compilation of silent comedy released a few years ago.

As the twenties drew to a close, Monte visited England. While there, he was asked to direct Gracie Fields in *Queen of Hearts*. As a result the two were married. His screen appearances became infrequent throughout the thirties but little Monte Banks had already carved his own niche in the annals of screen comedy.

Billy Bevan

The Mack Sennett comedians were always formidable competitors for top honors in their profession, and in the twenties few short-subject comics could claim the success of one Billy Bevan. Grim determination, a bushy twitching moustache, and the self-assurance of one who had succeeded in bamboozling the rest of the world characterized the little Australian. With his air of absolute confidence, Billy Bevan could impersonate a Wall Street banker and a hobo equally well.

Although Billy's screen career dated back to the early days of L-KO, where he had supported Neal Burns and Billie Ritchie, it failed to catch fire until he joined the Sennett organization in 1920. Billy's finest comedy was not one of action but reaction, and the rapid-fire slapstick of L-KO found no real use for his particular talents. But after coming under Sennett's guidance in 1920, Billy had his own series within two years, joining Ben Turpin and Harry Langdon as one of the top comedy attractions on the Sennett lot throughout the twenties. It was also Bevan's good fortune to have support from two of the most dependable comic foils available. Working with Andy Clyde (inevitably his cohort and crony) and Vernon Dent (usually his friendly enemy), Billy created some of the more interesting Sennett comedies of the period.

Billy's comedies were somewhat hampered by the slick and unfunny camera tricks that had become standard fare with Sennett: the extensive use of cartoon drawings, impossible gags like the camera that wilted amidst the odor of an unwanted skunk, and the floppy cap that came upright as a sign of fear. But in spite of these artificial gags, his reaction in most comic situations usually brought the house down with laughter.

Perhaps his most humorous comedies were also the most ribald. In one situation, Bevan was a photographer by the seashore, complete with view camera and black focusing cloth. Satisfied that he

45

had properly composed his scene exactly as desired, Billy bent down to pick up a film holder. At this very moment, an enormous lady, dressed in a voluminous blackskirted dress of the period, stopped by and bent down to peer into the camera. As smoothly as silk, Billy straightened up with holder in hand, and lifting her skirt, covered his head with the "focusing cloth." Unable to find the spring catch which held the film holder, Billy lifted the skirt, looked directly at the audience with a perplexed expression, shrugged his shoulders and returned under the skirt for another try.

Repeating this action a couple of times, Billy became more confused with each attempt. While he pondered another try, the fat lady, satisfied with what she had seen through his camera, left the scene as abruptly as she had appeared. When Bevan whirled around for a final try, he met with immediate success, a situation calling for a reaction of utter confusion. Although certainly a bit off-color, the entire scene was done so quickly and so well that few patrons were offended.

Bevan's impish roguery was a curious mixture of slapstick, burlesque and situation comedy, which seemed to fit into whatever situation he was thrown. And the Sennett writers created scripts especially for his happy-go-lucky character. In *Whispering Whiskers,* he made the transition to "man-about-town" and back to a hobo with ease, but more importantly, the audience believed in the transformation and accepted Billy. He was the bush league ball player pitching for the championship in *Butter Fingers,* and in *Giddap* he was the world's most inept polo player. But regardless of his role, the essence of Bevan was his ability to communicate to audiences that he was really just one of them, putting on a world which accepted him as the executive while remaining a man of the road. Accepting adversity as a matter-of-fact, Billy treated wealth or poverty with equal ease.

Later in the twenties, sophisticated drawing room comedy had pretty much become the order of the day. There were a few holdouts but the majority of screen laughs were artificially managed by situations and subtitles, a prelude to the stand-up verbal comedy that would overwhelm the art of pantomime once the screen learned to talk. Donning top hat and tails (as in the *Tired Businessman* series), Bevan had no difficulty fitting into the changing picture. Not dependent entirely on true pantomime, Billy's comedy style had been one of innocent response to the events around him, relying upon a quizzical look, wide rolling eyes and a jaunty side lift of his brush moustache to convey his feelings.

My Goodness, says Bert Roach, "I've caught Billy Bevan and Louise Fazenda in the act."

A genuine sportsman, Bill spared no expense with his car in *The Duck Hunter*.

It's *One Spooky Night* for Bevan and Billy Armstrong.

It's *Circus Today* for everyone except Billy and Andy Clyde, about to be unceremoniously dispatched by Kewpie Morgan.

Billy could never be certain where home would be found next. Sunshine Hart and Sid Smith aren't much consolation in *Galloping Bungalows*.

Billy's having a hard time choosing between the chief's daughters in *A Sea Dog's Tale*. He'd settle for Madeline Hurlock or Natalie Kingston if he could find either.

Billy was at home in the most unlikely circumstances. As *The Divorce Dodger*, he's about to get the good word from Barbara Tennant.

Billy Bevan's lopsided smile was accentuated by the oversized brush under his nose.

Bevan and Del Lord (his director) both agree on one thing—Sennett Bathing Beauties were the best kind.

Toward the end of his career in the silents, Bevan removed his inverted moustache for several comedies and the Billy Bevan loved by so many fans simply disappeared, to be replaced by a rather dumpy little fellow unknown to most of his audience. Even teaming up with new Sennett talent such as the youthful Eddie Quillan couldn't bring the rich comedy potential in films like *The Bull Fighter* into sharp focus. It just *wasn't* Billy Bevan without the luxuriant brush under his nose. The little comic was always at his best when equipped with moustache and garbed in a slightly shabby suit—the image of the dignified, businesslike hobo.

Billy's career survived the upheaval that sound created in the industry, and during the thirties he did both talking shorts and supporting roles in features such as *The Lost Patrol*. Billy Bevan's starring years had lasted well over a decade, a record not achieved by very many of the Clown Princes and Court Jesters, and he remained active in front of the camera for well over thirty-five years.

Billy Bletcher

The world of the silent screen was a most fascinating one for movie fans; while there were touches of fame, glory and instant glamor that swirled in and around the movie capital, the other side of the coin saw heartbreak, shattered careers and instant poverty. Both stories have been told countless times, but seldom has mention been made of the profitable obscurity with which many in the industry were greeted. Billy Bletcher was typical of the screen comedians who labored in a twilight of anonymity, virtually unknown to the public by name.

Billy entered movies via the stage in 1913 at the Vitagraph studio in Brooklyn. Working with and for a variety of Vitagraph stars (including John Bunny and Flora Finch), he acted, filled in as assistant director from time to time, and as he recently stated, "I did anything that anyone wanted done." In early 1916, Louis Burston brought Bletcher and his wife from New York to his Jacksonville, Florida, studio where the Vim Comedies were being filmed. Billy was put on salary and appeared in many of the Vim Comedies with Burston's two top comic teams, "Pokes and Jabbs" (Bobbie Burns and Walter Stull) and "Plump and Runt" (Oliver "Babe" Hardy and Billy Ruge). Billy's stay with Vim lasted almost a year and in that time, he "played heavies, but due to my size, smaller than the usual comedy heavy of that period, I usually played character parts of old men with big beards and moustaches—often a father or uncle comedy role."

Leaving Vim in late 1916, Bletcher headed back to New York City where he worked evenings as a cafe entertainer, singing to the accompaniment of a young pianist named Vincent Lopez, who was just starting the renowned musical career that would carry him to the top. Billy returned to the Vitagraph studio during the day as an assistant director and when Albert E. Smith sent a unit to the West Coast, Bletcher accompanied them. He left Vitagraph's employ soon after and journeyed over to the Sennett studio where Mack put him to work as a general all-around character comic from 1917 to 1919.

Billy's opportunity for his first starring series came in January 1920. A few months earlier, E. H. Emmick and J. L. Friedman had leased studio space at the old L-KO studio on Gower and Sunset Boulevard—the same lot on which Al Christie was filming his independent comedies. George Ovey had been hired as lead comic for the new Gayety brand, but business was so good that Billy Bletcher and Vera Reynolds were hired as Gayety expanded to include a second unit. The Gayety Comedies with Billy were several cuts above the average independent comedy of the period in conception, but uneven in execution, a fault which rested with his director (who was also Gayety's studio manager), James Clemens.

The second comedy in the series, *Dry and Thirsty*, began as a very clever Prohibition parody dealing with thirsty Billy's efforts to get his hands on a bottle, while law enforcement officers plagued his every step. The initial gags were very funny and well-executed, but before the reel was half over, it had bogged down in an aimless chase through a hotel, which gave the viewer the impression that the writers and director could think of nothing else to do. At any rate, Billy's Gayety Comedies were moderately well received— enough so that when they were completed, he signed in mid-1920 with Morris Schlank for a series of Spotlight Comedies, which Arrow released.

Billy was given the starring role in the Spotlights, with Violet Joy as his featured co-star. "The Spotlight Comedies starred myself and a girl by the name of Duane Thompson, whom I had brought over to work with me. I don't know why, but Schlank changed her name to Violet Joy. The Spotlights were somewhat like the Christie Comedies but we touched on slapstick just a little more—but still nothing like Sennett's!" Billy has admitted to borrowing (as many others had) a distinctly Sennett touch—The Bathing Beauties. "Like all of the comedies of that period, we had our own bathing beauties, but it was all a copy of Mack Sennett's original idea."

When the Spotlight Comedies were completed, Billy joined the troupe making the Bobby Vernon Comedies at Christie. "I looked a lot like Bobby," mused Billy in recalling his career, "and the scripts of our chief scenario writer, Scott Darling, often placed us in comedies of mistaken identity. Everyone loved working with Bobby. He was an 'actor's actor' and the days on the set were as much fun

Although he's *Dry and Thirsty*, Billy still has an eye for a cute figure. The Gayety Comedies brought Bletcher starring roles in 1919–20.

as the final comedies when they were shown on the screen." While much of Billy's previous work had been that of a utility man, filling in where and when needed, his stay with Christie gave him his first real opportunity for actual characterization in the much more closely delineated roles contained in the well-constructed Christie scenarios. "When most of the comedy studios of that period had a few gag men sitting around the sets who watched the progress of filming and stuck in gags and new situations during production, the situation was very different at Christie's. We had scripts and we followed them. At Sennett's, most of the comedies were made from scripts written on one page."

Throughout the twenties, Billy worked for so many different production companies that an accurate chronology of his screen appearances is a web far too tangled to straighten out here; the important thing is that he was caught up in a vortex of screen roles. At one point during the decade, he and his wife formed their own company in Long Beach to make a series of parlor (situation) comedies; at another, the two reappeared on the vaudeville stage as a break from the rigors of movie making; still a third found him in a starring series around 1925 at Universal, supported by Bert Roach. Sandwiched in between, over, under and all around were roles in comedies, feature dramas, feature comedies, scenics, travelogues and westerns. While he worked in about every type of film made, his feature roles were restricted generally to what Billy called, "All different character types—no one particular character—but really choice parts."

As the decade drew to a close with the introduction of sound, Billy Bletcher experienced much the same troubles with which the great majority of silent screen comics were forced to cope. Looking back today, he tends to shrug off his problems at the time in deference to the problems of those around him. "Really, the Christie brothers never paid me very much during the twenties—in fact, they didn't pay anyone much, except their top stars like Bobby Vernon and Neal Burns—but when sound came in, they really went broke. They lost everything they had, including all their property around Sunset and Gower and on north." But during the thirties, Billy continued to work steadily for a variety of studios, including

Billy Bletcher's long screen career found him working for almost every company in the business. This scene is from one of his Keystone appearances around 1917.

Paramount and Hal Roach. "I never knew exactly what Roach had on his mind, but he teamed me with Billy Gilbert, with some crazy idea in the back of his head to recreate another Laurel and Hardy. Of course, if he were really trying that seriously, then he was insane —no one could rival those two!"

During this same time, Billy began another career as a "voice man" for Walt Disney, numbering *The Big Bad Wolf* and *Peg Leg Pete* among the many vocal characterizations he dubbed in his twenty-five years behind the screen. He continued doing feature roles when available and is still active today; his latest screen appearance was in the 20th Century Fox's *Hello, Dolly.* Unknown to the public, Billy Bletcher has also been prominently featured in television commercials over the past few years. His particular favorite is the Keystone Kop routine which he did in behalf of Shasta Root Beer, but the competition is tough and growing tougher. "This commercial field is a very lucrative business, except for the fact that the big stars are beginning to realize this and have already started to invade the field."

And so life goes on for Billy Bletcher, still working as often and as hard as he did a hectic half-century ago. The anonymity associated with those days has continued to follow him closely across the pages of time. If you have seen more than a handful of films from the twenties, the chances are good that you've seen Billy Bletcher as the totally inept little butler, taxi driver, doorman or what have you. Only recently have his starring comedies started to appear on the collectors' market, making it possible for comedy fans to enjoy rediscovering one of the real "working" comics of the silent era.

John Bunny

In 1910, the man destined to become America's first
motion picture comedy star left a promising stage career to enter
the infant industry. While most of his generation viewed the "flickers" as a novelty that could not seriously threaten the legitimate
theater, John Bunny was perceptive enough to realize the potential
importance of movies and abandoned a twenty-five-year career,
which had carried him along from minstrel troupes to Shakespearian
roles. Almost alone among his contemporaries in feeling that moving
pictures had made serious inroads into the theatrical business,
Bunny foresaw the beginning of a great amusement enterprise and
the emergence of an aesthetically legitimate art form.

And so the summer of 1910 found the genial, rotund actor applying for work at the primitive studios in the New York area, but with
little success. None of the fledgling producers felt they could afford
this enthusiastic applicant. Exasperated, he finally offered to work
in one picture for no salary just to prove his point. Albert E. Smith
and J. Stuart Blackton of the Vitagraph Company agreed to use
Bunny in one film but insisted on paying him the regular wage of
$5.00 a day.

When Smith and Blackton saw the rushes of Bunny's trial film,
they were convinced that the portly stranger knew a great deal
about acting. Inquiring about his background, the producers were
amazed to discover that the man so eager to break into movies that
he would work for nothing was actually an experienced and successful stage comedian. While this first picture was being completed,
they offered John a part in another picture. Bunny agreed and
started production on the second film. As Bunny himself recounted
the incident years later, Smith and Blackton "plainly indicated that
they were pleased with my work, but when I broached a permanent
engagement, they advised me that it could not be considered." The

John Bunny at the height of his screen fame.

Vitagraph officials knew they could not come close to approaching Bunny's salary on the stage. "I insisted that they make me their best offer and after they apologized for doing so, they offered me $40.00, about one-fifth of what I had been receiving in the theater. To their great surprise, I readily accepted."

Bunny's films were an immediate hit with exhibitors, fans and critics alike. In fact, the *New York Dramatic Mirror* of January 18, 1911, pointed out the emergence of John Bunny as a new screen talent in their review of Bunny's comedy, *Doctor Cupid*, saying, "The character work of the cranky old father of the girl is a bit of acting worthy of the warmest praise. The old man could take no prize at a beauty show, but he has ability in picture expression of the highest order." Although it was not the accepted practice at this time to list players' names, the clever Bunny capitalized on his unusual name, managing to work it first into the subtitles and then the titles of his comedies, effectively creating a one-man star system long before Vitagraph and the industry generally accepted the idea.

While Vitagraph continued to raise his salary, Bunny knew he was worth far more than he was being paid, considering the huge financial success of his comedies, and unsatisfied with his progress, John took a shrewd step to correct this iniquity. Albert E. Smith recorded this incident in his memoirs shortly before his death in 1958, published here for the first time with the kind permission of his widow, Lucille B. Smith:

> One day, when I was at an important business conference in New York, Bunny called me on the telephone and said that he must see me for a few moments, on very important matters . . . I finally agreed to go down to the entrance of the building at three o'clock—he, faithfully, promising to be there.
> This building overlooked Longacre Square. Precisely, at three o'clock I excused myself and went down to the entrance of the building. There was no John Bunny there! I looked around and then saw him walking across the Square, toward me. When he arrived, he apologized for being a little late and commenced to talk about nothing at all. I was annoyed at his getting me to break away from the meeting and I finally said, "What is it you wanted to see me about, John?"
> Meanwhile, although I didn't notice it at the moment, he had manipulated me around, so that my back was to the street, and his back to the building. Then I commenced to hear a murmuring noise behind me, and looking around, there was the whole of the Square jammed with people who had gathered to see John Bunny! When I turned back to him, he said, "That was all I wanted you to see, Govenor." After which, he pushed his way through the crowd to a

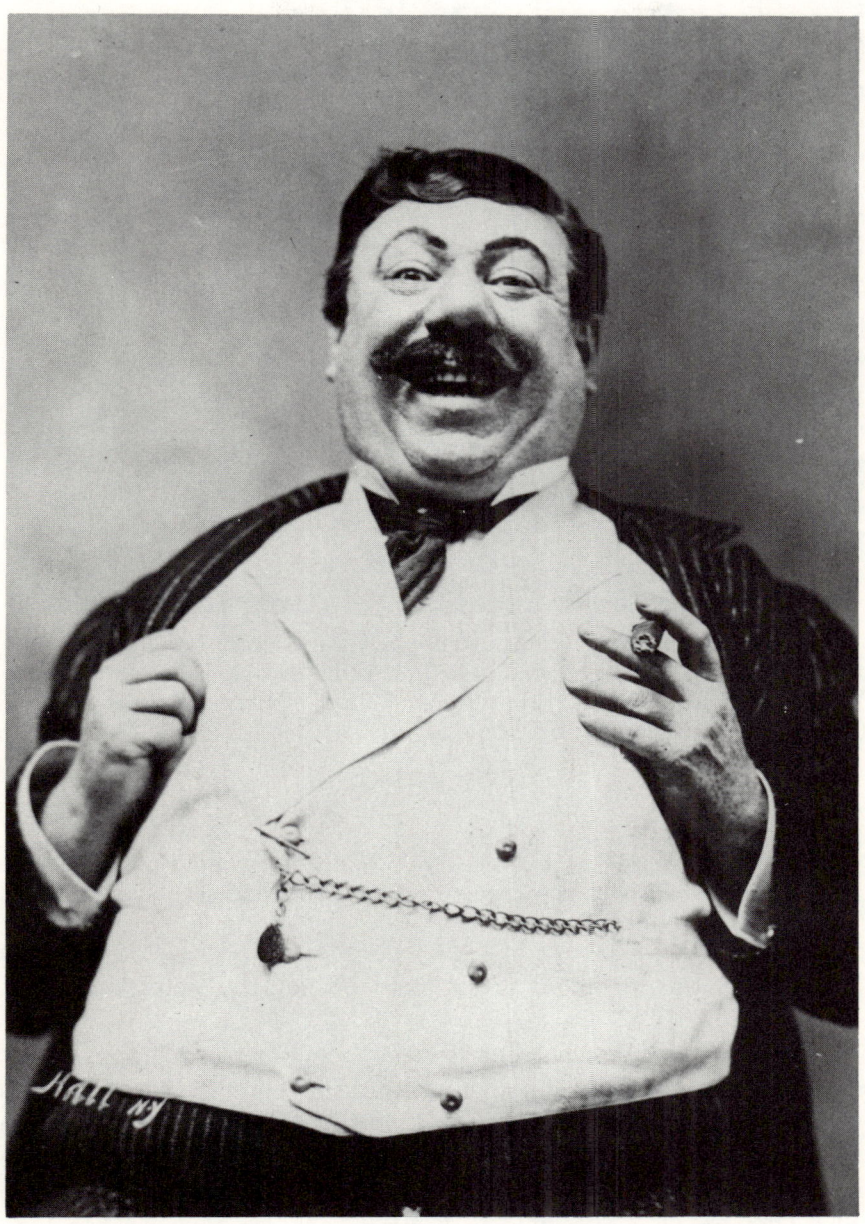

Bunny, as he appeared on the stage in *The City*.

In his early comedies, Bunny often played the gruff father and what a brood he ruled over here! Left to right—Edith Halleran, Norma Talmadge, Dorothy Kelly, Edith Storey, Lillian Walker and Julia Swayne Gordon in *The Troublesome Stepdaughters*.

car he had waiting and drove off. While I knew how popular some of the stars had become, it was the first time I had seen such a crowd gather to look at one.

Eventually, this strategic action paid off for the determined Mr. Bunny.

Engaging in what he regarded as a new art form, John Bunny believed the ultimate value of film would be centered in adaptation of the world's greatest dramas and stories, available to everyone in the simplified form of the moving picture. By May 1912, Vitagraph was apparently convinced enough to send Bunny to England to film Charles Dickens's *Pickwick Papers* on location. Mobbed by admirers wherever he went abroad, Bunny now realized the extent of enormous admiration and affection moviegoers held for his work in comedy. The most immediate benefit was a large salary increase—the result of English producers bidding for his services. Vitagraph did not want to lose their star comedian, so Bunny's $250 a week became $30,000 a year. A salary increase was not the only result of his extraordinary reception in England; along with Carl Laemmle's public advertising of his new star, Florence Lawrence, and Vitagraph's new attention to Maurice Costello, Florence Turner, Arthur Johnson and Jean ("The Vitagraph Dog"), John Bunny heralded the birth of the star system in motion pictures with a special position reserved for Bunny himself as the first comedy "star" in the American film.

John Bunny's mastery of screen comedy was the mastery of intricate facial expression and body movement. The Bunny comedies reflected John's concern for a natural acting performance and he attacked each one with a believable approach, exercising but a slight touch of exaggeration, and then only for comic effect. The memorable moments of *A Cure For Pokeritus* (1912) were not the clever quirks of plot or comic action but an almost indefinable overall impression—the smiles and handshakes among old cronies,

Vitagraph's company enroute to England in May 1912. The cameraman was George Bunny, son of the famous comic.

the unspoken request for enough money to get home from an old friend "spoken" only by glances out of the corners of his eyes and down to his empty pockets, the cautious and hesitant control of his bulk when mounting the squeaky steps at 2:00 A.M., and those infectious smiles of almost inexpressible self-pleasure as he tricked his wife in some childishly simple deception.

Instead of stagnating after two or three years of comedies ground out every few weeks, Bunny's films showed an increasing sophistication and subtlety in technique. The comic's concentration on more carefully delineated characters contributed to stories that became more polished, while improved technical knowledge and artistic attention to detail conquered the unreal, stage-like sets and harshness of direct lighting, characteristic of the early films. The extent of sophistication is well-illustrated by the technique of parallel editing used in *Polishing Up* (1914). This comedy was made contemporaneously with D. W. Griffith's *The Birth of A Nation,* supposedly the first film to employ parallel editing for dramatic purposes!

Bunny's comedies with Flora Finch were immensely popular with fans, who referred to the short comedies as "Bunnyfinches." In *Father's Flirtation,* John ends a carefree moment with Mary Anderson as Flora drags him back to the path of respectability.

An English caricature of Bunny as he appeared in *Pickwick Papers*.

Although she was hailed for her work as Bunny's co-star, Flora Finch's career faded almost overnight when Bunny passed away in 1915.

In many of his comedies, John Bunny was paired with Flora Finch, that marvelous character actress who looked and acted much like an emotional needle—the perfect opposite to Bunny in size and temperament: to his immensity, she was fragile and flighty; to his controlled emotion, she was one long emotional outburst; to his childlike playfulness, she was the school teacher disciplinarian. When attired in laces, ankle-length dresses and flowery hats, Flora looked much like those old spinster types so superbly described years later by W. C. Fields as "well-kept graveyards."

When Bunny arrived at Vitagraph, Flora Finch was already a recognized talent in eccentric comedy and character roles. Her teaming with Bunny was not a conscious decision, rather their work together seemed to make such a combination inevitable. The "Bunnyfinches," as their films were referred to by fans, were enormously popular, and by 1913 the team stood at the pinnacle of their profession.

Evidence of Bunny's popularity was no more apparent than on the studio lot itself. Apparently as well-liked off-screen as on, Bunny was father confessor to half the Vitagraph company and old and young alike greeted him as Uncle John. Bunny also performed all but the most dangerous stunts himself, despite his unusual size and weight. "He was also very patient and kind in instructing any-one unfamiliar with the making of movies," recalls Bunny's son, John Francis Bunny, "and when any new person had been hired by Vitagraph, my father's company was the training ground where they learned the movie business. He demanded only one thing—eagerness to learn."

John Bunny's screen career was brought to a close by his death in 1915. On leave of absence from Vitagraph to return to the stage in *Bunny in Funnyland*, the comedian found the overwhelming crowds, honorary banquets and formal welcoming celebrations physically exhausting. The result of this tour was a general break-down of Bunny's health, with the gradual development of heart and kidney complications, and finally Bright's Disease. Throughout April 1915, newspapers around the world carried reports of Bunny's progress in his struggle with death until the 26th, when the be-loved comic succumbed.

With Bunny's death, newspapers exploded into eulogies for the great comedian, but one of the finest was written for an English newspaper, *The Manchester Evening Chronicle*, on April 28, 1915:

> . . . . Bunny was lucky in having as a foil that acidulous female Flora Finch. Her sharp features and puritanical nose were an admirable contrast to the bulbous countenance of the inimitable John. When we saw him hen-pecked and dejected, seated at the breakfast table, withered by the bitter tongue of his formidable spouse, there was something more than laughter in our hearts. There was the least touch of pity, and this was a tribute to the truth and reality of his art.

With Bunny gone, Flora Finch was ruined. Vitagraph tried her in a series of her own, but the films were not profitable and she returned to character roles until 1917, when the Flora Finch Film Company opened business for a brief period. The resulting in-dependent comedies failed to meet with financial success and her career plummeted into the oblivion of minor and extra roles until her death in 1940.

John Bunny was a phenomenon of his times, and today his achievements are difficult to place into proper perspective. He prophesied the coming of color and talking pictures, recognizing the potential of an art form before it was an art and before it was given form. With an insatiable desire to raise the motion picture to the highest level of artistic integrity, he regarded moving pictures as more than a toy to amuse the ignorant masses. He brought to it a natural acting style in stories that did not rely on the low, physical humor of the burlesque stage but on the more sophisticated domestic comedy of the legitimate theatre, brought to a new intimacy by the motion picture camera. Moviegoers grasped Bunny as their first comedy "star," yet thousands of people in the world never even knew his name. It may not have been an exaggeration when a Dublin evening newspaper announced Bunny's death at the top of the front page with the words, in large black print, "John Bunny is dead, the best-known man in the world."

Neal Burns

The comedy that appeared under the Christie banner was essentially the comedy of situation with the everyday world as its real-life playground. The robust physical expression of burlesque and farce were severely frowned upon at the Christie lot. Unlike Mack Sennett, Al Christie permitted such comedy only when covered with a heavy veneer of order and general politeness. As pudgy Babe London once explained with succinct pride, "We looked down our noses at Sennett!" Christie comedians felt a mother's pride for their product and at Christie's, more than any other comedy studio, the relationship among players resembled that of a family clan. One of the oldest and most proficient members of this clan, Neal Burns, came to the studio in December 1914 and spent the majority of his career as a Christie comic.

For most comedians, the road to silent screen fame was paved with vaudeville houses and burlesque theaters, but Neal Burns came directly from the legitimate theater. Singing and dancing his way through innumerable performances in musical comedies, Neal had made his New York debut with *Just Out of College* in 1908, and by 1914 he was appearing at the Morosco Theater in Los Angeles. Invited to visit the Universal studios by Robert Leonard, a director, he met Al Christie and began a long and successful screen career in what Neal once called "those days of light diffusers when you went down with the sun and then off to the Alexandria bar."

In his first picture, a comedy starring Jack Dillon and personally directed by Christie, Neal found it necessary to unlearn everything he had acquired on the stage but achieved a satisfactory screen presence quickly and Christie immediately put the new comedian under Horace Davey's direction. A young but experienced director who had risen from property man for Nestor at the old Centaur studio in Bayonne, New Jersey, to full director for Christie at Uni-

69

versal, Davey—one of the original troupe to accompany Christie to California in 1911—was a highly gifted director of comedy. Neal joined an excellent stock company of comics and character players: the popular team of Lyons and Moran, beautiful Betty Compson and Billie Rhodes, hefty Harry Rattenbury, matronly Stella Adams, handsome Ray Gallagher and Neal's own brother, the versatile Eddie Barry.

During 1915, Neal Burns ground out comedies at the rate of one each week, playing a variety of eccentric comedy types that ranged from a Wall Street clerk to a destitute Negro. Although he had originally intended the stay with Christie to be but a short lark, all thoughts of returning to the theater were soon relegated to the back of Neal's mind. He began to write scenarios in response to Al Christie's need for more and better scripts, and in January 1916 Christie officially announced the formation of a new unit consisting of Neal, Billie Rhodes and Ray Gallagher, under the personal direction of Horace Davey. Gallagher had been chosen for his looks, Miss Rhodes for her demure beauty and quiet comedy and Neal for pure comedy. But a bigger announcement was in store for later in the year, when Christie separated from Universal to establish his own independent company.

Joining the new organization, Neal soon learned that Christie's ambition exceeded his financial backing. With most players on half-salary and the boss in New York searching for money, Neal's faith in movies and his future was temporarily shaken. He leaped at an opportunity to return to the stage for Morosco in *45 Minutes From Broadway* and went on to do *The Yankee Prince.* His work was well received by audiences, and the critics were kind. As George St. George, drama critic for the *Los Angeles Evening Express,* said: "Neal Burns has all the nerve in the world to tackle Percy and all the luck—or is it ability?—to get away with it. In any case he succeeds . . ."[1]

At the end of the theater season, Neal decided to return to Christie, although the company was still on somewhat shaky grounds. David Horsley (president of Nestor) offered Burns an attractive proposal—his own series of single reel comedies with Gertrude Selby in support—and Neal departed with Horace Davey for what appeared to be greener pastures. But World War I intervened and both men were drafted for military service.

---

1. October 11, 1916

Neal apparently never incurred the wrath of Al Christie by such moves (as other comedians did) for Christie, who was rapidly becoming one of the biggest comedy producers in the business, brought

Neal Burns came to the screen from the legitimate stage, a rarity in the days when most screen comedians were products of vaudeville and burlesque.

Neal began his career at Christie as the young male lead to beautiful Betty Compson. His brother, Eddie Barry, was also a talented Christie comic but never found the same fame that enveloped Neal.

his former comedian back into the ranks after the latter's discharge from the U. S. Army in 1919. But Al Christie had also changed his ways somewhat, for when other companies wanted Neal for a picture or two, the producer would now loan out his star to avoid forcing Neal to make another decision to leave. This policy began when "Smiling Billy" Parsons died unexpectedly in 1919 and National Film desperately needed a star comic to complete their Capitol Comedy contract with Goldwyn.

Throughout the twenties, Neal Burns was a featured star in Christie Comedies. The days of supporting roles and eccentric comic parts were now over—Neal was good box-office and had considerable control over his comedies. Leaving the direction to others, he wisely avoided the difficulties that trapped many comedian-directors. But Burns *did* have definite ideas of his own, believing that Christie's policy of polite situation comedy humor could easily lead to boredom if the situations were not funny in themselves. With tongue-in-cheek, he once dismissed a consideration of two of Christie's leading scenarists with these words, "W. Scott Darling was a writer who had but one plot—and the head of the scenario department? Well, I would say Frank Roland Conklin had two stories and just changed them around."

Neal had little faith in a strict, literal interpretation of Al Christie's proscribed comedy formula and his comedies bear witness. In *That Son of a Sheik* (1922), he was the comically dashing reflection of Latin Lover Rudolph Valentino. In *Soup to Nuts* (1925), more than half of the action centered around the hectic and chaotic efforts of Neal to save his ugly sister-in-law (Gale Henry) from his burning home, while having quite a time simply saving himself from the disastrous conflagration. In *Court Plaster* (1924), Neal seems to be one long blur of legs as he rushes away and into every person he would imaginably want to avoid. While he realized that movie fans no longer accepted the strong physical burlesque humor of the Key-

As *That Son of a Sheik,* Neal was a comically dashing reflection of the Latin Lover, Valentino, and is seen here on location during filming at Oxnard, California.

Be Yourself, Neal advised Babe London on the occasion of her first contract with Al E. Christie. Essentially a younger group, the Christie comedians enjoyed a camaraderie unknown to other comedy studios.

straight and trust upon the situation alone to bring the laughs. The fragile-looking glasses, stuck onto his face, gave Neal the appearance of a nervous jack rabbit. As problem piled upon problem, fans could almost detect a twitching nose and sharpening of all the senses. With face front, knees together, back stuck out and hands clenched in a nervous grip, Neal Burns was a creature bordering on panic, and his fast action was the product of desperation.

The most tragic event in Neal's career came with Christie's departure from Educational and his subsequent association with Parastone period, he refused to believe that audiences had changed so radically that they rejected everything but the most sophisticated, top-hat humor—and his perceptive analysis paid off in personal success.

Neal's popular comedies usually found him wearing the clothes of the everyday white-collar worker, with the simple addition of a pair of horn-rimmed glasses; but he refused to play the scenes

Neal believed that the polite comedy which became a Christie trademark could easily bore audiences unless the situations were extremely funny by themselves. Note Joan Marquis's wedding costume.

Neal's comic approach found a midpoint between the uncontrollable exuberance of Larry Semon and the overly subdued style of Eddie Lyons; he refused (as in this scene with Vera Steadman) to depend upon the situation alone for laughs.

mount in the late twenties. While Educational had really handled the Christie Comedies with loving care, Paramount treated them as fillers to their feature program. The final blow came with talkies. The hysteria that gripped Hollywood took its toll of silent screen comics, including Neal Burns. The fact that he possessed a fine voice and was an experienced stage actor was inexplicably insignificant to both Christie and Paramount. Within a few years, he and most of the well-known comedians of the silent era were but ghostly figures who paraded in a dim past, forgotten by an industry that never really cared.

The days of his $150 suits, $3500 cars, suite at the Stowell Hotel, the house he built on Holly Drive and his twelve-year membership at the Lakeside Country Club are days long gone to a man who now lives quietly without a telephone in a small cottage in North Hollywood. As he showed publicity photos of himself in his finery, Neal surveyed them for a while and then commented, "I sure would like to have some of the clothes I had then!" Then he added firmly and with unshakable conviction, "No! Though you might need money to pay the groceries; if you are a star, quit or don't do anything!"

Augustus Carney

The early days of screen comedy found few practitioners of the art who were outstanding in their ability, technique or public acceptance. Those who were accepted soon discovered that fame knew no boundaries; their popularity was assured wherever motion pictures were shown. One such comic who tasted the heady wine of success during this formative period was Augustus Carney, better known as "Alkali Ike." In the process, he also discovered that screen fame can be a short street, with obscurity just around the corner.

But of the early Essanay comedians, none were able at the time to achieve even a measure of the popularity that enveloped Carney. A decade later, Ben Turpin's stature would greatly surpass the diminutive comedian's, but to put Carney into proper perspective, it would have to be said that he rivaled John Bunny and Max Linder in popularity. Bunny and Linder represented the sophisticated situation comedy; Carney and Fred Mace led the school of broad burlesque humor.

Coming to the screen with the usual vaudeville background, Augustus Carney teamed with Victor Potel as *Hank and Lank* in 1910. Filmed at the Essanay western studio in Niles, California, the "Hank and Lank" comedies had a decided rural flavor and were quite popular with small-town audiences. This series led to a starring role for Carney in *Alkali Ike's Automobile,* a comedy of errors in which Alkali and his rival, Mustang Pete, romanced Sophie Clutts, the town belle. Alkali lost every round and audiences roared as he stomped away from failure—each time going down a new path with a tight-mouthed, squint-eyed determination. The comedy exceeded all financial expectations and gave a huge boost to the little comedian's career.

Essanay was in the process of creating a comedy series to follow

77

Augustus Carney (circa 1912) without his western makeup.

the adventures of a continuing cast in a rural locale and Alkali Ike became one whose exploits were explored in the subsequent Snakeville Comedies. Named after the mythical town in which they took place, the Snakevilles grew out of the Carney series. While Augustus Carney may not have been the innovator of this kind of comedy series, based on a specific locale and cast, his success was certainly influential in leading to the large number of such series to shortly reach the screen.

As Carney's fame grew, so, unfortunately, did his temperament. Before his death in 1967, Rollie Totheroh, a pioneer Essanay cameraman who later achieved his own mark of distinction as Chaplin's personal cameraman for over thirty years, recalled that "Carney became a pretty surly little cuss to work with." The ornery character of Alkali Ike quickly made an indelible impression on the once-pleasant comedian and all humility was thrown to the wind. "Star fever" had bitten Augustus Carney—perhaps with good reason.

When Carney left Niles in the fall of 1912 for his first trip to Chicago in three years, few people were on hand to bid him farewell. But upon his arrival in the Windy City, the train was greeted by hundreds of well-wishers and adoring fans. As word spread that Alkali Ike was in Chicago, Carney was mobbed wherever he went. Reporters followed his every footstep and photographers asked him to pose. After three years of steadily building a reputation, Carney now discovered that he had arrived.

There were other visible signs of success. At $1.50 each, "Alkali Ike" dolls were sell-outs at theater box-offices and novelty stores. While Carney was in Europe the following year, the reissue of *Alkali Ike's Automobile* returned a larger gross than in its initial release. The Chicago incident was repeated in city after city along his trip. After struggling for years to achieve success, a certain amount of self-pride could not be denied him.

But the reaction to a sudden discovery of his ascent to stardom was also the downfall for Alkali Ike and Augustus Carney. Upon returning from Europe, Carney asked Essanay for more money than

It seems as if just about everyone in Snakeville is enjoying a screening of *Alkali Ike and the Hypnotist,* especially Victor Potel, Carney and Harry Todd.

George K. Spoor felt he was worth. Spoor's refusal led Carney to exercise an option which Universal had proposed months before and he left Essanay.

Regarded by pioneer producers as a talent pirate, Universal let others spend the time and money necessary to develop a screen personality and then stole him away with a high salary offer. In Carney's case, he was given his own production company and a much

Universal Ike Has His Ups and Downs. Moving to Universal, Alkali Ike became Universal Ike, and from that point it was a short ride to obscurity.

While *Alkali Ike Plays the Devil,* the audiences roared in delight. Carney's popularity made him one of the unchallenged masters of the early comedy screen.

ballyhooed campaign was launched, allowing fans to choose a new name for Alkali. It came as no surprise when Carl Laemmle announced that audiences had overwhelmingly selected "Universal Ike" as a replacement for "Alkali Ike." Carney now had a new name at a higher salary, his own company and a new director, Harry Edwards.

Unfortunately, he had also retained an overestimation of his own abilities and promptly clashed head-on with Edwards. Laemmle, who stood for no foolishness on the part of his actors, quietly lined up beside his director and brought in an unknown who was cast as "Universal Ike Jr." Unable to run things his own way, Carney made a hasty decision in May 1914 and quit, virtually writing the finish to his screen career with this move. Aided and abetted by Laemmle, word of the little comedian's inability to work with others spread quickly.

Reduced to second-rate supporting roles—whenever he could find those—the degree of Carney's descent was reflected in *The Straw Man,* a 1915 Majestic comedy. Heavily made up and almost indistinguishable to audiences, he played the scarecrow tormented by

"If this is the only way to win the fair lady, I'll trade you my horse for that contraption." Gus Carney has a surprise in store for him in this scene from *Alkali Ike's Automobile,* the comedy which really put him on top in the very early days of the screen. (Courtesy George Marshall)

a group of small children. And so ended the career of one of the screen's earliest and best-loved comics.

Movie audiences of the 1909-13 period were not too terribly sophisticated, and as a result a large part of Carney's fame rested in his portrayal of a character with whom rural America could identify. His Universal comedies could have been a springboard to even greater success, but for his unyielding attitude that he alone knew best. One of the first screen stars to taste the power behind a studio's displeasure, Augustus Carney is virtually forgotten today.

Sydney Chaplin

Any number of reasons could have induced Mack Sennett to sign Sydney Chaplin for the Keystone screen. As an experienced stage comic from the English music hall, Syd's slapstick background was perfectly suited to success on the screen. Charlie's increasing popularity might have led Sennett to believe that there was still more gold to be mined from the Chaplin family, and it's even possible that Mack's practical nature told him Syd could be exploited on Charlie's reputation. As likely as each of these possibilities are, however, they were merely the reasons used by Charlie when he suggested Syd's employment as a means (unbeknown to Sennett) of repaying his half-brother for past favors.

Four years Charlie's senior, Syd had become the businessman of the Chaplin family at an early age: it was Syd who first reached the footlights of Karno's music hall troupe and then recommended Charlie for a part in 1906; it was Syd to whom the unsure little comedian had turned for advice and comfort in his formative years; and again, it was Syd who gave up a promising screen career to manage Charlie's business affairs after the public had made the younger Chaplin a million-dollar attraction. Although many of his contemporaries felt that Syd's potential was every bit the equal of Charlie's (a pronouncement with which Theodore Huff concurred in his definitive biography, *Charlie Chaplin,* when he commented that Syd's pantomime in *A Dog's Life* was as fine as Charlie's), Syd Chaplin has been overly neglected down through the years.

Joining Keystone in November 1914, Syd's comic style was more in the Keystone tradition than Charlie's had been. The emphasis on comic action above story made physical dexterity imperative. Gags were of primary importance, fitting into the framework of a character perhaps not so fully defined as Charlie would mentally outline his Tramp over the next few years, but outfitted memorably in costume.

A direct descendant from his music hall background, Syd's screen

Toning down the vulgarity that characterized his Keystone roles, Syd made a series of extremely popular features for Warner Brothers in the late twenties. Cross-pollination of costumes provided a comic hinge for Syd in *The Missing Link*.

comedy found its roots in the tradition of burlesque and farce. As "Gussle," his popular character in 1915 Keystones, Syd developed the immediately identifiable makeup of hair parted down the middle, raised eyebrows, and the German comic moustache that pointed up on the end. His costume almost always consisted of a high collar, exposed floppy ties and a well-worn pair of oversized shoes; the remainder of his garb would change from comedy to comedy. One of his favorite costumes was a tight-fitting coat and loose baggy pants pulled up high and padded to appear like a bustle. If the film called for a rakish individual—a common Syd Chaplin role—then a cane and low-crowned felt hat, tilted in cavalier fashion and with a small feather in it, was included for additional comic effect.

The humor of the English music hall during this period was far from the most polite comedy on the stage. In light of the suggestive and risque action that accompanied much of the comedy in this medium, it's not surprising that some of the practitioners were a bit rough in their comedy. Admittedly, much of Syd's humor, including the vulgarities, was really very funny but his penchant for low and

Syd Chaplin's Keystone screen roles were deeply rooted in the tradition of burlesque and farce. George "Slim" Summerville is going to pay for interrupting *Gussle's Day of Rest.*

As the wild waiter in *A Submarine Pirate*, Syd's low comedy portrayal became a minor classic among the early Keystone-Triangle Comedies.

vulgar slapstick was even more extreme than Sennett himself would allow; therefore dissatisfaction gradually developed between Syd and the King of Comedy.

Because of the abundance of wild, wacky and commonly vulgar humor that comprised the majority of short comedies of the period, a rescreening of Syd's Keystones today finds the viewer hard-pressed to believe that any effort had been made to censor the original footage. But Sennett was continually forced to order the reshooting, shortening or elimination of certain scenes he considered too vulgar or in exceptionally bad taste. Dixie Chene, who appeared with Syd in many of his Keystones, recalled that "Sennett just couldn't get along with him because every time Mack's back was turned, Syd was performing off-color stuff on the screen. Syd didn't seem to understand that Sennett was going to cut that out of the film. The next day, it had to be shot over and then Sennett had to sit there and watch it again."

Although the Keystone studio may have appeared to be a slapdash, carefree affair, the perceptive reader will have already concluded that from the purely practical standpoint of time and money, Sennett could ill afford to constantly reshoot footage or to devote too much of his time to policing Syd's on-screen portrayals. Keystone never could have succeeded as well as it did without an efficient and tight-fisted approach; Sennett never threw money away.

And so Syd Chaplin and Keystone eventually parted company, but not before Syd turned in a minor classic among the early Keystone-Triangle Comedies, *A Submarine Pirate*. As the devil-may-care waiter who overheard Glen Cavender and Wesley Ruggles plotting to destroy a battleship, Syd swiped a briefcase containing their plans and took command of a submarine. The result was absolute pandemonium. Over the years, *A Submarine Pirate* has been re-edited and reissued many times, gaining a prominence far beyond its original impact as fans discover and rediscover the "other Chaplin."

Early in 1916, Syd left the screen to take charge of Charlie's increasingly complex business affairs and was primarily responsible for the $670,000 Mutual contract his half-brother signed in February. Immensely successful in this capacity, the older Chaplin was exceptionally astute and shrewd. He represented Charlie in later negotiations with First National and landed the film immortal a $1,075,000 contract for eight two-reel comedies (Charlie's great wealth today pays silent tribute to Syd's acumen in the business of motion pic-

One of the most surefire laugh-provoking devices was female impersonation for comic effect. Especially adept at this form of comedy,
here's Syd in *The Man on the Box.*

tures). In addition to managing Charlie's career and occasionally playing roles in the Chaplin First National comedies, Syd also found time to undertake the production of a half-dozen features in Europe for Famous Players-Lasky in 1920.

During the twenties, Syd made a very triumphant screen comeback in *Charley's Aunt,* the famous stage play that Al Christie brought to the screen in 1925. Interestingly enough, masquerading as a woman for pure comic effect was a staple in both the American vaudeville and English music hall bag of tricks; but this low-comedy, farcical device—one of the most sure-fire laugh-provoking tricks in show business—had been considerably polished for the legitimate stage in *Charley's Aunt.* Syd toned down his wild acting and unadulterated vulgarity for the more sophisticated audiences of the twenties, but his popularity in this role also served to somewhat typecast him. Two other features—*Oh, What a Nurse* and *The Man*

Syd Chaplin's versatility was shown in the range of roles he portrayed—from Keystone slapstick to the sophisticated comedy of his Warner features. Perhaps the ultimate test was his wonderfully accurate caricature in *The Better 'Ole,* a well-worn stage play by Bruce Bairnsfather and Arthur Eliot.

on the Box—capitalized on Syd's comic talents as a female imper-
sonator. He was nevertheless sufficiently versatile to emerge as a
wonderfully accurate caricature of the famous hero in Warner's
adaptation of the well-worn theatrical by Bruce Bairnsfather and
Arthur Eliot, *The Better 'Ole.*

At the same time that sound began to revolutionize the industry,
Syd was running into difficulties with the Internal Revenue people.
Never having acquired American citizenship, he moved back to
Europe and gradually began to take over Charlie's affairs once more.
The screen lost one of its most brilliant but erratic performers, for
if Syd had decided to challenge Charlie on screen, it could have been
an interesting contest.

Charley Chase

Over the past decade, an increasing interest in the personalities of the silent screen has brought gradual recognition to one of comedy's finest practitioners—Charley Chase. After years of neglect, this comedian is finally beginning to receive the credit he deserves for his many contributions to the art of screen comedy. This reawakened interest in Charley can be attributed in large part to Robert Youngson and his silent comedy compilations of the past few years. In *The Golden Age of Comedy*, *When Comedy Was King* and *Thirty Years of Fun*, Chase was prominently featured along with Laurel and Hardy, Chaplin and Keaton—a position he easily held in the late twenties and early thirties.

A native of Baltimore, Charley was born Charles Parrott. Adopting "Chase" as a stage name, Charley was to use both in his show business career. He started in vaudeville with an Irish monologue, a few songs and a bit of dancing, but left the stage (a move undoubtedly for the best) to enter moving pictures when he turned twenty-one. Supposedly "discovered" by Al Christie during a very brief stay at Universal, Charley joined Keystone in 1914, and within a few months he was featured in several comedies. His portrayals were very similar to the famous character he would create in the twenties. He exhibited an almost total lack of concern for the exaggerated make-up or costume of the average Keystone comedian, reflecting instead the image of the struggling young man.

Chase soon made a decision that greatly affected his future screen career. Overloaded with well-known comics, the competition within Keystone was too great; Chase decided to learn directing. Feeling that his future was behind the camera, Charley talked Mack Sennett into making him an assistant to Ford Sterling, who was directing as well as starring in his own comedies. But progress at Keystone was not very rapid for the fledgling director and when Fox went into

Charley, as he appeared in the late twenties.

comedy production in 1916, Charley made the move. Over the next few years, he worked for L-KO, Bulls Eye and Paramount, directing many different comedians, writing scripts, absorbing techniques and evolving his own particular sense of comedy—its content, timing and pacing. By 1921, Charley Chase had acquired a reputation as an original and dependable comedy director and the Hal Roach organization beckoned.

Roach had promoted Harold Lloyd to a series of double reels, leaving Lloyd's supporting comic, Snub Pollard, to carry on the one-reelers. This expansion of his Culver City facilities made it clear that Roach was preparing an all-out effort to challenge Mack Sennett, his strongest competitor in the comedy field. Alf Goulding and Chase were brought aboard to help with the new comedy program and alternated with Roach in making the Pollard comedies.

Snub Pollard owed much of his success to Chase's direction. Charley highlighted Snub's talent and avoided those situations that would have revealed his shortcomings, thus making many of the Pollard films a sheer delight for comedy fans. But regardless of Roach's efforts his studio continued to remain a respectable second to Mack Sennett.

Toward the close of 1923, Roach offered Chase his own starring series, hoping to make the talented director a comedy attraction in his own right. Marie Mosquini (who had started with Roach as a secretary in 1916) and Martha Sleeper provided the feminine support for Charley as he embarked on the lengthy series that gave him the necessary experience. Chase became one of the most capable comedians of the period.

The success of the Chase comedies depended almost entirely upon Charley and his gags, as the stories were simple and quite often outrageously contrived. While some of his early comedies used slapstick to an extent, Chase soon developed his best portrayal—the innocuous young man who tried very hard to impress his wife, his mother-in-law and his boss, only to fail with all three. In *Crazy Like a Fox*, Charley, secretly in love with Martha Sleeper, was angry with his parents for insisting he marry a girl he had never seen just because she was the daughter of a very old and dear family friend. Charley decided to feign madness in order to avoid the marriage—only to discover in the end that his betrothed and Martha were one and the same, thus bringing the entire show in all its ridiculousness to a delightfully happy ending.

It was the gags, not the story lines, that counted and as Hal

Roach would remark years later, "Charley was a good gag man who worked on most of his own stories." Chase was crazy like a fox in another respect. Unlike other comedians who tried to write their own material, act and direct at the same time, Charley was wise enough to leave the directing to others, although he often offered his own thoughts.

This lack of the inflated ego so common to comedians brought him into close contact with some of the best minds in the business— F. Richard Jones, Fred Guiol, Clyde Bruckman, Leo McCarey and Charley's brother James. The latter, a comedian in his own right, was featured by Roach as Paul (or Poll) Parrott.

The Chase comedies of the late twenties showed a polish and precision seldom matched by others. *Movie Night*, a slight situation involving Charley and his family at the neighborhood theater, was interspersed with simple running gags such as a cough and the subsequent disturbance as Charley eased his way to the aisle for a trip to the water fountain. The results convulsed audiences and its basic premise was good enough to be repeated in 1936 as *Neighborhood House*.

With the transition to sound no company dealing in comedy shorts fared quite so well as did Hal Roach. With Laurel and Hardy, Charley Chase, Harry Langdon and Our Gang, Roach quickly surpassed the comedy efforts of Mack Sennett to become the real, if not acknowledged, "King of Comedy" in these final days before the animated cartoon and double features overwhelmed the comedy short subject.

Charley Chase became one of the most popular comics of the early thirties, but by 1936 the demand for short comedies had fallen off sharply and Roach decided to use his star comics in longer films. After only one starring feature, Charley surmised there was no longer a future for him with Roach and left to join Columbia, where he returned to the two-reel domestic comedies that had made him famous. But in 1940, Charley's health began to fail and on June 20 he suffered a fatal heart attack.

Within the motion picture industry itself, Charley Chase had become one of the most respected men to work in the field of comedy. As those who knew and worked with him are quick to point out, despite the fact that he was a seriously dedicated student of film humor and a man whose overiding concern was the creation of entertaining screen comedy, Chase was as personable an individual on the set as on the screen. His life was the world of show business and his work was a labor of love.

While this is a strange looking second-story man leaving the first floor window, the getaway vehicle and its operator also leave something to be desired. Comedy fans will immediately recognize a youthful Charles Parrott in a scene from *Love, Loot and Crash*.

After appearing in several Keystones (such as *Hash House Mashers*), Charley decided that his future lay in directing rather than comic acting. In the early twenties, he was one of the most creative directors working in the short comedy field.

Charley's early Keystone appearances seldom found him in the ridiculous makeup favored by Keystone comics. Fritz Schade and Slim Summerville supported him in *A Lucky Leap*.

Obviously, Charley doesn't want to "feed the kitty," even if it means pleasing Mildred Harris. Miss Harris had capitalized on her earlier marriage to Charlie Chaplin and was now one of the fading stars in Roach comedies.

Charley Chase and friend—anything for Pathé's publicity department.

In his screen roles, Charley often held jobs requiring imagination and skill, usually getting into trouble as a result.

Thus the curtain closed on a comic mind whose fresh and inventive originality had played an outstanding part in *The Golden Age of Comedy*. The two-reel comedy has also departed the scene. Three decades and many television series later, it has not been replaced by anything nearly so enjoyable or laugh-provoking as the ingenious situations brought to life with the gags of Charley Chase and others. Those days will never return.

Andy Clyde

Throughout the twenties, professional makeup men were virtually nonexistent on the comedy lots. Most comics were required to apply their own, learning the art from other more experienced comedians. On most studio lots, one comic would become the unofficial makeup artist, based more upon kindness and patience than on his available time. On Mack Sennett's lot, one of the best in the business could be found: Andy Clyde.

Even though he was one of the busiest comics Sennett ever had, Clyde spent untold hours with young extras and newcomers to the screen who did not know a "muff" from a "mo," or a tube of lipstick from an eyebrow pencil. Andy's proficiency in makeup also served a more practical purpose. By using Clyde's talents properly, Sennett found that Andy could play two or three roles in the same film, thus reducing the number of character actors needed for a particular comedy. In *Flip Flops*, Clyde played the supporting role along with three extra parts, and used entirely different makeups for each characterization. To Andy Clyde, the comedy lot became a testing ground for character experimentation and makeup virtuosity.

Jimmy Finlayson was responsible for bringing his fellow Scotsman to the screen from vaudeville in 1919. An old friend from stage days, Fin had just made the switch to movie comedy and invited Clyde to the Sennett lot to see how it was done. Andy was fascinated and Fin got him a job playing bits and small roles. Soon after, Jimmy left the Sennett lot in a bid for fame at Hal Roach's, but Clyde remained at Edendale for over a decade.

In his earliest comedies, Andy appeared most often as the slippery villain, slinking into the small town from the corrupt city. The long sleek moustache of his melodramatic villain was most often twirled amidst the innocence of the calico-dressed, pigtailed Louise Fazenda. By the mid-twenties, Clyde's face had become a bulletin

Andy Clyde's career began in 1919 and ended with *The Real McCoys* television series.

board for tacked-on beards and moustaches. With the long two-foot beard, he became the mad scientist, an old gouty-footed uncle, or Harry Langdon's perplexed father. With his short fuzzy beard, Andy became Ralph Graves's harrassed employer or Alice Day's fuming father, enraged by his daughter's elopement. Reducing this to a dark stubble of a bum, he became Billy Bevan's tricky companion.

By the late twenties, Clyde had finally developed the famous comedy character and makeup of countless sound comedies and endless westerns. Beginning in the *Smith Family* series, and growing to perfection in the Daphne Pollard-Carol Lombard comedies, Andy Clyde formulated his portrayal of the old man whose zest for life was unmatched by his physical ability. Females flustered him, and no matter whether he was caught by young flirtatious flappers or experienced sultry vamps, Clyde registered a blush that seemed to redden the black and white screen. Filled with youthful exuberance brought on by a naughty tickle under his chin, Andy would gather up enough energy to trip over chairs, tables, park benches or anything else within the path of his crashing love-blindness. His awkward but defiant determination to succeed inevitably surmounted the mountains of difficulties he encountered.

The comedy character was reflected perfectly in his makeup: the tousled hair and stubble of a beard-to-be (typically the product of absentmindedness), a large "gay nineties" moustache, and a pair of bifocals that emphasized both his age and embarrassment as he raised his eyebrows, peering sheepishly over the rims.

Although Clyde was Mack Sennett's personal favorite—his fair-haired boy and real money-maker in the thirties—after a decade on the Sennett lot, Andy and his boss no longer saw things eye-to-eye. The comic's dissatisfaction had grown gradually until the split was firmly wedged and he left for work at the Educational studio. Clyde's unhappiness had started with a dog and ended with an unsatisfactory contract. While working in the *Smith Family* series, Andy became increasingly irritated by the use of Raymond McKee's talented but viciously temperamental dog. After alternate pleas and complaints to Sennett, Andy ultimately walked off the set, refusing to return until the dog had been replaced. With typical Sennett stubbornness, the dog remained and Clyde was replaced in the series by Arthur Stone, who copied Andy's makeup and style.

The final break came with a new but unsatisfactory contract. When it came time for renewal, Andy asked for the right to refuse to do stunts he considered too dangerous; with his usual distaste for

In *Bow-Wow*, Clyde was Teddy's prisoner while John Henry Jr. clapped his approval. Without his make-up, it was difficult to tell Andy from any number of other comedians busy in the early twenties.

A grown-up Harry Langdon can't bear being parted from *His New Mama* on Christmas Eve. Andy heartily disapproves.

By 1930, Andy's screen character was well-founded and he would play the role for another three decades. This scene is from Sennett's feature for Sono Art World Wide Pictures.

"Your choice of weapons, sir." But *The Prodigal Bridegroom* (Ben Turpin) isn't certain that Madeline Hurlock's worth a fight with the aroused Clyde.

This is the moustache to end all moustaches. Behind it, a careful viewer can spot Andy Clyde as Alice Day pleads in behalf of Danny O'Shea in *Pass The Dumplings*.

Andy's character makeup began to mellow in the "Smith Family" series, In spite of Raymond McKee's admonitions, Mary Ann Jackson was determined to make life miserable for the Scotsman.

individual exceptions, Sennett resounded with a firm *no* and Clyde departed. Andy's professional career extended through comedies in the thirties, comic sidekick roles in westerns of the forties, and television in the fifties. His last work was done in *The Real McCoys,* Walter Brennan's long-running television series.

But Andy missed the spirit that had accompanied the making of comedies in the silent days. In a career that spanned more than four decades, Andy Clyde was constantly in demand and few other character comedians contributed so much to the entertainment of millions.

Chester Conklin

Almost simultaneously with its founding in 1912, the Keystone Film Company began to expand and a large number of comedians passed through the Edendale studio gate in 1913. Among these was a small ex-circus clown from Oskaloosa, Iowa, who had tired of painting stringers during the off-season and decided to leave the Al G. Barnes show to try his luck in the movies. For over a decade, Chester Conklin's rise in the entertainment world had been the result of a brash self-confidence and when Mack Sennett inquired if Chester could be funny performing in front of the camera, Conklin's brusque reply was simply, "I'll leave that up to you."

Hired on a daily basis, Chester answered every work call, usually earning his $3.00 in a Keystone Kop uniform. Although the work was steady, Conklin left Keystone to spend six months at Majestic, where he was quickly moved into supporting roles. With this experience behind him, Chester returned to the Keystone lot and Sennett put him back to work, this time in supporting and featured roles.

Ford Sterling's coaching helped to improve the new comedian's screen pantomime and Mack Swain took a hand in helping Chester develop a camera presence. The essence of his old stage act, Chester's ill-fitting comic garb was essentially complete when he rejoined Keystone, but over the years, it would become somewhat more refined. Reflecting his own self-confidence, Chester's screen personality became identified with three similar characters during his Keystone years. The most descriptive was "Fish Face," in recognition of a wide-eyed sullen glare over the droopy moustache. An extension of this portrayal, the belligerent little "Walrus" became his most famous character and one which most often found him matching wits with Mack Swain's "Ambrose." Equally popular was his inept, fumbling bungler, "Droppington." But regardless of which character he chose to portray, Chester's magnificent melodramatic exaggeration of evil stood out above all else.

Loveable little Chester Conklin.

The town's best-dressed bank clerk is carrying on an affair with the president's wife, Alice Davenport. Wait until Ambrose hears about this. Of course, he's pretty busy with Chester's wife right now in *The Home Breakers*.

Relying heavily on fast moving action, the Keystones were pure farce and required very little real effort on Chester's part. As the wife-stealing wolf in *Love, Speed and Thrills,* he simply drove away on his motorcycle with Minta Durfee in the sidecar, eluding both the Keystone Kops and Mack's desperate chase on horseback for a full ten minutes before the final denouement. As a bank president and his clerk in *The Home Breakers,* Mack and Chester flirted with each other's wives on the side until the janitor (Slim Summerville) decided to profit by the extramarital affairs. Only after leaving Keystone was Chester able to give much dimension to his screen work.

Regarded by most as a hard but fair man to work for, Sennett usually enjoyed a good relationship with his comics and Chester was no exception. But as Keystone grew and Mack's attention turned increasingly away from production to the business aspect, he became almost inaccessible, preferring to leave personnel relations in the hands of his studio manager, J. A. Waldron. Naturally oriented to what he considered to be Keystone's best interest, Waldron's aloof attitude gradually alienated many of the comics who had worked side by side with Sennett during the early days. Mack upheld his studio manager religiously (especially in money matters), and as a result Al St. John, Hank Mann and Chester left the fold.

Conklin moved over to Fox and the Sunshine Comedies, but his real ambitions lay in feature comedy and after a short stay with Fox, Chester began to freelance. The late twenties became the busiest and most creative period of his career. Teaming up first with Charlie Murray and then W. C. Fields, Chester made his greatest impact in feature comedies such as *McFadden's Flats* and *The Old Army Game.* In addition, he found time to make a dozen two-reelers for Standard Cinema's Blue Ribbon Comedies in 1925-26 and teamed with Hank Mann in 1926-27 to make a series for Tennek Film Corporation.

Almost perfect travesties of Chester's earlier Keystones, the Blue Ribbon Comedies, were produced by Joe Rock, who had gained brief starring fame in Vitagraph's Montgomery-Rock comedies of 1915-16. Departing from the situation comedy prevalent toward the close of the silent period, Chester's work in *Lame Brains* was typical of the entire series. As a new graduate of detective school (by virtue of a correspondence course), our hero was trying to locate a notorious bootlegger suspected of operating from a hotel.

Suspicious of Conklin's behavior, a deaf hotel detective constantly interfered with his investigation, but Chester finally hit upon a foolproof scheme and tied a small bell to his shadow's coattails. The

Walrus abducts Ambrose's wife (Minta Durfee) and the chase is on in *Love, Speed and Thrills*.

"Well girls, you're a bit overdressed," Chester has his own ideas for Mollie McGowan, Elsie Ware and Marvel Rea as Peggy Cloud prepares to shoot the footage in this 1919 publicity still.

Chester always maintained he left Sennett because of a low salary, but if Kalla Pasha had given him many more treatments like this one from *The Village Smithy*, Chester might have had other reasons.

Chester was Chester, regardless of the makeup. This fine little comic's ability kept him busy for over a half century in show business, working in short subjects and features. This one was First National's *The Duchess of Buffalo*.

"*A Bird's a Bird,*" thinks Minta Durfee as Chester prepares to make hash of the parrot.

real humor lay in the comic interplay between Conklin and the detective as our hero prowled the lobby after attaching the tinkling bell. His extremely baggy suit, huge moustache and highly over-exaggerated pantomime all added up to a caricature of the Keystone sleuth not seen on the screen for well over a decade, and a welcome treat for devotees of slapstick's earthy humor.

Chester's career began to fade in the forties, and by 1954 he was working as a department store Santa Claus in Los Angeles. In 1961, he moved to a cottage at the Motion Picture Country House in Woodland Hills but the greasepaint of over fifty years in show business would not wash off that easily, and in 1965 the eighty-year-old comedian came out of retirement to step back in front of the camera with a small role in *A Big Hand for the Little Lady*.

Clyde Cook

Although most successful screen comedians had a vaudeville or stage background, not all of the stage and vaudeville comics were successful in their attempts at a starring screen career. Some, like Sammy Burns, failed miserably. Others managed to hang on without ever creating a definite public impression; Clyde Cook fell into this category.

A career which began when he was twelve led the little Australian comedian to a London tour and then to Paris and the Folies Bergère. Eventually arriving in the United States, Cook met with some success on the American stage, first with the Ziegfeld Follies and then as Charles Dillingham's principal clown and pantomimist at the New York Hippodrome.

Induced to become a part of the expansion program that Fox was underwriting, Clyde Cook came to the screen in 1920 with visions of stardom, but his early pictures were far from sensational. Jack Blystone and other Fox directors couldn't seem to communicate properly with their new comedian and a lack of suitable material compounded their difficulties. As a result, Blystone, Cook and many exhibitors were quite unhappy with the comedy series.

Enter Hal Roach, still searching for the answer to match Mack Sennett's success. Roach decided that Clyde had talent and could become a comedy star. With the very capable stable of writers and directors in his employ, Roach had no reason to doubt that his people could not materially advance Cook's career. And so Clyde Cook went over to the Hal Roach lot where he hoped for better days.

Cook's initial picture for Roach was unacceptable to Pathé, which reserved the right to refuse release to any product they felt did not live up to the rather high standards established in earlier days by the Pathé Film Committee, which met in judgment of all films before they were released. Roach realized that Cook's problem once again

115

Clyde Cook, as he appeared in the Fox Sunshine Comedies.

The script writers had a field day with Clyde and these gadgets.

was director trouble and called in Stan Laurel to doctor the footage which had been shot and reshot by various directors. Stan was able to come up with an idea that salvaged the film, but it was now apparent to Roach that Cook presented an unusual problem.

Although a natural comedian, Clyde Cook required a strong, experienced and decisive director to guide him. The days of outlandish comic costumes had disappeared and Cook presented a very neutral appearance to the camera's eye. Possessing no outstanding physical features (other than a brush moustache he twitched with a simple, slow-witted expression) by which he could be distinguished from any one of the other minor comedians romping before the camera at the time, Clyde Cook's entire success had to be measured not only by his material, but by his execution of it.

This presented a challenge to Roach's best writers and directors —one which they met sufficiently well to keep Cook on the payroll almost three years, but not well enough to make him a comedy star. In fact, it became an everyday occasion for Jimmy Finlayson, in supporting roles, to steal Clyde's entire picture out from under him. Fin hardly even tried.

Of all who attempted to direct Cook, only James Parrott seemed confident in his ability to work with the comic and immediately set about revamping the comedian's image. New writers were called in to develop material that would accent Cook's acrobatic talents. Story lines were given unusual twists to establish an abnormal situation within a ridiculous setting and Finlayson, who had come on too strong in a competitive way, was replaced by Noah Young. Young, who had previously supported Lloyd and Snub Pollard, was the epitome of the comic bully and Cook's screen character was given a dash of the meek, mild-mannered victim of circumstance. The results were most gratifying, especially to Cook and Roach.

The peculiar story lines set up a comedy framework, and given free rein, Clyde Cook's acrobatics resulted in some very funny comedies. *Should Sailors Marry?* was a good example of the Parrott-Cook collaboration. The plot was simple, but absurd. Behind in collecting overdue alimony payments from his ex-wife, Noah moved into her boarding house and the two schemed to marry her off to a wealthy man.

An agency recommended Clyde as a rich sailor and the wedding took place posthaste. Although introduced to Noah, Cook had no idea that when he retired for the night, his bedmate would be the ex-husband. At this point, the absurd became the ridiculous. Informed by Noah that he was to work and pay up the back alimony, Clyde gracefully accepted the idea and settled down for the night. A wrestler by profession, Young's peaceful rest turned into a nightmare and he attacked Clyde in his sleep. This turn of events opened the door for Cook's real talent and he put on a fine display of acrobatics in evading his attacker.

The next morning, the schemers took out an insurance policy on Clyde's life and tried to dispose of him on a construction site. This set the stage for additional breath-taking acrobatics as he fell from beam to beam, heading for the ground below. The film closed as Cook fell into a passing balloon, conveniently headed for Reno and a divorce.

Clyde Cook's career pulled out of its tailspin, but never did catch fire. After holding up his end of the release schedule in a respectable manner, Clyde went to Warner Brothers and worked well into the thirties, playing character comedy roles in features. In many respects, his work paralleled that of Lupino Lane, another fine acrobatic comic who failed in a bid for stardom. Comfortable while doing his stage skits, the apparently disconnected shooting of a

Clyde drew on his stage experience for a hoofing sequence with Warner Oland in *Good Time Charley*, a Warner Brothers story of the theater.

Cook dropped comedy to do serious supporting roles. *Beware of Married Men* found him working with Audrey Ferris.

Cook moved to Warners after his stay with Roach expired. Here he's chained to Louise Fazenda in *A Sailor's Sweetheart*.

screen situation required a great deal of effort on Clyde's part to retain spontaneity.

Curiously enough, Cook's name continually appears in conversations with other comics of the era and it is evident that those in the business held a lot of respect for the little Australian's talent. Many of the Roach comedies still prove to be a delightful romp, with a comedian who really deserved more attention from the public than he received.

Vernon Dent

The most neglected heroes of silent comedy history have been those actors who forfeited their own stardom to become straight men in support of the lead comedians. Although this was seldom an altruistic gesture on their part, the very nature of screen comedy required comic foils and many talented men directed their careers towards that goal, knowing full well that while comedy leads come and go with the breeze, the good supporting character comic works forever. If honors were to be passed out in that category, the title of "King of the Character Comics" would have to be given to Vernon Dent for his work in the twenties.

Although surely not true, it seems that Dent appeared in every other comedy of the silent and early sound period. Despite the injustice of his obscurity, Dent's activities as a supporting comic embodied the duties of any top-quality straight man. His responsibility was to center as much attention as possible upon the lead comedian, working constantly to emphasize all of the comic action.

Vernon arrived at the Mack Sennett Studio in 1921, after completing a series of Folly Comedies for the Pacific Film Company in which he had the leading role. Although Dent was quite experienced in the art of screen comedy (he had also supported Hank Mann at Arrow in 1919-20), Sennett viewed him as a straight man from the very beginning of their association. Vernon's first role for Sennett was as Mabel Normand's small-time lover in *Molly O*. While he did attempt starring comedy leads occasionally (as in *The Lion and the Souse*), these isolated attempts never flowered into a regular comedy series.

Dent's greatest value had been immediately and correctly judged by the shrewd Sennett. If a comedian tripped over a bench, all the qualities of that bench had to aid the eventual laugh. In the same way, Dent's comic function was closely parallel to just such a bench. The bench might look funny or be situated in a peculiar

122

Vernon Dent was the perfect foil for Billy Bevan and Harry Langdon in their Sennett comedies.

An early Dent villain bribes the jockey in *The Barnstormers*, a Fox Sunshine Comedy of 1922.

position, but it had to be solid and immovable. In order to serve successfully as a comic vehicle, it had to present a villainous obstacle to the comedian.

To the impish roguery of Billy Bevan, Vernon Dent became the law-enforcing chief of police or the enraged and jealous husband. In response to Andy Clyde's awkward embarrassment, he was the suave fellow with a smooth mastery of the situation. To Harry Langdon's child-like innocence and hesitant inefficiency, he appeared as the world of experience and an impatient man with a job to be done.

In *Don't Get Jealous*, Dent was caught up in a typical comic situation—Billy Bevan was making passes at Vernon's girl (Carmelita Geraghty) in a cozy corner of a restaurant. Plastering himself with a wild burst of hair in the mad Russian tradition, Dent assumed the role of maitre d' to observe the illicit affair closely. Since he was made up in a wild disguise and wielded a pair of wicked carving knives, Vernon had all the necessary requirements to draw laughs to himself. But instead, Dent threw the laughs Bevan's way by becoming the gravely serious villain who spelled disaster for the little "man-about-town" Billy. Creating suspense through straight-faced villainy, he allowed Bevan to indulge in the laugh-getting devices of comic tension—the unexpected and deception. Dent created the atmosphere of hovering disaster, permitting Billy to play along in his roguish innocence before the eventual awareness and unavoidable fall.

Dent did not play absolutely every scene straight. Unquestionably, he sometimes used makeup that ranged from huge beards to dapper little pencil-thin moustaches to comic advantage. And at rare times, he would use his weight for comic effect—as in *Picking Peaches,* when he skipped across the room as playfully and skillfully as Ferdinand the Bull sniffing flowers in a spring meadow. The comic action in *The One-Mama Man* was divided equally between Charley Chase and Dent during their mad, uninhibited punch-throwing fight, delivered in grand mock tragedy style.

Dent's success was not based upon an identifiable character, but rather in the very absence of a constant personality. Unlike Andy Clyde, whose films showed a talented comedian groping toward a

Although he occasionally played comedy leads, as in Sennett's 1924 *The Lion and the Souse,* Vernon Dent's only starring series was made for the Pacific Film Company in 1921.

As Harry Langdon's sergeant in *All Night Long*, Dent provided the strong shoulder little Harry needed.

Dent's lack of definite comic personality contributed to his success as a supporting comic in comedies like *East of the Water Plug*, with Alice Day and Ralph Graves.

Although Billy Bevan is determined to bring back a souvenir from *"Hoboken to Hollywood,"* his traveling companion (Vernon Dent, of course) questions this particular one.

The masculine symbol of authority which tried his best to keep impish Harry Langdon under control, Dent faced competition from Ruth Hiatt in *"Saturday Afternoon."*

successfully established character through a myriad of miscellaneous funny comic types, Vernon Dent discarded any intention of developing a single character. Versatility proved to be his most valuable asset.

Dent's career continued in the thirties, when he worked in countless Columbia short subjects with Clyde, Chase, Langdon and The Three Stooges. But in Mack Sennett's world of make-believe during the twenties, Vernon Dent almost yanked the cuckoo land back to reality, with his apparent impatience with all the clown and burlesque characters romping through the endless number of crazy comedies. Dent's emotions of anger, jealousy, greed and intolerance were thoroughly real when compared to the simpleton shenanigans of the Billy Bevans and Harry Langdons. Dent supplied the unpleasantries of the real world from which the make-believe comics struggled humorously to extricate themselves.

Although maintaining a state of mental alertness, Vernon's last years were spent in the dark world of the blind, a cruel injustice to one who had created so much entertainment for the eyes of millions. Dying in near-total obscurity in 1963, he had been forgotten by all but an ever-diminishing few and virtually ignored by the compilers of cinema history.

Dorothy Devore

Seemingly born with acting blood in her veins, Inez Williams began her show business career when she was only fifteen, staging amateur theatricals that used her own musical compositions. Acting as her own manager, the young actress secured a producer and dispensed with her real name for the new *Dorothy Devore Revue*. With additional appearances on the stage, Dorothy was a headliner at Al Levy's and other top Los Angeles night spots for almost three years. The next step was the vaudeville circuits, but these ambitious plans for such a young girl were countermanded by a worried mother and an insistent film producer named Al E. Christie. Under the pressure of both, Dorothy finally acquiesced and accepted stardom in movie comedies at a beginning salary far below that she could have made on the stage. But within a few years, Dorothy Devore had become one of the brightest young stars in silent screen comedy.

Dorothy Devore arrived on the scene as a new movement in silent screen comedy was unfolding—the two-reel romantic comedy. While Madge Kennedy, Mabel Normand, Dorothy Gish and Connie Talmadge were investigating the box-office potential of feature-length comedy-dramas, Christie intensified his efforts to explore the possibilities of shorter films. Billie Rhodes, Ethel Lynn and Betty Compson had already participated in earlier experiments in this direction, but Dorothy Devore was to become its leading exponent in the twenties.

In so many of the World War I period comedies, love and romance had become an unbelievable affair, with cartoon characters striving for the fair maiden's hand in a carnival atmosphere, but it was Christie who began to clear the air of burlesque romance with a more believable world of love. "I played as young and petite a thing as possible," recalls Dorothy today, "and was often teamed

Dorothy Devore, as she appeared at the peak of her fame in 1928.

Dorothy's romantic comedies at Christie ultimately made her one of the highest-paid comic heroines of the twenties. In this scene from *Kiddin' Kate,* she has Jimmie Harrison wrapped around her coy little finger, as Eugenie Forde and Babe London look on.

with Earl Rodney, whose height and mass made me look even smaller and younger than I was." In *Naughty Mary Brown, Saving Sister Suzie, Fair Enough* and other Devore-Rodney pictures, the tone of her comedies was subdued, the action believable and the world was the everyday life of two young Americans. "We had none of that slapsticky stuff like Sennett," Miss Devore still notes with conviction, "we did not rely upon wild moustaches and funny clothes, but on situation and the story."

Never simply a plot device or pretty nonentity, Dorothy—and a beautiful, talented lady whose personality bordered on vivacity— was often the instrument of the story. Quite often, she exchanged impish liveliness for a calculated firmness, when rather than being the creature of impulse she would be the lady of decision. More than any one else in the Christie studio, Dorothy fitted Al Christie's ideal of a comedy heroine, for her screen image encompassed youth, good looks and a healthy reserve of energy, which carefully skirted the extremes of straight drama and pure comedy.

With few exceptions, the film world of Dorothy Devore was the world of romance, and the comedy situations revolved around

"You think this will melt the fat off sis?" Dorothy can't believe her eyes and even Babe London is a little dubious. That's Billy Bletcher in the background (with moustache) in *Kiddin' Kate*.

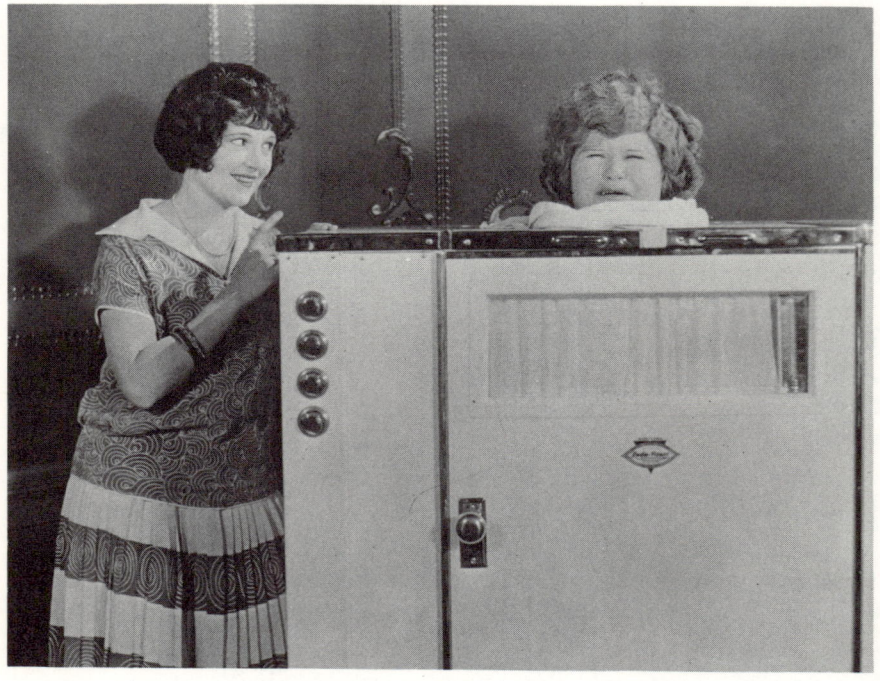

"You asked for it, troublemaker," Dorothy tells Babe London.

the comical ineptitude or mischief of the persons who surrounded her. A perfect example is *Kiddin' Katie,* in which Dorothy's plump kid sister (Babe London) hoped to win a suitor (Jimmie Harrison) through the mail by sending him a picture of her beautiful sister. When Jimmie announced an intended visit, Babe began a rigorous weight-reducing program, while Dorothy was forced to adopt the role of a child, complete with high-waisted fluffy dresses and curls. *Kiddin' Katie* was a comedy of deception that fitted neatly into the framework of Christie's comedy format. By herself, Dorothy did not precipitate the audience's laughter, but she was the cute and charming love interest (who eventually won Jimmie, of course) caught up in the comical activities of Babe, the monstrous family cook who acted as Babe's athletic trainer (Blanche Payson) and the inept little butler (Billy Bletcher).

Directed by the big guns of the Christie directors—Scott Sidney, William and Harold Beaudine and Christie himself—Dorothy's comedies rapidly became one of the industry's most sought-after series, and accordingly she quickly reached Christie's top salary of $1500 a week. As Babe London has pointed out, "Dorothy was the most valuable comedienne Christie had in the twenties; in fact, she was pretty hot property for all producers interested in comedy or light dramas." Before long, recognition of her own worth was made painfully evident to her boss, as the star comedienne requested a $1000 weekly increase in her pay envelope. After the Christie brothers' laughter had subsided, Dorothy delivered her ultimatum —either pay the extra salary or consider her unwritten contract to be cancelled. The Christies balked and Dorothy Devore walked out of their studio and into Warner Brothers—at $2500 weekly.

But Christie was to encounter the ambitious Miss Devore once again. After receiving the check for her first week's work at Warners, Dorothy entered the Christie studio business office and asked comptroller Fred Porter to cash the check as a favor. "I knew the office would never have such cash on hand," Dorothy admits today, "but within a couple of hours, everyone on the lot knew the extent of my new success. It was a beautiful example of childish spite, but in later years, Al was to think back on it as one of the most humorous incidents in his long career."

Her situation at the Warner studio was ideal for the rising young actress—a high salary, stardom in feature-length pictures and a contract written to order. She was even teamed with one of her favorite directors at Christie's, William Beaudine. But this dreamland was short-lived. "I adored Harry Warner, who was a very

The charming Miss Devore in a pensive mood from *The Prairie Wife* (a 1925 Eastern Production released by Metro-Goldwyn), in which she played the title role.

Dorothy (at left) posed for this group shot on the Christie lot at a
time (1923) when the biggest names in polite comedy worked for the
studio. Top row: Bobby Vernon, Neal Burns, Jimmy Adams, Earl Rodney, Jimmie Harrison and William Irving. Below them sit Dorothy
Devore, Vera Steadman, Charlotte Merriam, Natalie Joyce, Hazel Deane
and Babe London.

kind, soft-spoken and gentle man; but Jack and I began a long
series of clashes that eventually led to my departure from the
studio." The "last straw" was the studio's intention to cast Dorothy
in a supporting role with Rin-Tin-Tin. "Before I signed the contract,
I stipulated that I would have the right to refuse appearing in any
picture made by Warners. When I was offered the supporting role
to a dog, I knew it was time to enact the special clause in my contract. I refused and June Marlow was secured for the part." After
that incident, Dorothy examined every possibility of getting out
of her seven-year contract, which had begun to assume the char-
acteristics of an enslavement. Finally, she realized that there was
only one avenue open and so Dorothy Devore bought up her own
contract to escape into freedom.

Having worked for a variety of studios in the twenties (usually on loan from Warners), Dorothy was ready to return to the short-reel comedy form and a studio that would offer relative stability. Financially and temperamentally, Dorothy would never have returned to the Christie studio, so she proceeded to sign with the one person who could be considered Christie's boss, Earle W. Hammons (president of Christie's releasing company, Educational Film Exchanges) and his Educational Comedy studio.

Within the realm of two-reel comedy, Dorothy Devore's association with Educational was an actress's Valhalla. She was given the greatest degree of control over production that any star could possibly exercise—including the power to choose her own director and accept or refuse any story, supporting cast, wardrobe, etc. The average time allotted to production was *three* months per comedy and the production values of photography, sets and stories were among the most desirable in the entire short comedy field. Best of all, the salary was a staggering $5000 weekly!

The Educational Dorothy Devore Comedies were produced from 1927 to 1929 and within that period, Dorothy enjoyed all the benefits of her enviable position. While Mabel Normand and Billie Rhodes faded from the scene after unsuccessful attempts to return to two-reel comedies, Dorothy had returned to the romantic comedy short with an unimprovable contract and a public acclaim to match. With two of Educational's finest comedy directors, Charles Lamont and Norman Taurog, Dorothy worked at a welcomed, leisurely pace, appearing in a series of box-office successes—*Kilties, Little Rube* and *Up in Arms* in 1927; *Rah, Rah, Rah!, Cutie, Companionate Service* and *Circus Blues* in 1928; and *Auntie's Mistake* in 1929. But with the coming of sound, Dorothy Devore joined that scarce number of individuals who wisely avoided the struggle to survive in a new medium and gracefully bowed out of the silent era and motion pictures with an untarnished fame.

Sidney Drew

While slapstick of the Keystone variety was gradually dominating screen comedy in the years before the twenties, one man successfully fought the trend and emerged triumphant. This most unlikely practitioner became the model against which all other situation comics of the silent screen have been measured. One would hardly have expected an uncle of the Barrymores, half-brother of John Drew and successful leading man associated with Charles Frohman on the legitimate stage to have achieved fame as a leading motion picture comedian, but Sidney Drew was an unusual performer.

Drew and his first wife, Gladys Rankin, left the stage in 1911 to enter movies with Kalem. As with so many other stage personalities, his initial films consisted simply of his own stage sketches, familiar to all who had seen his act but unknown to the multitudes of screen audiences who had never set foot in the legitimate theater. Kalem proved to be loads of fun, but hardly the place for the Drews to build a reputation and so they went to work for Vitagraph in 1913; he as a light comedian and she as a writer.

Although in ill health, Mrs. Drew wrote a group of highly praised features before she succumbed that December. Six months later, Sidney married Lucille McVey, a scenarist and sometime actress who worked under the name of Jane Morrow. Drew began his Vitagraph career working with Anita Stewart, Dorothy Kelly and other aspiring young actresses, but real fame was to await his teaming with the second Mrs. Drew.

Sidney's early Vitagraph films defy analysis, as there seems to have been no definite pattern of characterization. In some, he played the rather sedate husband content to let the wife rule the roost; in others he was seen as the original razz-ma-tazz college kid. But almost all of his stories did contain one common element—he was cast as the nephew of a cantankerous uncle.

The husband and wife team of Sidney Drew and Lucille McVey was extremely popular between 1914–19 with their "drawing room" comedies.

Sidney Drew's earlier screen roles were somewhat out of keeping with the "polite" comedy style for which he is best remembered. Here his is in Vitagraph's *Goodness Gracious* with Clara Kimball Young at the exact moment Cupid's arrow struck. (Courtesy Blackhawk Films)

Two releases of January 1914 demonstrated the variety of his early roles. In *Goodness Gracious,* he wooed and rescued the beautiful Clara Kimball Young in the finest of melodramatic fashion, but *Jerry's Uncle's Namesake* found him borrowing three babies in a scheme to con L. Rogers Lytton out of a donation to their welfare.

By 1915, Drew and his wife had formed a team that was to offer formidable competition in the "drawing room" or situation comedy domain. Using Mrs. Drew's skill with the pen, they wrote, directed and starred in weekly comedy releases for Vitagraph until 1916, when Louis B. Mayer's newly formed Metro offered them $90,000 for a series of fifty-two single-reel comedies.

Successful in their portrayal of the typical family, the Drews played on the foibles and follies of married life. Although their stories were often built around the slightest of situations, realism was the keynote. What husband could not identify with a man who would rather walk into the sea and disappear than listen to his wife's incessant chattering? Or step into Sidney's shoes as he returned from a college reunion and discovered a glove in his coat pocket, right before his wife's eyes (who had planted it there as a reminder

His Wife Knew About It and Sidney wasn't too much of a gentleman to let the neighborhood gossips know she knew. The Drews won a large following of fans with their delightfully simple domestic comedies.

Charley Sharp, con man extraordinaire, lets the wife in on a secret in *A Safe Investment*. He's hit paydirt this time.

But wifey blew it again. Sid awaits the arrival of the police with a sigh of relief; at last he'll be alone for awhile. No policeman in his right mind would arrest Sid's beautiful but dumb wife, the cause of all his troubles.

to come home early)? Feeling trapped, who would not respond as did Drew, who concocted an elaborate story for her benefit and became so immersed in it that he persisted in his tall tale even after she revealed the truth. Such small incidents as these were woven from the fabric of life and served to place the Drews at the top of their profession.

Sidney and his wife continued their immensely successful formula at Metro for two years, but left in 1918 to appear once more on the stage. By the time their engagement was over, the pair had enjoyed a lengthy rest from the daily rigors before the camera and formed their own company (the VBK Corporation) to produce comedies for the expanding Paramount program. The clean, wholesome comedy of marital misunderstanding was their forte, and without pratfalls or pies the Drews stood out against the backdrop of slapstick that dominated the silent screen around World War I. Had Sidney Drew lived to work another decade, he would have undoubtedly been at the very top of the field in the twenties, when situation comedy came into its own.

But Sidney was not in good health and the news that his son (by his first marriage) had been killed in France just before the Armistice was signed dampened his will to live. Young Sidney Rankin Drew had followed his father's footsteps into motion pictures as a director and left a highly promising career to volunteer for service in 1917, much against Sidney's wishes. In April 1919, just six months after learning of his son's death, Sidney Drew passed away. Mrs. Drew would actively continue in the industry until her death in 1926.

The two had provided many moments of laughter for screen fans and had successfully proven that there was a place on the screen for sophisticated comedy as well as slapstick. It is not surprising that the Drew comedies remain as interesting today as when they were first shown over a half century ago, for the substance of their comedy came from real life—and marriage remains a battle of the sexes.

Jack Duffy

The silent comedy screen was alive with talented character comedians who failed to reach the heights of fame and thus slipped rather quickly into obscurity with the advent of sound. Jack Duffy was the perfect example of this species.

Jack achieved his greatest popularity in Al Christie's comedies. He was a good example of the comic whose talent was widely acknowledged by those within the business, but whose popularity with the public was limited. Small but dedicated, his informal fan club was much like the ones that have formed around such television personalities as "Schultzy" on the *Bob Cummings Show* a few years back. Few t.v. viewers know that Ann B. Davis played the part, but many quickly recall "that funny secretary" who was present in every episode. In a similar vein, most moviegoers of the twenties knew Jack as "that funny old man with the fuzzy beard and no teeth," rather than by name.

Coming to the screen in 1916 after a decade on the New York stage, Jack Duffy was in that line of screen comics whose wrath knew no bounds—Eric Campbell, Jimmy Finlayson, Billy Gilbert, et al. His usual character was the stingy Scot with the temper of an Irishman. In *Loose Change*, one of Jack's "Sandy MacDuff" series, he played the role of a Scotsman so cheap that he feigned death to let an ambulance transport him from one place to another rather than pay the bus fare.

A favorite image of Duffy remains from his 1926 comedy, *Hold Still*, as in which he played the part of an old Scottish goat pantomimically venting his fury about youth's disrespect for the elder members of society while he was dwarfed in the splendiferous surroundings of his palatial mansion. Jack was always plagued by the people around him—an inept valet (Billy Engle), and an ungrateful daughter (Ann Cornwall), who refused to marry her father's choice, a worthless son (Neal Burns), or a total boob (Billy Dooley).

Regardless of his supposed afflictions, Jack could always appreciate a pretty girl, in this case, Dorothy Devore.

Eddie Baker is in real trouble unless Walter Hiers can persuade Jack to reconsider his intentions.

The youthful Jack Duffy—in real life.

Although Jack Duffy worked with Vitagraph, L-KO and Universal, he made more comedies for Christie than for any other company, and where he was the perfect violation of Christie's basic concept of comedy. Al Christie was the leading proponent of situation comedy, but Jack was a combination of the exaggerated clown of burlesque and the obsessed figure of Jonsonian drama. As a result, the story was relegated to a secondary position by Duffy's old Scottish cheapskate.

There was also a large amount of the lecherous old goat in Jack's screen character, with the humor accentuated by the periodic shedding of infirmity in his wild acrobatics. Audiences were so amazed by the agility of this character that they refused to believe the "old man" did not use a double. Disguised by a brilliant makeup job, Jack Duffy was really a young man who performed the stunts himself. One of Duffy's greatest aids in making himself appear to be a man of seventy or more was his set of false teeth—the toothless look *was* real.

As he appeared on the screen.

On-set at the Special Pictures Corporation (circa 1920–21). Left to right—Jack Duffy, Charlotte Merriam, Neely Edwards, Margaret Cullington, Eddie Baker, Jack Ackroid and Fay Bunny. Sitting in front with the pith helmet is the director, Reggie Morris.

As Jack's acting career faded during the early thirties, he was able to fall back on his proficiency in the art of makeup, and created an entirely new career for himself. The talkies had brought an influx of stage personalities to Hollywood and the demand for skilled makeup men had mushroomed almost overnight. Thus Jack was able to remain active in the business until his death in 1939.

Louise Fazenda

Few comediennes of the silent screen were as beloved, both on- and off-screen, as Louise Fazenda. After a lengthy and successful career was brought to a close by the advent of sound, Miss Fazenda turned a considerable talent to the plight of her fellow man and even such notoriously unpleasant individuals as Hedda Hopper and Louella Parsons could not conceal their enormous admiration and respect for Louise's charitable and social work. Turning her back on a posh retirement, she devoted untold hours to the work of various non-profit organizations. In fact, finding anyone who could ever bring themselves to speak a harsh word about Louise Fazenda seems to be a near-impossibility, a most unusual commentary on the Hollywood scene.

As a youthful veteran of the stage, Louise made her first screen appearance in *The Cheese Special*, Universal's initial Joker Comedy released in October 1913. Starring Max Asher—the popular Dutch comic turned movie comedian—the Jokers were one of the most successful of the early comedy series and featured Louise, Lee Morris and Sylvion de Jardin (Bobby Vernon) in supporting roles. Louise found it necessary to match her appearance with the different location and time period of each Joker Comedy, thus the development of a fixed costume, makeup and character was ruled out at that time.

If cast in a western setting, she dressed in the boots, chaps and wide-brimmed hat befitting a filly of the wild west. Wearing high heels, full-length dress and flowery hat, she also portrayed the much-desired fair maid of the city who played for the affections of Max and his friendly enemy, Harry McCoy. But in occasional "rube" comedies, Louise did approximate the farm girl appearance and personality she later made famous as one of Mack Sennett's prized comediennes.

147

Louise Fazenda was typecast in Sennett comedies as the poor farm girl struggling to overcome her surroundings.

Louise, as she appeared in Warners pictures of the late twenties.

Louise Fazenda as the destitute and harrassed wife of Max Asher in *Lazy Louie,* a Joker Comedy of November 1913.

This rustic character was overshadowed by a variety of other roles in the Jokers—as the Queen in *Mike and Jake Among the Cannibals,* Max Asher's destitute and harassed wife in *Lazy Louie,* the fair young catch in many Mike and Jake (Asher and McCoy) comedies, the pretty flirting cashier in *The Headwaiter,* and the kind young lass who fed pies and cakes to hobo Bobby Vernon in *Jam and Jealousy.* In a word, the Joker Comedies demanded versatility from Louise, and she was certainly capable of it.

By 1914, a remarkable cast of funmakers had been assembled for the Joker Comedies. In *Love and Electricity,* Louise appeared as Max Asher's daughter in a cast that also included Vernon, Gale Henry, Billy Franey and Sam Kaufman. From this cast of six principals, five later had their own starring comedy series.

The following year, Miss Fazenda was caught up by Sennett to play leads in his Keystone Comedies and rapidly became a favorite among the gallery of Keystone buffoons and clowns. Soon perfecting the famous farm girl costume and makeup, she was seen almost constantly in callico or gingham dress, a well-worn pair of man's working shoes, homely pigtails and that obnoxiously homespun curl plastered against the middle of her forehead. Although physically strong (an asset to her typed role), Louise added a touch of the sweet, calm and pathetic feeling to an otherwise complete burlesque comedy type.

While not in the same league with the whimsical Mabel Normand, Louise managed to avoid the buxom roughness of Polly Moran, whose coarse humor contained none of the sensitive aspects which Miss Fazenda's personality and acting brought to the screen. A sympathetic character, she was usually seen trying desperately to remain loyal to a father (Dave Anderson or Bert Roach) outraged by the affections showered by some simpleton (Billy Bevan or Baldy Belmont) who appeared to represent her only escape from a dull life on the farm. Sneak elopements were a common theme in Louise's comedies.

After Sennett joined Triangle, Miss Fazenda's roles became somewhat more varied. She created a series of eccentric comedy characters, which were well-received by the fans. Louise played the ugly princess in *A Game Old Knight* with a rare sense of humor and ap-

Louise Fazenda resisted the blandishments of Fritz Schade in *A Hash House Fraud,* one of her earliest Keystone appearances.

"Come away with me," says Phil Dunham, "and you'll never go *Back to the Kitchen.*"

Joseph "Baldy" Belmont has second thoughts about taking an excited Louise *(The Gingham Girl)* with him to the city.

Father (Dave Anderson) has it in for the city slicker (Billy Armstrong) who wants Louise in *It's A Boy*.

"*Let 'Er Go*," screams Bert Roach but Billy Armstrong and Louise are too taken with each other to let Bert distract their attention.

Mack Swain bestows the well-aimed kick that starts Louise out into the cruel world in Al Christie's 1928 remake of Sennett's earlier hit, *Tillie's Punctured Romance.* Only the title and Swain remained from the original—the rest of the cast and plot had no connection with the 1914 version.

peared in *The Great Vacuum Robbery* as the worldly lady crook, extremely knowing and fascinating. As Sennett's comedy style became more sophisticated, the softer aspects of her character were emphasized. Not all of her comedies took place on the farm, but wherever she did turn up, Louise always seemed to be in the midst of a struggle against a strong, oppressive social and financial environment. Audiences were forever pulling for Miss Fazenda to overcome her surroundings in the finest Horatio Alger tradition. She rarely made it.

During the twenties, Louise drifted into choice roles in feature dramas, the dream of many character actresses and comediennes who preferred the smaller feature parts over leading roles in short subjects. But even as late as 1928, she was still appearing as the poor farm girl struggling with life, as in the Paramount-Christie remake of the 1914 Sennett hit, *Tillie's Punctured Romance.* Finally able to shake the stereotyped role of her Sennett days, she made a few features at Warner Brothers and then talking comedies for Christie, but her popularity had diminished greatly and her career really came to a halt with the introduction of sound.

To say that she lost success would be a gross error, for the vast amount of social work to which she dedicated herself after leaving the screen lifted her from self-pity and lost fame into the realm of truly great humanitarianism. The famous character Louise developed on-screen was indicative of her own, for as her friends are quick to point out, Miss Fazenda was not only a charming and distinguished lady, but one whose humility and total lack of vanity was reflected in her casting aside the proverbial beauty aids of Hollywood for the homely garb and makeup of the low-comedy farce comedienne.

Jimmy Finlayson

When James Henderson Finlayson walked through the iron gate that separated the Hal Roach lot from the rest of the world, he must have done so with considerable trepidation about his future in motion pictures. The year was 1923 and although Fin had been very successful on the stage (both in Scotland and later with a touring company of "Bunty Pulls the Strings" in the United States), his earlier comedy work for Universal, Metro and Mack Sennett had not flowered into his original expectations. While Sennett had elevated him from two-reelers to the ambitious feature-length comedies of 1919-20, Fin still seemed to be denied the opportunity to break away from supporting roles.

Instead, he was consistently cast as "second banana" to Sennett's top stars—Ben Turpin, Louise Fazenda, Ford Sterling, Charlie Murray and Billy Bevan—all of whom had secured seemingly unshakeable positions. By the time Fin left Sennett in 1922, the prospects for his own starring series seemed dim and the work that immediately followed at Metro and in Universal's Century Comedies looked about as promising as his past association had been with L-KO and Sennett. A realist at heart, Jimmy Finlayson knew that the only direction was up.

Fin's fame finally came at the Hal Roach studio, but ironically, this fame hinged upon two things—the success of Laurel and Hardy and Jimmy's return to supporting roles. While eventually winning his own starring series at Roach during the mid-twenties, the spark necessary to set off comic stardom was rarely present, even under the excellent supervision of F. Richard Jones and the direction of Stan Laurel. In *Yes, Yes Nanette* (1925), Fin's lead role as the bridegroom brought home by Lyle Tayo (a girl) was no more than an excuse for the comic disgust of her old boyfriend (Oliver Hardy) and the spirited tomfoolery of her brother and sister (Grant Gor-

This dapper young man about town? None other than Jimmy Finlayson, who rarely posed for a studio portrait in his comic makeup.

This scene from *Don't Weaken* perfectly exemplifies Jimmy Finlayson's dilemma while working for Mack Sennett. Caught between Ford Sterling and Charlie Murray, Fin's chances for success were very slight.

man and Sue O'Neill). In his series, Jimmy was simply a funny-looking stick figure pushed through comic situations and gags.

But as Roach began to place the little Scotsman back into supporting roles, first with Clyde Cook and later Stan Laurel and Oliver Hardy, the fun and fame started to blossom. His well-trimmed moustache grew into a bushy forest of hair and the facial expressions loosened up into that unforgettable facile display of his famous "double-take and fade-away." His starring roles as an undesirable suitor or flirtatious husband gave way to a choice selection of eccentric character parts and the well-tailored clothes degenerated into an ill-fitting assortment of comic costumes, the best of which was the high-buttoned cutaway suit with vest, which gave Jimmy Finlayson an appearance somewhere between an oversized scissor-tailed flycatcher and a yellow-bellied sapsucker.

A marvelous cartoon character, Fin was a caricature of man in all his shortcomings who embraced The Seven Deadly Sins with melodramatic glee. Gluttony was reflected in his common usage of the gouty foot and Covetousness in his Simon Legree intolerance and greed. While Envy, Sloth and Lust were grasped only intermittently, Wrath became his specialty. Joining the ranks of Noah Young, Tiny Sanford, Edgar Kennedy and Billy Gilbert, Fin became a member of Roach's celebrated legion of character actors whose wrath knew no bounds. Yet his anger was of a very special brand. While Young (the traditional "heavy" of evil incarnate) and Sanford (the inescapable law and order of society) tolerated no foolishness from the comedians, Kennedy and Gilbert endured such indignities up to point, registering unfathomable irritation along the way. But Fin was a soul who could only look quizzically upon his fellow man in staggering dumbfoundedness. The incredible errors in the reasoning, thought and action of a Clyde Cook or Stan Laurel met Jimmy's uncomprehending stare—that one-eyed squint of disbelief that melted into the aforementioned "double-take and fadeaway." While one eyebrow arched high above a wide-open globe, the other furrowed low over the tightly squinted eye as Jimmy scrutinized his opponents. Like the sight of a submarine periscope under attack, his double-take was the reexamination before firing.

Ben Turpin introduces *Love's Outcast*, the durable Jimmy Finlayson, to Kathryn McGuire. Fin played second banana to most of the Sennett stars before leaving to seek his fortune with other production companies.

Fanny Kelly has the goods on Jimmy now, but we're certain that Marie Prevost can explain this compromising situation to Fanny's satisfaction—or can she? If not, *The Dentist* is going to need another "able employee" to take Marie's place.

Jimmy outdid his competition (Arthur Stone) this time. But only Katherine Grant can answer the question, *Are Blonde Men Bashful?*. Fin's leading roles at Roach failed to give his career the boost it needed.

"Sugar Daddies" found the venerable Scotsman supporting the popular new team of incompetents who billed themselves as Laurel (in dress) and Hardy.

Despite his previous starring roles, Jimmy Finlayson was not star material. The great comedy of Fin was the overexaggerated comedy or reaction. A star comedian was usually either the cause of various comic misadventures or the victim of circumstance who comically fought his way out of the predicament. Fin's forte in comedy was not as cause or victim, but as the incredulous bystander forced into participation. He was the proverbial husband away on an African hunting trip who arrived home to find his wife in the arms of another man, or as in *Big Business* a man whose quiet, restful Sunday afternoon at home was interrupted by two idiots selling Christmas trees in Southern California during the summer. Fin was forever yanked into a comic melee by individuals meddling in his own private affairs. But despite his usual role of unwilling participant, Jimmy was always the exaggerated burlesque character. When he did return home from the big-game hunt to find his wife making love to another man, he entered his home still fully attired in the garb of his jungle adventure, complete with safari hat and wide-bore elephant gun.

In the Laurel and Hardy comedies of the late twenties, Fin was usually an individual attempting to perform his everyday duties in the most normal fashion possible—normal, that is, until the appearance of Mr. Laurel and Mr. Hardy. At that point, Fin's comic reactions to the absurd activities of the two master fools evolved from initial disbelief through slight irritation and gradual aggravation to total red-faced exasperation and eventual chaos. This comical route was followed most completely and devastatingly in *Big Business*. In this film the simple knock of two salesmen upon the door of Jimmy's home led eventually to shredded trees, an axe-splintered piano, uprooted shrubbery, ripped-out windows and a demolished car. Whether playing a normally contented businessman at home, a judge *(Do Detectives Think?)*, a rich oil tycoon *(Sugar Daddies)*, a stone-age father *(Flying Elephants)*, a prison warden *(The Second*

It was with Laurel and Hardy that Jimmy Finlayson became an institution to movie audiences. The pair brought out the best in Fin and he played his roles with an obvious relish, as in *Big Business*, one of the most popular two reels of organized destruction ever filmed.

Hundred Years), a store owner (*Liberty*) or a simple soda jerk (*Men O'War*), poor Jimmy was always the unsuspecting soul forced against his will (and better judgment) into an inescapable adventure with the screen's two greatest simpletons, whose incredibly moronic activities so easily peeled off that thin veneer of politeness which lightly covered Fin's immeasurable wrath.

An examination of the Laurel and Hardy comedies of 1928-29 discloses a noticeable absence of Jimmy in a considerably large portion of this team's work; the First National studio had discovered Fin's excellent character acting potential for feature film work and Jimmy engaged in a healthy series of character roles under the direction of William Beaudine. While many other character roles followed throughout the thirties and forties, and even television appearances in the early fifties, no roles ever commanded the public's attention and affections more than his work with Stan and Ollie.

Working with Laurel and Hardy, Fin's character underwent a transformation and his mannerisms loosened up into that incredible mobile facial display of his "double-take and fade-away," directed here toward Noah Young and Stan Laurel.

Fin's versatility as a character actor was recognized by the bigger studios and he did quite a number of feature roles in the declining days of the silent film. This is from First National's *Show Girl*.

In his last years, Fin began to see a revival of interest in his Laurel and Hardy comedies and before his death in 1953, Jimmy frequently attended the Silent Movie Theater in Hollywood to watch comedies he had appeared in more than two decades earlier, sitting very quietly among the children and teenagers who were laughing just as hard as their parents had many years before.

Billy Franey

Slouching along with hands in pockets, bowler jauntily perched on the back of his head and his nose, bushy moustache and chin jutting skyward with a squat cigar butt stuck in the corner of his mouth, little Billy Franey projected a studied air of defiant ignorance. There *was* a way to beat the rap known as life and Billy just *knew* he could find it. In a search for the magic formula, Franey romped from comedy to comedy throughout the twenties but he never quite found it. Always appearing to be around the next corner, success and fame managed to elude him, whether as chef, paperhanger or hobo. But in the process, Billy Franey created gales of merriment for comedy fans.

Billy first came to the attention of movie audiences in 1913 with the Universal Joker Comedies, co-starring with Louise Fazenda, Gale Henry and other comics who would rise to stardom within a decade. The Joker Comedies weren't spectacular in their humor, but filled a definite void in the rough, rugged and slightly ribald fashion of the L-KO and early Keystone tradition. Knockabout comedy of a somewhat vulgar nature seemed to prevail and Franey strutted through several years of Joker Comedies before leaving Universal to make his own series for independent release.

Often referred to as Poverty Row, the independent market seldom sent a comic upward: in fact, the direction was usually downhill. Comedians like Billy West managed to make a good living and retained their second-class comic status, but by and large, independent release seemed to be a one-way ticket to obscurity. Why then did many comics make the decision to appear in the "quickies"? The answers are as varied as the number of comedians who made the independent comedies: some felt it possible to buck the trend and rise above the supporting roles they had played for so long; others, lured by the offer to star in their own series, ignored the con-

sequences; then there were those who simply had no other choice—
if they worked at all, it had to be in independent comedies.

Billy Franey made the move late in 1920, signing with the
newly formed Reelcraft Film Corporation to do his own series of
single reels. Independent producers tended to cut every possible
corner to maximize their profits—a sad fact of life and one that made
this type of release so precarious. Their main interest was in disposing of the territories for their product, leaving the bulk of advertising and promotion to the exchanges, which would eventually
distribute the films. Such exchanges were in no financial position
to properly exploit the films, relying instead on word-of-mouth and
market demand for their sales. As a fair share of stardom resulted
from concentrated advertising and exploitation, because of this system many good comics never received their just due.

The Reelcraft Franey Comedies were directed by George Jeske
and Tom LaRose, who kept the quality at a high level for independent productions. There's no way of knowing how much money was
spent on these films, but the writing, as well as Billy's comic im-

Mother-in-laws aren't too smart. For that matter, neither are wives.
Billy always got a kick out of wash day but Gale Henry didn't think it
humorous.

Is this our Billy Franey about to take a bribe from Milt Uhl as Eddie Baker keeps watch?

provision, provided some very humorous situations as jumping-off points for a comic follow-through and Franey was equal to the challenge. This series of independent comedies is gradually coming to light today, one or two films at a time, and each new discovery serves to buttress the opinion held by the many Franey fans of a generation or two ago—Billy was a darn good comedian!

Much of Franey's material was clever, and as such was a refreshing change from the average comedy offerings of the twenties. Billy seems to have been at his best when the script called for a bunko artist or confidence man. Never too well dressed, he nonetheless came across on-screen as one who could con a little old lady out of her life savings or part a youngster from his all-day sucker with equal success. His air of self-assurance that he was more than capable of the task at hand came across very well on the screen and in comedies like *The Water Plug* (1920), the viewer felt compelled to sympathize with Billy in his attempt to extract a few fast dollars from the local suckers, using a phony water hydrant and a tin badge. Satirizing ticket fixing, seemingly as prevalent in the twenties as it is today, Franey created an empathy with his audience immediately, as they hissed the police and cheered the little con man.

Billy's first series did not make him a star, nor did the other independent comedies he made during the twenties, but they did serve as a showcase for a talent that might well have shone far

Somebody lost money when they hired Billy Franey, *The Paper Hanger.*

Every now and then, Billy would spend a night out with his friends, *Fixing Lizzie.*

brighter had lady Luck chosen Franey for one of her smiles. Nevertheless, his talent was sufficient to guarantee him supporting comedy roles in major features for Universal, First National, Metro-Goldwyn-Mayer and Paramount. Although lacking the artistry of Chaplin or Keaton, Billy was far above the average silent screen comedian of his period. It was his misfortune to operate within the framework of independent production. In the shadow of overpublicized comedians who had armies of press agents beating their drums, Billy Franey has been long overlooked and nearly forgotten by film historians. Only the aging fans who once cheered and laughed at the antics of this funny little man really remember this clever screen comic today.

Ham and Bud

(*LLOYD HAMILTON and BUD DUNCAN*)

The ultimate success of any screen comedian rested in the depth of the character he portrayed and the universality of its appeal; Chaplin, Keaton and Lloyd all developed comedy characters that deeply touched the *common* man. Other comics of the silent era managed to reach him to some degree, and the extent to which they moved their audience determined their ultimate success or failure.

Lloyd V. Hamilton and Albert Duncan provided a fine example of the possible variations which fame took. Already cavorting on the screen in 1914 when Hamilton reached Kalem via musical comedy, burlesque and Frontier Films, Duncan was hired from Apollo to help support the reigning Kalem funmakers, Johnny Brennan and Ruth Roland. Writing, directing and acting in these short comedies, Marshall Neilan (who later became a well-known director) soon realized that he actually had two comedy units working in one group. The newcomers seemed to hold more promise than his stars and so the team of Ham and Bud was born.

Ham and Bud began working together in their own comedies in mid-1914, but the "Ham and Bud" series began officially with *Ham at the Garbage Gentleman's Ball* in March 1915. Both comedians dressed in the ill-fitting clothes regarded at the time as standard comic garb, but over 6 feet tall and weighing more than 200 pounds, Hamilton appeared colossal in comparison to little (4' 11") Bud Duncan. This great contrast in size played a very prominent part in their Kalem comedies. For example, after surviving a series of misadventures with an irate Moslem prince and his bloodthirsty servants in *Ham and the Harem*, Ham and Bud were captured as trespassers and brought before the prince. While in the presence of the villain, Bud nervously gripped Ham's lower pant leg for

Lloyd Hamilton, the star of Educational's Hamilton Comedies.

security, giving the effect of a small child beside his protective father.

Ham and Bud soon became adept at working such scenes into their single reels and a typical ending would find the two admitting failure in strange but touching ways. Before resigning themselves to a watery grave, Ham would bid fond farewell to his little partner by bending over and lightly kissing Bud on the top of his forehead, with Bud reciprocating on tip toes in this final gesture of friendship.

As with most single-reel comedies of this period, the Ham and Bud films were slapdash affairs filmed in a few days. They consisted of the most simple of plots, which were highly contrived to allow the team to become involved with the widest range of characters in an equally varied number of locations. But Neilan had been correct; Ham and Bud quickly became the most popular Kalem comedians. Ruth Roland went on to fame as a serial queen but John

Lloyd Hamilton's real break came when he left Kalem to join Fox, where he met Henry Lehrman. Lehrman put him on the road to prosperity in comedies like *A Twilight Baby*.

Hamilton (holding blanket) had not completely developed the character that would bring him fame when he joined Jack White in 1920.

Brennan's brief fling in the limelight had turned to almost instant obscurity.

During 1916-17, the team's popularity suffered because the Kalem product was being handled by the General Film Company, the distribution arm of the Patents Trust. General Film had lost considerable ground before the determined onslaught of independent firms and public exposure to Ham and Bud lessened each month as fewer exhibitors dealt with General Film. Their association with Kalem came to an end just before Frank Marion sold out to Vitagraph in 1917.

Although Ham and Bud appeared in over two hundred single reels for Kalem, most of which were reissued after World War I by Jans Producing Corporation, only a few of these had been located until just recently. Viewing the increasing number of Ham and Bud Comedies today, a first impression of Ham is the interesting similarity to Buddy Ebsen's "Jed Clampett" of television's *Beverly Hillbillies* fame. When compared to Ham's later comedies, it is clear

Ham and Bud are in trouble again. Perhaps Marin Sais will plead for their lives in *Ham in the Harem.* Little Bud Duncan never again achieved the success he knew in the Kalem Comedies of 1914–17.

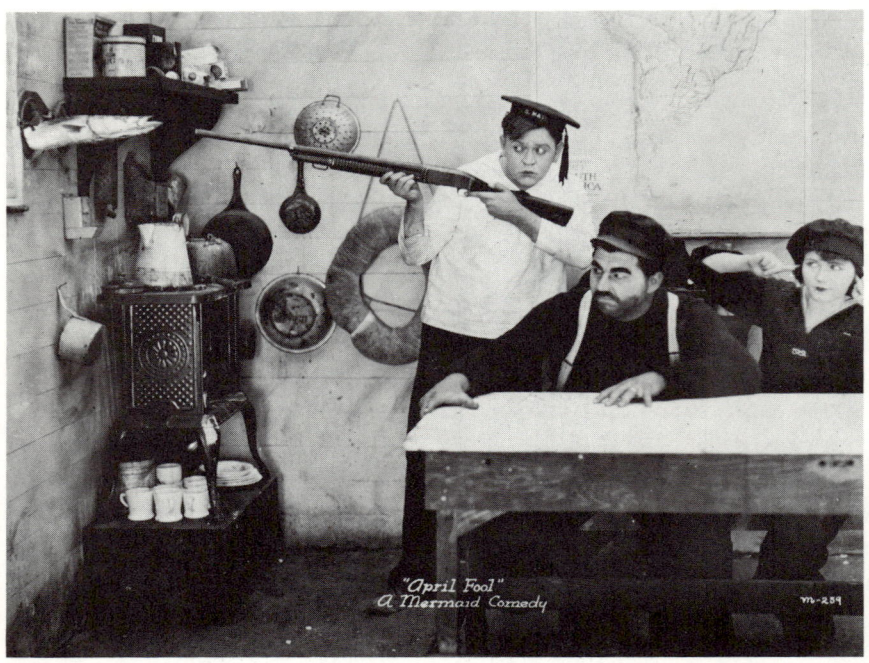

The Mermaid Comedies were so successful that Lloyd opened his own company.

that Hamilton retained little of the Kalem character in his later success and that Duncan was little more than a shadowing foil for the ubiquitous Ham.

Bud, who had carried the Kalem comedies by himself for six months in 1915 while Hamilton was sidelined with a broken leg, attempted a change of scenery with National Film's Clover Comedies, but his efforts were short-lived. Duncan's comedy character was firmly attached to that of Hamilton and his subsequent career proved almost as bleak as had Brennan's.

Bud Duncan had no distinctive identity or characterization of his own sufficient to stand by itself and no one else seemed to need a runt for a partner. Working when and where he could, whenever something came his way, Bud's one peak in an otherwise fading career came in August 1920 when he signed to make a series of single-reel comedies for the Shiller Production Company, with release through the independent Reelcraft Film Corporation. Entitled the "Bud and His Buddies" series, Duncan and Nancy Deavers worked hard but the results did nothing to halt a sliding career. While Ham met the challenge of change, Bud Duncan soon became only a memory in the pages of screen history.

Joining the Fox Sunshine Comedies being produced by Henry Lehrman, Hamilton was able to make the switch to more substantial comedy work. Lehrman spent weeks and several thousand dollars to make a two-reel film. Given the additional time and money with which to work, Ham's stay at Sunshine proved to be a transitional step from the formative years at Kalem to a full development of his comedy characterization as it appeared on the screen under the Educational banner during the twenties.

Equally important to his career was the association with Jack White, soon to become head of Mermaid Comedies and a fine director of short comedies. Together, White and Hamilton worked to develop a bumbling character that can be best compared to Jackie Gleason's "Poor Soul." Complete with pancake hat and ducklike walk, Hamilton's portrayal was in this same vein and by the time he left Lehrman's employ to join White at Mermaid in 1920, Ham had become the epitome of the fumbling hero who tried to do his best, but somehow always managed to fail. It was a portrayal done by numerous other comedians with varying degrees of success, but stamped with the popular personality of Lloyd V. Hamilton, it won him a growing body of fans.

By 1924, Hamilton was confident enough in his ability to form

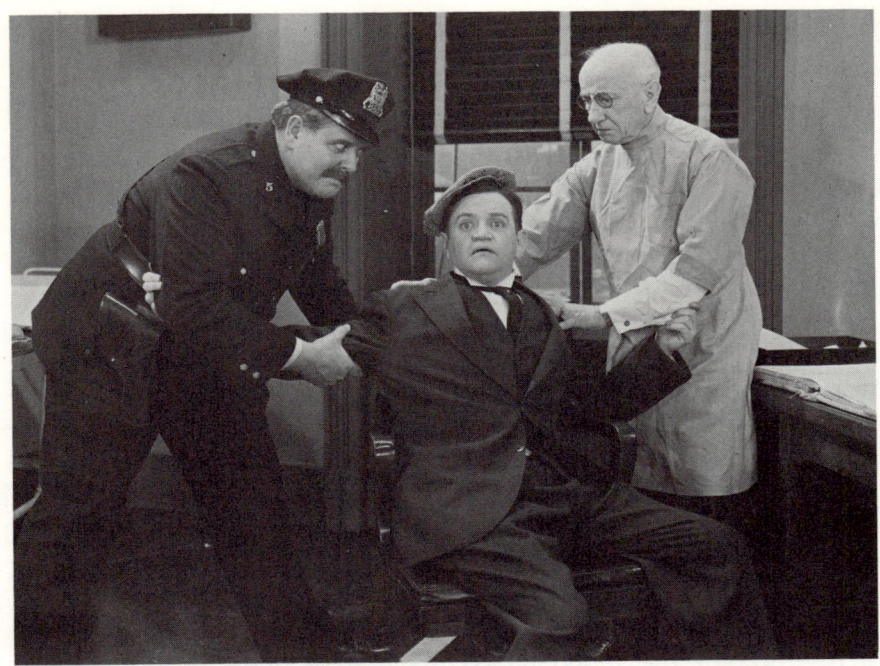

The Depression, financial reverses and failing health forced Hamilton to give up his own company in 1931. But Ham continued to make comedies like *Too Many Highballs* until his death in 1935.

Making the transition to sound without difficulty, Ham and Marjorie Beebe are about to settle a score with Dorothy Granger in Sennett's *False Impressions*.

his own company. Released through Educational, the Hamilton Comedies resulted from this most creative period. These were also his most popular years. With his screen character honed razor-sharp during a full twenty minutes of clean and solid fun for all, these two-reelers carried Ham into the sound era. But under the gathering clouds of bad times, financial reverses and failing health, Hamilton was forced to give up his own company in 1931 and went to work for Universal and then Mack Sennett, where his popularity with the audiences continued unabated until death ended his career in 1935 at the age of forty-eight.

Gale Henry

From opera diva to screen comedienne; if this sounds like an ideal story line for a slapstick comedy short, you've captured the feeling for the kind of comedy we've been discussing. But for our purposes, it's a capsule career of Gale Henry, one of the most clever and popular of the early screen comediennes. After a three-year engagement with the Temple Opera Company in Los Angeles, Gale joined Universal's Joker Comedy Company in 1914, replacing Harry McCoy who had moved over to Keystone. The Joker Comedies were cranked out fast and furiously, averaging one a week, and Gale was kept busy, most often seen on-screen as the hen-pecking wife who interrupted her slaving over a hot stove or washtub long enough to hurl a few dishes at her irresponsible husband (most often Max Asher).

Miss Henry's histrionic talents were considerable and although the Joker Comedies were not really an ideal showcase for an actress, Gale quickly impressed those with whom she worked. As Max Asher's widow, Hazel, recently pointed out, "Gale was really a consummate actress but she could make pictures quickly and well, which certainly made her a valuable property for Universal and Joker." When the Joker comics gravitated to other studios Gale fell heir to the role of lead comic, sharing the principal starring roles with Billy Franey.

In 1915, Asher rejoined Gale at Powers to make *Lady Baffles and Detective Duck,* Universal's successful parody of its own popular Grace Cunard-Francis Ford cliff-hanging serials. For the next three years, Miss Henry continued to turn out a variety of one- and two-reel comedies under the Joker and Powers banners, working quite often with a young, energetic comedy director, William Beaudine, whose early efforts at screen comedy also happened to be some of Gale's best-received comedies of the period—*The Man With*

Gale Henry successfully transferred her talents from the field of opera to Universal's Joker Comedies. Her unusual resemblance to Olive Oyl of the Popeye comic strip, both in appearance and comedic style, is impossible to overlook. Here she feeds Lee Morris as an irate Max Asher prepares to clean house.

a Package, The Boss of the Family and particularly, *When Damon Fell for Pythias.*

By.1918, Gale Henry's reputation as a screen comedienne had become firmly established and she left Universal for a few months of rest before organizing her own production company to make two-reel comedies. Supported by Milburn Morante, Hap Ward and Eddie Baker, Gale's Model Comedies were produced at the Bulls Eye studio on Santa Monica by Bruno J. Becker (Gale's husband) and released by Reelcraft Pictures Corporation. With her very first film, *A Wild Woman* (May 1919), Gale entered the rarified atmosphere of featured comediennes; very few women of that period (or any other) ever secured their own starring comedy series. The ever-present "heavy" in these comedies, Eddie Baker, recalled those days shortly before his death in 1967. "Gale had her own comedy writers, but most of the scripts were of the 'boy-meets-girl' variety and we followed them pretty loosely. If we thought of a gag on-set, we'd work it in." Eddie also recalled a practice not unusual for comediennes of the time: "Gale also performed her own stunts. She had to. We had stuntmen for something very extraordinary, but half your battle to be a comic in those days was the ability to do your own falls—and Gale did, too!"

Miss Henry's popularity as a Reelcraft comic was matched only by their Billy West series, as the Alice Howell and Billy Franey series had just started to catch on with the public. Measured by the standards of most independent comedies of this time, the Model Comedies had a surprisingly long life and Gale kept busy for almost three years before Reelcraft finally collapsed financially. Faced with the innumerable problems of refinancing and restructuring her Model Film Company, as well as obtaining a new distribution outlet, Gale took the easy way out by graduating to character roles in feature comedies. Her first work in this capacity came at Metro in *The Hunch* (1921) and *Quincy Adams Sawyer* (1922), followed by

Gale's eccentric comedy abilities were well used in the Joker Comedies, which also featured Louise Fazenda, Bobby Vernon (center) and Max Asher.

a seemingly infinite number of other eccentric character roles for a lengthy list of studios.

Gale's approach to comedy had an amazingly strong resemblance to the Olive Oyl of Popeye fame, an analogy that may seem far-fetched to those who have never seen her on-screen. The tall, lanky form of Miss Henry and the spindly arms and legs of Olive Oyl matched each other in their towering awkwardness; their heads looked like enlarged eggs with tight little mouths, long pencil-thin eyebrows and beady little eyes painted onto the smooth, oval surface. With the amazing receding chins and ugly pig-tails, the portrait of each was complete and a perfect match of two essentially cartoon characters.

Despite an increasing number of parts in features, Gale refused to discard the two-reel comedy format that had brought her fame and she periodically returned to the small comedy studios to appear in films like *Soup to Nuts,* the Neal Burns Christie comedy of 1925. Playing the tall, aloof sister of Neal's wife (Vera Steadman), Gale

When Gale left Universal in 1919 to appear in independent comedies, Eddie Baker, Billy Franey and Milburn Morante left with her. Within a few months, Franey and Morante also had their own starring series for Reelcraft.

Curious to find out *How Max Got His Raise,* Gale dropped into the office only to discover that now her husband had his own secretary. It looks as if Max is about to take a long business trip for his health.

Running for Fire Chief, Gale's campaign goes rather badly. . . .

Until she gets to the issues in *Her First Flame*, a model comedy of 1920.

was marvelously expressive as she looked down figuratively and literally upon the unimpressive and awkward Neal. She had replaced the usually ugly, unkempt clothing of her earlier comedies with the fashionable dress of the twenties, but when Gale registered the whole gamut of emotions upon her face as she sipped a horribly ill-prepared bowl of soup in one of the oldest sight gags on film, it was readily apparent that the "new" Gale Henry had lost none of the comic abilities so successfully demonstrated in her comedies made a decade before.

As is the case of numerous others in the ranks of The Clown Princes and Court Jesters, Gale Henry's obscurity today results not so much from a lack of talent as it does from a scarcity of prints of her work. While Gale's particular artistry does not qualify with the supposed timelessness of the Kings of Comedy, it does have many entertaining moments and stands out as some of the finer female comedic work of the silent era. As this is being written, several of Miss Henry's comedies are in the process of being made available to those interested in silent films and if you've never seen Gale in action, we heartily recommend investigating this fine comedienne and her eccentric comedy style—laughter is always worth the effort.

Alice Howell

Between the genius of Mabel Normand and the bevy of beautiful but untalented girls supporting most silent screen comedians lay a promised land occupied by only a handful of females. Looking back today, the comedy screen appears to have been a man's domain, for while many women tried, relatively few succeeded in scaling the heights to comic stardom, achieving both the status of comedienne and carrying the comic action in leading roles. One who rose from the ranks to delight movie-goers of the twenties was Alice Howell.

At twenty-two, Alice was a veteran of the vaudeville stage when, breaking up the popular act of Howell and Howell, she joined Keystone in 1914. Relegated to roles that most often found her appearing as a scrub woman, her stay with the Sennett organization lasted but a year. Needing a female comic to do leading parts and unable to sign Mabel Normand, Henry Lehrman beckoned and Alice moved to L-KO. Cast opposite Billie Ritchie, she had no competition from either Louise Orth or Gertrude Selby, both beautiful girls but not real comediennes. Although the L-KO Comedies were virtually imitations of the Keystones, this time Alice had the leading roles.

Alice Howell practically outlasted L-KO, remaining with the company until the spring of 1917, when she became the leading lady in Jack Blystone's new Century Comedies. Formerly an L-KO director, Blystone had decided to form his own company for independent release, and interestingly enough the Stern Brothers eventually bought into Century. This again gave Universal release of Miss Howell's films just before L-KO was closed down in 1919. But Alice was a comedy star in her own right and no longer supported male comics. She didn't feel like supporting animals either and when the Sterns decided to make the Century Comedies a showcase for animal antics, Alice left.

Alice Howell at the height of her popularity in the early twenties.

How had she done it? Mainly by hard work, talent and a wild comic appearance. Two large and prominent eyes filled her small round face, which was usually set in a vacuous stare and framed by a fuzzy hairdo piled high on her head, giving the impression that she was taller than her 5′ 3″. Compared to the majority of comediennes active at the time, her sense of comic timing was unusually well developed and a penguin-like shuffle moved the entire absurd character around in just the manner her appearance suggested. Not above a pratfall or two, Alice Howell rode an empty-headed portrayal to the top.

Her departure from Century was not unexpected, but for her to have signed a contract with an obscure and independent production company in Chicago was surprising. Ordinarily, this was the fastest way to the bottom, but the Emerald Motion Picture Corporation merged shortly with Bulls Eye to form Reelcraft, a production and distribution unit that proved to be one of the most solid independents in the business during 1920-21. The Alice Howell company was transferred from Chicago back to Los Angeles in

June 1920, and the following month Alice went before the camera again to continue the series that had made her one of the two leading Reelcraft attractions.

Directed by Richard Smith, the Alice Howell comedies were low-burlesque charades and as such were slanted toward the neighborhood and second-run houses, where they found receptive audiences. Comedies such as *Lunatics in Politics* and *His Wooden Legacy* utilized Alice's years of slapstick experience in a variety of roles. As the unemployed maid in *Cinderella Cinders,* Alice won out over a score of applicants in what was surely the most humorous race to an interview ever put on film. Her new job lasted just long enough for all aspiring maids to pick up sufficient hints on how to stay permanently unemployed.

By late 1921, Reelcraft had stumbled into the same pit-falls that

It's Alice Howell and friend in a scene from *One Wet Night,* an hilarious comedy that also featured Neely Edwards and Bert Roach. Two of Alice's trademarks are shown here—the frightful hairdo and her wide-eyed look. The third, her manner of walking, can't be shown in a photograph but several good Howell comedies have recently been made available to the public and should be seen by all comedy fans.

Alice can't believe it! Her husband is *Under A Spell* but the doctor is confident he can break it. Pity poor Neely Edwards when he snaps out of it; Alice has a grievance list two miles long.

so many independents before it had discovered—every series had to be a money maker. The Reelcraft releases included several unprofitable series, which sapped the financial strength provided by Alice Howell and Billy Franey. However Alice departed before the inevitable crash occurred and surfaced again at Universal, in what was probably her finest series.

During the early twenties, Universal was a barren wasteland for comedy fans but before his departure to M-G-M, Irving Thalberg had set out to recapture the once-profitable market. Alice Howell reappeared on the lot, this time sharing billing with Neely Edwards and Bert Roach. Half of the vaudeville team of Flanagan and Edwards, Neely entered movies as one of the Hallroom Boys, a cartoon strip brought to life by the Cohn brothers. Roach had been a supporting comic on the Sennett and Christie lot.

Neely and Alice usually portrayed a married couple with Roach as their faithful butler. The three comics worked together perfectly and out of this collaboration came some of Universal's most memorable comedies of the twenties. Starting with the usual framework provided by the situation comedy format, directors William Watson and Richard Smith inserted a sufficient amount of subdued slapstick to flavor these single reels with laugh after laugh. *One Wet Night* depicted the adventures of Neely, who lost in his race against a rainstorm on his way home from work. Arriving completely soaked, he asked the butler (Roach) for a dry suit and was lead to the window, to see all of his clothes airing on the line in the downpour.

Company appeared for dinner and in the process of fondling Neely's new shotgun, one guest blew a four-foot hole in the ceiling, filling the living room in a deluge of water. From this point on, Alice and Roach took over and each of their attempts to stem the tide ended with increasing failure as one laugh multiplied into others.

Under A Spell cast Alice as the doubting wife who hired a quack to check out her suspicions by hypnotizing Neely. Demonstrating his abilities, the quack mesmerized Neely into believing himself a monkey and was promptly laid out cold by a vase shattered over his head. Escaping in the confusion, Neely led Alice and Bert on a merry chase involving speeding autos and antics on a high tension line, giving Alice the opportunity, among others, to perform a perfectly ludicrous dance scene at the foot of a tree. These Universal comedies added up to an ideal showcase for Miss Howell's talents.

Alice Howell's career as a leading comedienne extended well over a decade, an unusual accomplishment for a female comic. Brains (or the apparent lack of them) rather than beauty kept Alice in this enviable position and the sight of her wide-eyed, innocently blank expression brought many well-deserved laughs from appreciative audiences. Few other comediennes enjoyed such popularity during their careers. Even fewer enjoyed the accolade given her only a few years ago by the late Stan Laurel, who when asked to name the ten greatest comediennes of all time, ranked Alice Howell among them without hesitation.

Lupino Lane

The success of many screen comedians was due in large measure to the material with which they had to work, and comedy gag writers were increasingly hard-pressed in the twenties to keep up with the great demand for fresh and original ideas. Like Clyde Cook, Lupino Lane was a stage comic whose screen material often failed to do him justice, but unlike Cook, his films were quite popular in the closing years of the silent screen.

Lane, whose forte was acrobatic comedy, came from an illustrious English stage family, and long before appearing on the American screen, Lupino had been popular in English films. In 1915, he had rented studio space at Clapham Park and formed his own company, Little Nipper Films. *Nipper's Bank Holiday* introduced Lupino's stage character to the screen in an interesting, if not altogether successful, series of one-reel comedies. Two years later, he joined the Homeland Company to do *The Blunders of Mr. Butterbun* and then made a series of "Kinekatures" for Hagen and Double in 1918.

His two-reel novelty numbers used distorting mirrors to give the actors a bizarre appearance and were popular for a short time. Typical of such celluloid caricatures, "The Blunders of Mr. Butterbun" (a series) followed the misadventures of Lupino and a mysterious Babylonian ring, which, when rubbed correctly, reproduced everything in an unusual manner. As its popularity quickly waned, this series of longer novelties was soon replaced by one of single reels, which also used the distortion technique (i.e. *The Haunted Hotel*). Although Lupino was an extremely versatile comic (as he demonstrated in 1929 with *Only Me,* in which he played all twenty-five roles), something was clearly lacking. The English producers had misused his talent and as a result, few of these pictures fairly represented Lane's real abilities.

189

The little acrobatic tumbler came to America in 1920, making his Broadway debut in September with the English production of *Afgar,* which was a smash hit, and by October 1921, Lupino had been approached by Fox representatives who wanted him for their quiescent screen comedy program. Unable to join Fox until his stage contract expired, Lane's first American comedy (*The Broker*) did not appear until March 1922.

The youthful Lupino Lane came from a distinguished family prominent in the English theater since the time of Charles I. When this picture was taken in 1926, he was the fourteenth member of his family playing on the stage or in pictures.

A rare production still taken on the set of Lupino Lane's *His Private
Life*, written and directed by William Goodrich. Lupino was one of the
few individuals to give Roscoe Arbuckle work after the tragic scandal
of 1921 had died out.

Lupino's Fox comedies brought no great stampede to the box-
office and after two seasons, he went back to the stage and the
Ziegfeld Follies. The Fox program, which had started off so well
in 1917 under Henry Lehrman, was now rapidly losing its head of
steam, and although Clyde Cook, Al St. John and a variety of
lesser comics were working under the Fox banner at this time, the
decline was well underway. Fox did not seem to be comedy conscious or even committed to the art of laughter at this time. Interestingly enough, none of the major studios ever really excelled in the
production of short comedies.

The most popular one- and two-reel comedies in the twenties
were those produced by Sennett, Al Christie, Hal Roach and an
organization with the unlikely name of Educational Film Corporation of America, headed by Earle Hammons. Educational had been
Hammon's brainchild in 1919, formed with the avowed purpose of

distributing films to schools, but his original idea proved to be highly unprofitable—the educational establishment did not beat down Hammon's door, and he turned to the production and distribution of short subjects. In the latter twenties, much of the originality on the comedy screen appeared under the Aladdin's lamp trademark, truly "The Spice of the Programme."

Lupino came back to the American screen in 1925 with a series for Educational that lasted through 1929. This time he had guidance from the skilled direction of Charles Lamont, William Goodrich (Roscoe Arbuckle's pseudonym) and Norman Taurog, as well as excellent support from his brother, Wallace Lupino (who also had his own series of Cameo Comedies released by Educational) and that thoroughly "heavy" heavy, Glen Cavender. Scripts were written around Lane's acrobatic comedy style although he developed a more definite screen character as time passed. Norman Taurog later described these comedies to the authors as, "A little more story, a

Lupino Lane, as *Monty of the Mounted*—the grimly determined nitwit who was his own worst enemy—about to set out on the trail of Black Pete and disprove the famous NWMP slogan. (Courtesy John Hampton)

There are *Hectic Days* ahead for dude gamblers, as Lupino is about to discover. (Courtesy John Hampton)

little more situation, combined with a certain flavor of wild gags. If Lupino threw something and he thought he was aiming at you and hit a policeman instead, he never knew it until the cop came up and touched him. Then you saw the black eye on the cop and then Lupino realized it. Lupino Lane was always the cause and the effect would happen to somebody else." The Lupino Lane of *Maid in Morocco, Monty of the Mounted* and *Sword Points* was a grimly determined nitwit who proved to be his own biggest enemy, yet always managed to emerge triumphant in spite of himself.

Lupino played every role with a faint trace of a smile and a touch of the childlike Harry Langdon was present in many of his portrayals. But unlike Langdon, none of the vindicative appeared, for Lane's screen character was of a more adult persuasion. Understanding feminine advances, he even encouraged such, but it was his own ineptness that stood in the way as the major obstacle to be overcome.

"Gosh, it's nice of you fellows to wait for me." Our hero Lupino is in trouble in *Sword Points*, his 1928 burlesque of the Three Musketeers theme. (Courtesy John Hampton)

While much of Lupino's material was uneven and one-dimensional, occasionally a near-brilliant parody such as *Roaming Romeo* (released in England and often referred to as "Bending Hur") would emerge from the Educational lot. (Courtesy John Hampton)

The acrobatic virtuosity of this stage comic turned screen hero was complemented by a variety of amusing props. Perhaps the most popular was "Yellow Streak," a rubber-jointed facsimile of a horse that appeared in several of his comedies. Actually a pair of contortionists clothed to look like a horse, "Yellow Streak" provided the perfect foil for Lupino's uncanny acrobatic stunts and Lane became the logical successor to a fading Larry Semon's mantle.

Lupino Lane combined his Hollywood career with stage appearances; while filming the season's releases in 1928, he appeared on the same bill at Los Angeles's Orpheum Theater with a young Jack Benny. Although many reviewers praised his screen work, most agreed in print that Lupino was even better with his role in the stage spectacular, *Play Bits,* and as sound overwhelmed the industry in 1929-30, Lupino left the screen and returned to the stage, always his first love.

The few of his comedies available today reveal Lupino Lane as an extremely interesting and often very funny comic whose material seems uneven and one-dimensional too much of the time, allowing his full potential to shine through only occasionally in near-brilliant parodies such as *Roaming Romeo.* This poses the fascinating question of how best his myriad talents might have been used, for while not approaching the timeless quality of Chaplin, Keaton or Lloyd, Lupino Lane's countless acrobatic antics have weathered the test of time much better than the work of many of his contemporaries.

Harry Langdon

Few comedians ever made it to the top and re-
mained there for very long without the help of a healthy degree
of self-confidence. But that very factor which often made success
possible was also capable of destroying its possessor. Harry Langdon was one comic whose misdirected faith in his own abilities
ruined his career just when it appeared to be shifting into high gear.

Harry came to the movies in late 1923, directly from a headline
vaudeville act, and it was his good fortune to enter the business
with the Mack Sennett studio; it's doubtful that any other producer
could have harnessed his comic ability as well as did Sennett. The
newcomer was turned over to Erle Kenton and Roy Del Ruth, two
of Mack's best directors, but it was with a third one, Harry Edwards,
that Langdon really clicked. Beginning with *Smile Please* in 1924
(although his second film, *Picking Peaches*, was released first),
Harry worked his way through comedy after comedy, his career
gathering additional momentum with every new release. Reacting
very favorably toward the antics of the bewildered and naive screen
character which Langdon portrayed, audiences little realized that
it was a mirror reflection of the man himself.

The essence of humility, Langdon's screen character was always
anxious to be accepted by others—willing to go to any extreme for
approval, but forever doubting his own worth. The hesitant wave
of a hand, unbelieving blink of the eyes and uncomprehending raise
of the eyebrows signified a man unsure of both himself and the
world around him. Audience identification with Harry Langdon
proved to be quick and easy, for he represented the doubts and
fears common to all humanity. In so doing, he created a portrayal
filled with life, equal in all respects to Chaplin's Tramp.

Charlie's Tramp was a man—one who chased girls and met the
world on adult terms. Harry's character was a child—women chased

Seriously challenging the Kings of Comedy in the late twenties, Harry Langdon was one of the true comic geniuses of the screen.

him for reasons he could not begin to understand. But this infantile characterization won him thousands of fans—women who wanted to mother the baby-faced innocent and men who immediately felt superior to his ridiculous behavior.

This was basically the same character he had played in vaudeville when his act consisted of helpless frustration with a balking automobile. The costume and makeup came from the stage—tight-fitting waistcoat, slightly enlarged pants and shoes, and the white face of the pantomimist. Having created this humble being and certain routines in which to use him, Langdon was not quite certain what else could be done with the character. This was the role to be played by Harry Edwards. Working with Frank Capra's scripts, Edwards took the basic character and coached Langdon on its relationship with each new environment. Out of these sessions came some of the finest visual comedies ever made.

An intensely serious practitioner of comedy developed beneath the simpleton exterior of Langdon's character. Harry himself re-

Although it was released as his second film, *Smile Please* was actually Langdon's first screen comedy. Alberta Vaughn and Jack Cooper supported the sad-faced clown.

A characteristic Langdon situation that brought both laughter and tears from the fans. Harry was given a "political" job in Chinatown in a futile attempt to keep him out of trouble in *Feet of Mud.*

garded the very creation of comedy as a "tragic" responsibility and once admitted he felt a comedy studio to be the saddest place on earth, with "more worry, more disappointment, more genuine heartbreak" in the achievement of comedy than tragedy. He considered the four greatest stimuli to laughter to be rigidity, automatism, absentmindedness and unsociability. This theory was reflected in his blank amazement of the world around him (rigidity), hesitant wonder of repeatedly confusing action (automatism), continual neglect of responsibility (absentmindedness) and infant conception of love (unsociability). Yet, Langdon's comedy was not the comedy of serious satire endeavoring to push man into virtuous action, but comedy that would permit the audience to briefly forget its troubles.

Harry's films for Sennett were short—never over three reels long—and many of them were filled with Sennett tricks that had already become clichés—cartoon drawings, impossible gags, slightly

"Oh, oh, what comes next?" Natalie Kingston has designs on our soldier boy in *All Night Long* but he doesn't recognize it. This infantile reaction was typical of Harry's on-screen encounters with women.

unreal endings, and concentration upon speed and action instead of pantomime. Yet, viewers were still brought to a state of sympathy for the little fellow, punctuated periodically with laughs. He might be garbed in a doughboy's uniform *(All Night Long, Soldier Man)*, Scottish kilts *(The Sea Squawk)*, or a lumberjack's wool clothes *(Boobs In The Woods)*; but the uncomprehending raise of eyebrows of the simpleton, the stiff gait of an infant learning to walk, the child-like confrontation with the opposite sex, the endless, almost imperceptible hesitancies, and the innocent extension of his hand in a combination greeting and feeble handshake were all present in the essential Langdon comedy character that emerged full-blown in the last Sennett comedies and First National features.

Langdon was slow getting into a gag—slower even than Chaplin, who had greatly exasperated Sennett a decade earlier with his lack of concern for speed. A good part of any Langdon situation began with his soulful stare at the camera, blinking eyes cautiously moving from one side to the other as emotion began to well up and envelop his pallid little face. But Harry's screen character also had its own special streak of childish savagery. He could stand by and watch his trunk willfully destroyed by a careless baggageman, shrugging his shoulders after neatly placing his key in the center of the ruins; but he could also lie to a representative of the law and then threaten to throw rocks at the unsuspecting officer before beating a hasty retreat to safety.

Langdon's stubbornness began to assert itself as his comic stature grew. Gag-writer and director James Gruen worked with Harry and recalled him as a difficult comedian to direct. "He had a set of mannerisms that he used over and over for every picture and these tricks were funny, but to deviate from them at all was terribly hard for him. It was almost impossible to convince Harry that an action different from ones he had used before would be funny. If he couldn't 'feel' it, he would refuse to try it."

As confused as his on-screen adventures, Harry's personal life

Fireman Harry to the rescue in *His First Flame*. The odds are even that he'll burn the house down saving it.

was complicated by five marriages, and as his fame increased so did his salary—and so did his alimony payments. Mack Sennett reputedly paid Harry $7500 a week, and unfortunately the little clown realized his own importance. When First National offered him $6000 weekly plus 25 percent of net profits, Langdon leaped at the opportunity to become his own producer. Sennett once described Harry's business acumen as comparable to that of a backward kindergarten student—and Langdon appears to have deserved the description. He spent his entire production budget ($150,000) before his first story was ever written.

Over the years, Harry's failure as a producer has been blamed on his attempts to function as writer, director, producer and star of his own features. Langdon may have been able to carry such full responsibilities in the creation of two- or three-reel comedies, but certainly not in the staggering production requirements for the six- or seven-reel feature films. After several confidence-boosting features for First National—*The Strong Man, Tramp, Tramp, Tramp*

"The First Hundred Years" are the hardest, Harry tells Alice Day and Louise Carver is living proof that he's right.

and *Long Pants*—regarded today as some of the finest masterpieces of silent screen comedy—Langdon unfortunately attempted to assume the role of Frank Capra, who had served as Harry's most brilliant story and gag mind (as well as director) since the Sennett days.

Despite the immense artistic success of the first full-length comedies, each of Langdon's six features earned less than the preceding one, and First National refused to renew his contract in 1928. Dismayed and bewildered, Harry was unable to comprehend what had happened to his lucky star and he returned to vaudeville to appear in New York City's Coliseum Theatre. After a short and successful booking, Langdon returned to Hollywood, hoping to reactivate his own company and movie career.

The best Harry could do was to secure a job at that eventual home of all near-greats and former stars, the Hal Roach studio.

Harry's final short subject for Sennett, the 1927 *Fiddlesticks* found him as a dejected sidewalk musician too dumb to be frustrated by his unsuccessful attempts to make a living.

Considered to be one of his best films, Harry's first feature found him a contestant in a transcontinental foot race. If he just starts off in the right direction, there's hope.

When Harry started to New York for the opening of *Tramp, Tramp, Tramp*, the First National publicity department presented him with a fur-lined overcoat and snowshoes.

Roach put him to work in a series of talking shorts that failed to renew the public's interest. Langdon had retained the pantomimic technique and artistry of the silent film, but like other silent comedians forced into talking pictures, he neglected to retain the "no talk" law of pantomime. When all concentration on dialogue should have been avoided, a good part of the action and supposed humor

Both Langdon and Mack Sennett were in their forties when this picture was taken and within a few years, Harry's makeup would no longer cover the tell-tale signs of age.

actually hinged upon a verbal base. The effect was disastrous. In addition, Langdon's baby face was slowly disappearing, aided unmercifully by the impersonal tactlessness of the camera closeup. Despite the most professional of makeup jobs, the camera revealed the inevitable wrinkles of Langdon's increasing age.

Harry played whatever roles he could find, wrote routines for other comics and appeared in a series of unsuccessful comedies for Monogram. His last work was at Columbia, where he exhausted himself rehearsing a musical comedy scene. Falling into a coma, Harry Langdon suffered a cerebral hemorrhage and died on December 22, 1944, still dreaming of the comeback he was so certain lay just around the corner.

Harry may have contributed blindly to much of his own downfall, but the greatest tragedy was the disintegration of his comic talent. Intensely disillusioned as each new venture became another in a long line of failures, Langdon must have wept while viewing his own unfunny films of the 1930s and 1940s. While he feebly acted out what he thought were those safe, sure-fire comedy mannerisms, the real genius flickered and died. The sound two-reelers show a comedian who is detached from his own comic art—not necessarily a lack of concern, but a tragic inability to once again grasp the methods of making people laugh. Harry Langdon was the legendary clown overwhelmed by tragedy.

Laurel and Hardy

In the midst of a pop art and culture boom, two fine gentlemen named Stanley Arthur Jefferson and Oliver Norvell Hardy are enjoying a renaissance three decades after their prolific screen careers slowed to an eventual close. One wonders why it took so long. Film historians now rate Laurel and Hardy among the very top in their field, but the general public somehow tends to forget. The public loved their films but the label of greatness escaped the two comedians for years. Everyone agreed that Laurel and Hardy were good—few classified them as great. It took the younger generation to bring Stan and Ollie back for the long-over-due accolades they so richly deserve.

What is it about these two that turns the kids on? Perhaps this new attention is a response to Ollie's marvelous aplomb in the face of lost dignity; or Stan's fantastically direct and childishly simple approach to any problem, complex or otherwise; or because each took turns playing straight man for the other, a realistic approximation of life other comedy teams have overlooked. But these are probably all parts of a larger whole, which includes the complex interplay of little bits and pieces that comprised their comedy, such as Ollie's tie-twiddle as he tried to postpone the inevitable disaster, or Stan's wince and pucker before breaking into tears. Regardless of the outcome, or who was at fault, they possessed an unswerving confidence in each other—a factor that life seems to lack for youth today, and one that has made these two comics of a day long past favorites once more. In short, television has resurrected Laurel and Hardy and the youngsters recognize Stan and Ollie as comic geniuses.

Although basically slapstick in nature, the Laurel and Hardy comedy routines were classically simple and methodically created. They were not forced to rely on the sight gags used by other com-

Oliver Hardy in the 1916 Vim Comedy, *Hungry Hearts*. Too large and boyish-looking for leading roles, Ollie's early career was unspectacular until 1918, when he donned a heavy mustache to begin a long line of comic villain roles, which would lead directly to Hal Roach and Stan Laurel. (Courtesy Blackhawk Films)

edians; instead, they created extensions of themselves, exaggerating both the virtues and frailties of human nature. Ollie became the boy who believed he was an adult while Stan remained the eternal child. It did not all come about that easily, nor were the boys an instant success as a team. Each took his share of hard knocks over the years before Hal Roach brought them together by accident in his "Comedy All-Stars Series."

Stan's origin was in the English music hall, and as a member of the Karno troupe that toured the United States in 1913, he understudied Chaplin in the "drunk" role. The Karno touring company folded soon after Chaplin left to join Keystone. To support himself, Stan then turned to the American vaudeville circuit. Changing his name to Laurel, Stan managed a living for the next few years. His screen debut came in 1918 with *Nuts in May*, a single-reel comedy backed by Adolph Ramish, owner of the Los Angeles Hippodrome.

The film was sold to Nestor, and as a result Stan signed a one-year contract with Universal. It was soon cancelled in a studio reorganization.

Back in vaudeville, Stan compared his short film career with his life on the stage and decided that movies held the better future. In the next few years, he bounced in and out of films—substituting for Toto the Clown in a series of Roach comedies and supporting Larry Semon in his Vitagraph shorts. His big chance came in a pilot comedy made by G. M. Anderson. Entitled *Lucky Dog*, this one found Stan working with Oliver Hardy. When this film is screened today, the viewer finds a rough but surprisingly close approximation of the future Laurel and Hardy.

Lucky Dog finally sold to Metro and Anderson produced six more before his lack of business acumen caught up with him. Stan was out of a job again, but not for long. A lengthy series of single-reel comedies for Hal Roach followed, then twelve two-reel shorts for Joe Rock at Standard Cinema in 1924. By this time, Stan's

Leave it to our Stan. What other bootlegger would display his wares in front of detective Eddie Baker?

comic character had evolved from the brash slapstick used by other comedians to a wistful form, reminiscent today of the fine work of Harry Langdon. This is not to say that Stan was an imitator, only that he was coming ever closer to the true comedy genius of Stan Laurel.

Primarily a creator of comedy, Stan found his greatest success behind the camera in the mid-twenties. Developing comedy routines was his special forte and it was as a gag man and director that Laurel excelled. Many of his contemporaries owed at least a portion of their own success to the excellent routines he devised for them.

Oliver Hardy's screen career began about 1913 with the Lubin Jacksonville studio, where he started as a bit player and worked his way through comedy stooge roles to comic heavy. Jacksonville was also the home of Wizard and Vim Comedies and Ollie repeated his rise in their ranks during 1915-16, earning a starring role in

Some of the early Laurel comedies betrayed a touch of the sorrowful character Harry Langdon would bring to fame later in the decade. Here Marie Mosquini and Max Asher support Stan in his effort to free himself from the unwanted companion.

"Come on, Stan," pleaded Jimmy Finlayson, "You can do it."

the "Plump and Runt" series with Billy Ruge. By 1918, he had reverted to a comic heavy in support of Billy West, Chaplin's foremost imitator. After the first few King Bee Comedies, he masqueraded behind a heavy makeup similar to that used by Eric Campbell, Chaplin's comic menace. In the next half dozen years, he worked as foil for Larry Semon and many other producers, doing both straight and comic roles.

Hardy's career progressed along somewhat different lines from Stan's. Not particularly concerned with the conception of comedy, he worked quite steadily through the years—most of the time for a public that failed to recognize him. Ollie was hampered throughout this period by his extremely boyish appearance in relation to the roles he was called upon to essay. Hardy appeared without makeup in the early Billy West Comedies, but as Billy told it, they later had to hide his youthful features behind some kind of makeup to give him the maturity that his screen roles required—hence the heavy moustache and sometime beard.

Almost completely unknown to each other, Stan and Ollie turned

Oliver Hardy in *Rex, King of the Wild Horses,* Hal Roach's feature of 1925. Before teaming with Stan, Ollie played villains of every ilk.

Helpful Stan did it again, but Ollie bears the brunt of Charlie Hall's anger in *Two Tars*.

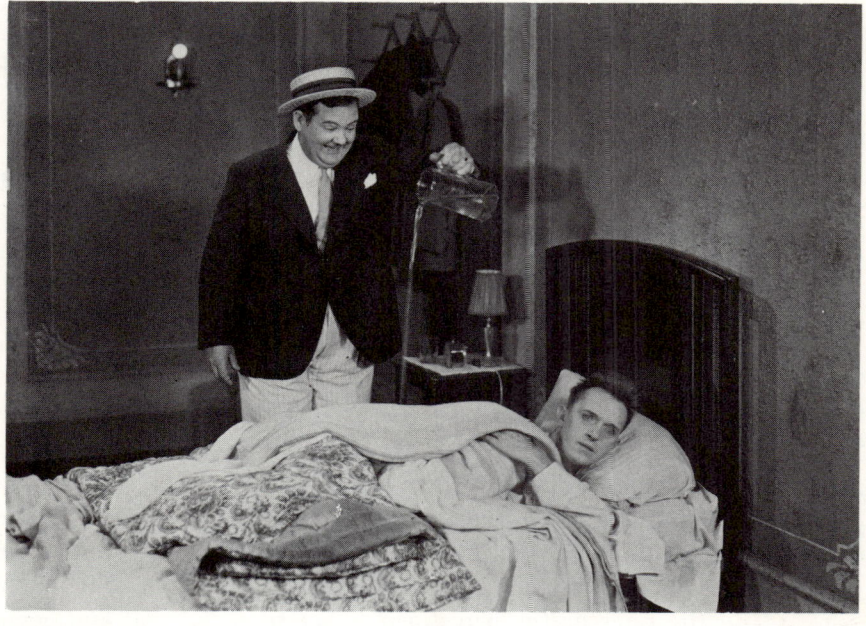

Who needs an alarm clock with playful Ollie on the scene? From *Early to Bed*.

Stan's famous pucker and pointing finger can only mean more trouble for Ollie as a determined "Tiny" Sanford asks the usual question, "Which one of you nuts started it this time?"

up on the Roach lot in 1926 and were cast in small supporting roles in the "All-Star Series." Gradually, their parts increased in size until Laurel, Hardy and Jimmy Finlayson were carrying the comedies all by themselves. By the time Roach moved his release from Pathé to MGM in 1927, the boys had established their basic screen characters and were given star billing together in several films. Roach had stumbled onto his biggest asset almost by accident.

The early Laurel and Hardy comedies were rather violent slapstick, but as film after film rolled out of Roach's factory, the team refined their characterizations, developing a suitable pacing and timing. They reworked and reused gag after gag, each time improving on its previous use. The comedies caught on slowly with exhibitors, but by 1928 Laurel and Hardy were firmly entrenched as box-office material who could draw crowds simply by their marquee billing.

Laurel and Hardy made the move to sound films with comparative ease and after a few hesitant comedies went on to greater heights. Interestingly enough, their repertoire of material was basically limited and simple in nature, but its reuse and refinement had an infinite number of variations and possibilities. The sound comedies had hoary plots that duplicated incidents from the silent shorts, but the boys had a firm grasp of the material and audiences responded with heartier laughs than ever before.

Max Linder

For decades now, Max Linder has been the forgotten father of screen comedy. Lip service has been paid to his genius by critics and historians as a sort of required ritual even though few of them have ever seen much of Linder at work on the screen. For many years, it was assumed that the bulk of his films had been long gone, destroyed by the ravages of time and circumstances. After all, the majority of his work was done in France for Pathé; the remainder in the United States for his own company and Essanay, a firm not noted for its interest in the preservation of negatives. World War I and Pathé lab fires, combined with the state of the art between 1905-14, should have made this a safe assumption; but as has been the case with other obscure screen personalities, countercurrents were at work during this time and the reawakened interest in silent comedy has brought film collectors across the world into close contact for the first time. Suddenly Max Linder's early Pathé comedies are reappearing, not only at the national film archives of several European countries but also in the hands of private collectors. In the near future, Linder will have to be reconsidered in depth for his contributions to screen comedy.

Born Gabriel Leuvielle in 1885 at St. Loubes (near Bordeaux), Max left his family's vineyards for the stage after winning a contest at the Bordeaux Conservatoire. Coaching by Charles le Borgy, then secretary to the Comedie Française, led to a role in the Varieties, where Charles Pathé happened to see his act in 1905. Pathé told Linder he could make a fortune in front of the camera; shortly Max was creating comedy films during the day and working in the theater evenings. Strangely enough, theaters and clubs did not wish their patrons to know that the entertainer was also a screen actor and so his screen name (which was the legal property of Pathé) stayed behind at the studio.

Dapper Max Linder was the screen's first real comedian.

The urbane Linder was equally at home, whether waiting on tables or picking pockets.

His initial appearance on the screen, *The Collegian's First Out-ing*, was followed by hundreds of split-reel comedies. By 1909, Max's fame had spread beyond the borders of France; he had become an international figure, copied by some and applauded by all. When Linder left Pathé in 1914 to go to war, he was earning over $40,000 yearly.

Possessing the first distinct motion picture comedy style, the dapper dandy portrayed by Max anticipated the slapstick of Mack Sennett in both manner and treatment. Wearing a small moustache, the French comic usually appeared in evening clothes or a neatly cut morning suit, complete with cane. Popular enough to merit the added production expense of hand-coloring, Linder's Pathé films made extensive use of trick effects, which also helped set his work apart from that of his contemporaries.

Writing and directing many of his Pathé comedies (a not-un-common feat in the earliest days of the screen), Max also worked under some of Pathé's best directors of the period—Gasnier, Capel-lania and Zecca. His sense of comic timing was complimented by extensive use of the stage comedian's bag of tricks—contrast, exag-geration, ludicrous situations, et al—and the character he developed bore remarkable similarities to the tramp Charlie Chaplin would make famous. Chaplin later acknowledged this debt. Perhaps the greatest point of divergence between Linder and Chaplin rested in the reversal of their characters—while Max's dandy often stooped beneath his presupposed status in life, Chaplin's tramp strove for the respectability his position lacked, but seldom achieved it.

After the war, despite repeated attempts, Max was able to regain only a fraction of his former fame. Gassed in the early part of the war, Linder was reassigned from the front to a diplomatic mission in Italy, but suffered a serious breakdown. He was then sent to Switzerland for recuperation and discharge. In the meantime Chap-lin had risen to fame, first with Keystone and then Essanay. When it became apparent that Chaplin would leave for Mutual in 1916, Essanay signed Max, bringing him to the United States amidst great fanfare.

Historians have stated that Linder had lost his touch and that Essanay misused the little Frenchman's talents in bad films, but contemporary reviews of these comedies were quite good and the major reason for Linder's failure to recoup his position on the screen apparently rested with Essanay, a dying organization whose distribution facilities were faltering badly. Essanay did not mis-use Max, rather it misexploited his films. Between 1916-23,

Unable to pick up his career after a severe gassing in World War I, Max passed into premature obscurity with a handful of films before committing suicide in 1925.

Linder's poor health allowed him to make only a few pictures. After parting company with Essanay, Max formed his own production unit and made three feature comedies in 1922: *Seven Years' Bad Luck, The Three-Must-Get-Theres* (a brilliant parody of Fairbanks's *The Three Musketeers*) and *Be My Wife*.

Max Linder in 1922, just before leaving for a return trip to France.

Unfortunately, Linder's war experiences affected both his mind and body, setting the stage for later tragedy. His poor health, accentuated by a failing career, combined to drive his spirits alternately between despair and elation. Returning to France, he made *Help* and then went to Vienna where he made one final picture. In 1925, he and his wife committed suicide in a Paris hotel, leaving behind a baby daughter. Like Charles Pathé and George Méliès, his death was hardly noted, for by this time, Max had become one of the forgotten pioneers of the comedy screen.

Maud Max Linder grew up quite unaware of her father's exalted artistry until one day some twenty years ago she accidentally came across his name on a film society poster in Versailles. Going inside, she saw her father on the screen for the first time and determined that day to restore his name among the greats of screen comedy. Much of the renewed interest in Max Linder today has resulted from her efforts in locating Linder's final trio of American comedies, which provided the basis for a compilation *En Compagnie de Max Linder*, shown at the Venice Film Festival some years ago. Intrigued by the talents he exhibited at the supposedly low ebb in Max Linder's career, collectors have now taken up the challenge of locating and preserving the early work of the screen's first real comedian.

Eddie Lyons and
Lee Moran

Motion picture comedy was a wide-open field in 1912, with fans clamoring for more and better comedies. Into this setting came two ex-vaudevillians, to begin developing the routines that would make Eddie Lyons and Lee Moran one of the most popular and profitable partnerships on the early screen. Born in Beardston, Illinois, Eddie Lyons had joined the Newsboys Quartette in 1901 when he was just fifteen. This led to work with both the Marlowe and American Stock Companies, but by 1911 Eddie had made the same trip down to Biograph's East 14th Street studio taken by so many other stage actors. After a few extra and bit parts at Biograph, he joined IMP, an association which finally brought him to David Horsley's Nestor. Lee Moran's career followed a similar progression, also leading to Al Christie's stock company at Nestor.

When Lyons joined Nestor, the Christie unit was just beginning a group of western comedies with Donald McDonald and Louise Glaum. Eddie and Lee's teaming was not immediate, nor was it the result of a moment of supreme inspiration. They were to work together in supporting roles for some time, just as Laurel and Hardy would work together as members of the Hal Roach stock company in the late twenties. The partnership was officially formed in 1915 while Eddie was directing one of the new Nestor units under Christie's supervision. Nestor's New York office had decided that Lyons and Moran would work well with each other and so the two were paired under the direction of Horace Davey.

The boys proceeded to polish a comic style that had resulted from their early association with Al Christie. Successfully resisting the trend toward slapstick, Christie always insisted that the best

Lee Moran and Eddie Lyons, Nestor's popular comedy team of the World War I era.

Conquering drama as well as comedy, Lee Moran eyed Marie Wal-
camp in an early Nestor.

comedy came from a situation instead of the comic himself. This
concept explains why so few of the talented Christie comedians
ever rose to fame by themselves. In effect, Christie operated his
own stock company of comedians, almost any of whom were inter-
changeable to a large degree with one another.

In her early pictures in Hollywood, Babe London appeared in
the comedies of Lyons and Moran as a character actress, a fact of
which she is rightfully proud. "The comedy of Lyons and Moran
was very different from the usual style of the period. Lee was a very
good comic, but their humor was more story-oriented, which
showed their earlier training with Al Christie. They were more
'high class,' situation comedies." Although Lyons and Moran developed a relaxed combination of slapstick and polite humor within a
situation setting, their stage training had stressed the cardinal rule,
"Keep it moving," and the boys applied this with rigor in their
screen work. The slow pacing of many situation comedies had led
to the early demise of numerous careers and these two profited
from the mistakes of others.

Sylvia Ashton and Billie Rhodes have nothing to fear from Neal Burns, as long as Lee doesn't drop the gun. *It Almost Happened.*

Although not the best nor the most inventive of the period, their comedies were light, snappy and pleased their fans with off-beat plots such as *Little Egypt Malone,* which found Eddie and Lee as college men needing money to get home. Joining a tent show, Lee impersonated an Egyptian dancer as Eddie tried to coax patrons into contributing to their trip. *Eddie's Little Love Affair* cast Lyons and Moran as professors at a girls' college who secretly carried on with the students behind the dean's back. By 1916, the team was firmly established as Nestor's top attraction. Eddie gradually took over the direction of their work and when Christie left Nestor in 1916, the team left with him.

But Christie had not counted on Nestor's unusual reaction. Dave Horsley wanted them badly enough to offer Lyons and Moran their own unit, Star Comedies, to be supervised and directed by the boys themselves. Packing their bags once more, Eddie and Lee returned to Nestor, continuing their popular series until 1920 when they broke up the team to go their separate ways.

Remaining at Universal, Lee Moran's starring career stalled, but he soon entered the profitable realm of character acting and became one of the most popular supporting players in the features of the twenties. Eddie Lyons landed a contract with the newly formed Arrow Film Corporation, soon to become one of the leading independents of the twenties. Eddie produced, directed and starred in his own series of clever two-reelers from 1921 through 1924.

The first Lyons Comedy was typical of the bulk of Eddie's Arrow films. *Oh, Daddy!* was the story of a confirmed bachelor who was also president of a mens' club opposed to marriage. At its annual meeting, he received a telegram announcing that he was now the guardian of a dead friend's child. Reassuring his friends that this family situation would in no way affect his status in the club, Eddie prepared to meet his new responsibilities. While Eddie thought his new ward would be a boy, it was actually a college girl (Virginia Warwick), providing the comedy twist in the plot. Warned in advance of his expectations, she disguised herself accordingly and attempted to break up his relationship with a stuffy society girl (Helen Darling) who wanted Eddie's hand in marriage. The disguise was revealed in the end and Eddie renounced his bachelor vows to court this pleasant surprise.

Delightfully innocent in approach, Lyons's comedy was mainly reaction to the situation. Its success can best be measured by the four years he spent filming such disarming comedies for the independent Arrow release. But Eddie's real love was directing and

By 1914, Lee Moran was firmly entrenched as a Nestor comedy star but if he doesn't watch out, Jack Dillon will steal Billie Rhodes away.

Eddie Lyons gets a goodbye kiss from Lee as Victoria Forde, Billie Rhodes and Jack Dillon look on. Almost every comic attempted a female impersonation at one time or another in his screen career.

the opportunity to supervise and direct Bobby Dunn and other comedians for Arrow proved to be too enticing. Giving up his appearances before the camera, Lyons invested in the new Mirthquake Comedies and took over responsibility for their production.

It soon became apparent that the comedies of Eddie Lyons and Lee Moran were prototypes for the humor of an entire era as the twenties brought a changing face to the moving picture comedy scene. The pure, unadulterated slapstick was passé. Following the domestic comedy of John Bunny and the Drews, the situation comedy of Lyons and Moran found a new expression in the twenties with Mr. and Mrs. Carter De Haven and the struggling young husband types like Harold Lloyd and Charley Chase in the comedies of Hal Roach. Mack Sennett "went sophisticated" by putting Billy Bevan in tuxedos and bringing Harry Langdon to the screen. Al Christie's old policy of situation comedy with a dash of slapstick, so perfectly exemplified by his disciples Lyons and Moran, had set the general tone of screen humor. Everyday life of the

By 1920, Lyons and Moran were doing features as well as short subjects. *Once a Plumber* found the boys eying Ethel Ritchey and friend with obvious delight.

A fellow certainly can lose time—Eddie opened the door on July 4 and in walked Halloween.

American white collar worker became the starting point for comedies, out of which the gags and laughter came naturally. If there was an unnatural amount of abundant energy, physical action or slapstick, it was tied more closely to plot and characterization. A stout harness was put on all comic horseplay and pure slapstick, with the reins held by the influential and cautious producers of the big Hollywood studios.

While a large number of early Sennett comedies have been made available, representative samples of Al Christie's formative years and his concept of comedy are sadly lacking. The majority of the Lyons-Moran films have yet to be unearthed. Although the Nestor master negatives are rumored to be still intact, nothing has yet been done to preserve or reproduce the pictures of these two comedians. If their films really do exist, today's comedy fans may have the pleasure of rediscovering the work by one of the most popular comedy teams in American movies of the First World War period.

Fred Mace

For many early screen personalities, stardom had all the elusive qualities of a will-o-the-wisp. Just when they became convinced that the mantle of fame and fortune was about to be draped around their shoulders, fate stepped into the game and reshuffled the cards. Such was the tragedy of Fred Mace, one of the most popular of the early comedians.

An 1898 graduate of dentistry school, young Fred practiced his trade for thirteen months in Erie, Pennsylvania. Discouraged by the long Erie winters and the prospect of spending the rest of his life peering into cavities, Mace decided to throw it all over and indulge his nagging desire for the stage. The Wilbur Opera Company hired him and a few months later, Fred celebrated the arrival of 1900 by joining the cast of *Floradora*. This show took him to London for over a year, and after returning to the United States he was an established figure in stock and musical comedy for the next decade.

Fred's travels around the various stage circuits brought him into contact with a lot of unusual people; one of these had changed his name and gone to work in the movies. Apparently, the fellow had done pretty well for himself, for when Mace ran into him again in early 1911, Mack Sennett was wearing a new suit. Sennett still talked a mile-a-minute about comedy and cops—his favorite topic and one that caused most people to yawn.

But Fred Mace listened attentively this time. Sennett was now a director in the movies and he needed comedians for his new Biograph unit. Tired of the road, Fred decided he had nothing to lose and so joined Biograph in 1911. Immediately, Sennett and Mace put their heads together and evolved two new characterizations which proved to be big money makers—"One-Round" O'Brien (a punchy boxer) and the Two Sleuths (a double takeoff on Sherlock Holmes).

This picture of Fred Mace was so popular that the comedian gave away over 10,000 to his fans in 1913.

One of the rare comedy makeups worn by Fred Mace. From *My Valet*, the initial Keystone offering on the new Triangle program, 1915.

Biograph privately frowned on Sennett and his production unit, but the resulting films were very profitable, so the company was restrained in dealing with Mack and his unusual collection of clowns. Mace soon adapted his stage training to the different requirements of the motion picture and became the most popular comedian in Sennett's Biograph unit. In later years, Fred would tell interviewers that it took him many long hours of practice to become accustomed to the camera as a substitute for a live audience.

Mace left Biograph a year later and went West to California, joining Universal's Imp brand as director-actor. Shortly after his arrival on the lot in Edendale, the new Universal combine began to fall apart at its seams. Kessel and Bauman, its largest producers, parted company with Carl Laemmle, and in the ensuing uproar all Universal contracts were cancelled. Left without a job, Fred was stranded, but within hours a wire arrived from New York advising him to "hold tight, salary will continue." The Keystone Film Company was being formed and Mack Sennett wanted Mace on his payroll.

In the fall of 1912, Mace, Sennett and Mabel Normand turned

My Valet won new acclaim for Mabel Normand, Raymond Hitchcock and Fred.

out comedies as fast as film would run through the camera. Fred's popularity with audiences zoomed skyward and his fan mail overwhelmed the studio. As a result, he left Keystone to go on his own in April 1913.

The next two years seemed to be just one disaster after another. Comedian he was; businessman he was not. When Mace rejoined Sennett in July 1915, he explained his failure to *The Moving Picture World* as a lack of ability, coupled with a swelled head. "When I started directing, my troubles began; perhaps it was because I had succeeded so well and was in demand that my head began to expand. I thought I could write, produce and star in my comedies.

"I did but the result showed I was only kidding myself. When I started, D. W. Griffith told me I was attempting the impossible but my ears were locked with my Keystone success. At that time three years ago, I was at the top of the comedy world. John Bunny, Max Linder and myself were the big ones. Sennett and I were just about two years ahead of the times. My mistake was to think I could carry the whole burden by myself. Now it's time to try and retrieve the ground I've lost."

As a charter member of the Keystone troupe, Mace shared in the immense popularity that Sennett's films enjoyed, but ranking himself in the same class with John Bunny and Max Linder was somewhat of an exaggerated personal opinion that should not be accepted without question.

Regaining the lost ground was not so easily done. Although Fred did win new acclaim with his roles in the early Keystone-Triangle Comedies, he never again matched his earlier popularity. At that time, Mace had played many supporting roles that were necessary for comedy but not necessarily funny in themselves—such as the irate father whose refusal to allow his daughter to marry advanced the story but left the comedy to others.

He had also done numerous leading roles, usually being seen as Chief of the Fire Department, the villainous Spaniard (sometimes an Italian for variety) or one of the Keystone sleuths. As a result, he had appeared in almost every one of the early Keystones. Sheer exposure seems to have been a large factor in his earlier success, for Fred seems never to have developed a genuine comedy character with a set makeup and costume.

Extremely well versed in the school of broad burlesque comedy and primarily an exponent of farce, Fred now found himself out of step with the changing face of screen comedy. During his early

Fred Mace robbing the poor box? He looks as if he could use some help in *A Janitor's Wife's Temptation.*

"Look, dear, I've got a winner this time." Alice Davenport looks as if she almost believes Fred in this scene from *His Last Scent*.

"I'll give you a cigar for that little lady," purred Earl Rodney. But it looks as if Fred figures that Louella Maxam is worth at least two.

Keystone days, Mace had shared the screen with only Sennett or Ford Sterling and Mabel Normand; three leading characters had been a sufficient number to carry the primitive plots. In the few films he had made while on his own, Fred had also been the focal point, but when he returned to Keystone in the summer of 1915, things had changed.

Sennett was busy producing for the opening of the new Keystone-Triangle program. Now the comedies were all double reels and in addition to serious attempts at characterization, casts were larger. In essence, where Mace had once been a large fish in a small pond, things were just the opposite now. In a number of the Keystone-Triangles, Fred held star billing but had very little to do.

Audiences had also changed in the interim. Better educated and more sophisticated patrons required an emphasis quite different from the tastes of 1912 and Mace had pretty much been out of touch with the scene as the new flavor of comedy evolved. In short, his ill-fated attempt to succeed on his own now meant that he was suffering from under-exposure on the screen. The fans had simply forgotten him.

Discouraged with his career and his personal life, Fred Mace left the Keystone fold a second time in December 1916. Ostensibly, he was to return to the legitimate stage. There were also rumors that he was again attempting to secure financial support to underwrite his own film company; but whatever his intentions, he did not live to see them fulfilled. While staying at the Astor in New York City, the thirty-eight-year-old comic suddenly died. Although his death was recorded as a heart attack, there were some who felt that his personal relationship with Marguerite Marsh had led him to commit suicide with poison. Removed from a fading career while still in his prime, Fred Mace is now only a shadow in the dimming history of the early days of screen comedy.

Hank Mann

The world of screen comedy was an open avenue for many and varied backgrounds. While the majority of comedians could claim experience ranging from the legitimate theater to vaudeville and the circus, such was not a necessary prerequisite. All that any comedy producer asked from his comics was that they create laughs, and so an ex-steeplejack and sign painter was able to find his calling on the screen.

David Liebeman was at the end of his financial rope when he applied to Keystone for work in early 1913. As Hank Mann, he had worked a tumbling acrobatic act on the Sullivan-Considine circuit until it closed down, leaving the "high-lofty" artist stranded. Sennett soon found Hank to be more than willing to risk life and limb for art and a strong bond of friendship developed between the two. It would be broken only by money. Mack also discovered that Hank's absurd sense of comedy lent itself perfectly to the farcical Keystones, for underneath the dead-panned exterior was a highly creative comic whose unusual finite touches often stole an entire comedy from better-known comedians.

By asking to be last in a Kop sequence, Hank found a place for his little bits and pieces and soon became known as one of the best "fly-catchers" (scene stealers) in the comedy business. As the last Kop out of a burning building, Hank skidded to a smoking stop, searched his pants for a cigarette, which he nonchalantly lit by leaning forward to catch a wisp of flame from the burning building and continued madly down the street. A protective railing served as a backdrop for a rooftop chase and the Kops raced across the screen; Hank brought up the rear, scampering across on the railing. A courtroom scene with Chester Conklin pleading for his very life contained the ubiquitous Mr. Mann in the jury box, solemn as a statue. While Conklin wrapped up his eloquently exaggerated plea

It looks as if Grover Ligon is serious about spanking Hank in *A Bird's a Bird*. Alice Davenport and Minta Durfee look on in this 1915 Keystone.

Hank and Madge Kirby in the first of the Hank Mann Arrow Comedies, *When Spirits Move.*

for mercy, Hank's hand moved quietly to the knot on his tie, which he loosened and slowly moved up and down: a silent hangman's noose.

Spontaneous comic touches like these soon made Hank an invaluable asset to the Keystones, but Sennett continued to use him only in supporting roles. When L-KO offered more money in 1915 than Mack was willing to pay, Hank left to continue his droll antics with Keystone's most determined competitor. But like so many other Keystone comedians, Hank Mann returned to the fold a year later—this time with better roles and more money.

Accentuated by a pushbroom moustache and his hair cut in bangs, Hank's doleful comic appearance was reminiscent of a sad-eyed basset hound. The deadpan appearance concealed his intentions from the audience, helping Hank to avoid telegraphing his next move, as Ford Sterling was fond of doing. The versatile Mr. Mann was a highly visual but subtle comedian whose presence on screen required the close attention of his fans, who otherwise would have missed much of his best material.

Hank and Keystone parted ways for a final time in 1917, when

Hank climbed up the stairs to Sennett's office to ask for more money. Mack was not about to raise any salaries if he could help it, but he did agree to let Hank out of his contract. Mann went over to Fox, where he was given leading roles and the opportunity to direct. The Fox Sunshine Comedies occupied his attention for awhile but by August 1919, Hank stuffed a contract from Morris Schlank in his back pocket and confidently went to work at the Horsley studios. Madge Kirby provided the feminine interest in these independent single-reel comedies marketed by Arrow.

Just before Christmas 1919, Schlank reorganized his company and the series was changed to double reel comedies. Vernon Dent signed on as a supporting comic along with Jess Weldon and Jack Richardson; and Herman Raymaker, one of Sennett's better directors, replaced Tom Gibson, who had moved over to Gale Henry's Model Comedies. To Hank, it was just like "old home week." He got along fabulously with Raymaker, and the Hank Mann Comedies became one of Arrow's most popular series.

Vernon Dent (r) supported Hank in the Arrow Series. It's time for sad farewells from Dorothy Vernon as our heroes embark for the wicked city.

Hank's boxed in this time. Ordinarily, two would be no match at all for Mr. Mann, but Dorothy Vernon holds the equalizer in *The Bell Hop*.

Hank's in trouble now. Dorothy Vernon and company have him dead to rights. There'll be no more flirting with Madge Kirby.

A comic version of Mata Hara, Madge Kirby romances our foolish hero in *The Janitor,* an Arrow comedy of 1919.

Hank and Madge Kirby in one of his Arrow Comedies, c. 1919–20.

Hank Mann in comic pose.

Much of Mann's best work as a lead comic was done in this group of comedies. Whether cast as a paper hanger's assistant in a girl's gymnasium *(Paper, Paste and Poultry)* or managing a hotel *(The Bell Hop)*, Hank managed to squeeze every laugh possible from the rather conventional story lines. Occasionally, a plot came along that was out of the ordinary—Hank Mann would make the most of it. Such was the case with *Mystic Mush*, subtitled "A Cereal in Two Bowls"—a satire on the melodramatic serials, which had reached their peak of popularity in 1920. While protecting her father's invention, Madge Kirby was kidnapped. Coming to her rescue, Hank encountered sliding panels, trap doors, hectic chases, electric chairs, fiery pits, contracting walls and dynamite. All the elements of the popular chapter plays were included in two reels as Hank triumphed over villainous Vernon Dent in a comic tour de farce.

After completing his contract with Schlank, Hank began to free-lance, appearing in Metro's *Quincy Adams Sawyer* and other features. In 1926-27, he went back to the short comedy field briefly, joining forces with Chester Conklin in a dozen two-reelers for Tennek Film Corporation. As the silent period drew to a close in the late twenties, Hank did some of his best work with roles in *The Patent Leather Kid, Broadway After Midnight* and *The Garden of Eden*. A long career in talkies followed, until illness forced his permanent retirement from the screen. Respected in the business as a comedian's comedian, Hank Mann never achieved his full measure of fame with the critics and historians, but provided laughs galore to the unsophisticated but golden days of comedy.

Milburn Morante

Like any other business in the twenties, the movies had their own social structure. Features, serials and comedies all possessed differing degrees of acceptability. Within each genre, a reasonably rigid social order had evolved according to talent, popularity and financial status. Many at the bottom of the order never rose above supporting roles, for any number of reasons. Milburn Morante, however, was one of those who became their own masters but nevertheless remained at the bottom of the social heap—making a lot of money and ignoring the lowliness of their position.

Before coming to the screen, Milburn had been a member of The Three Morantes, touring the vaudeville houses with his brother Al and father Joe. First appearing in Universal's Joker Comedies with Max Asher and Gale Henry, Milburn worked with virtually every other comic on the Universal lot during 1913-18. Specializing in eccentric comedy, fans never knew what disguise Morante would show up in next—a factor that held back his development as a recognized star. The most successful screen comedians had developed an easily identified character; Milburn played them all.

After leaving Universal in 1918, Gale Henry organized her own company in 1919 to produce two-reel comedies for release on the independent market through Bulls Eye. Miss Henry hired Milburn to play supporting roles in her Model Comedies, and within a few months Morante also organized his own company. Produced at the old Balboa studio in Long Beach, his Mercury Comedies were also released by Bulls Eye.

An occasion to celebrate, the Mercury Comedies meant a family reunion and the beginning of a lengthy and profitable family association. Joe Morante became technical director and self-appointed master of his son's destiny. Al was assigned to learn the art of directing as Grover Jones's assistant. A lighthearted group, the Morante unit was forever playing practical jokes on each other.

Detective Morante investigates Gale Henry's cries for help.

Milburn's first Mercury Comedy found him cast as a henpecked husband whose wife had ordered the wash done. Calling in Charles Everett, Jones told his prop man to locate some clothes to be used when the laundry scene was shot the following day. Without telling anyone on set, Everett brought in his wife's laundry and by the time Jones was satisfied with the scene, Milburn had finished Everett's wash (under the gentle prodding of the prop man, who cautioned the comedian from time to time to scrub all the clothes, not just a few).

Three comedies had been completed and released to the independent market in December 1919, when Joe Morante sold his son on the idea of a reorganization and expansion. Milburn finally agreed with his father, and renaming his company Morante Comedies, Incorporated, he issued $100,000 in stock to finance the new venture. Another and more profitable releasing arrangement was secured with Reelcraft, and in March 1920 production began on location in San Francisco. Milburn had cut back his plans for the year to an even dozen two-reel comedies, giving more time to produce each one and the resulting films were considerably more polished than his previous Mercury Comedies had been.

But Morante Comedies, Inc. was overextended financially. The life of a "Poverty Row" producer was usually a series of crises separated by dollar signs. Most rented both studio space and equipment, trying to abide by a tight shooting schedule to conserve enough of their funds for lab fees and release prints once filming ended. Often there was no money left in the purse to begin another film until the last one had been sold. Credit was a scarce commodity for these producers and this fact of life forced Milburn to close up shop.

The remainder of Morante's career was quite amazing. After giving up his own company, Milburn followed the trend to sophisticated situation comedy in the twenties and made a series for Federated release in 1922-23. The following year found him starring in Crescent Comedies for Morris Schlank and then in a series for J. C. Cook, released by Sovereign Feature Productions. Although not a

Gale Henry's Model Comedies gave Milburn (second from left) the boost to his own production company.

name comedian, he managed to stay active throughout the period, making comedies for various producers and directing independent westerns.

Even more amazing is the fact that his comedies actually sold to exhibitors, for their quality had dropped off greatly after Morante Comedies went out of business. Milburn's eccentric style had given way to situations that were basically not funny in themselves, and in some of his films he actually played a relatively minor role, with more screen time devoted to the supporting cast than to the star. *Down to the Sea in Cabs* was a typical example, with Milburn and Cliff Jones cast as cabbies and Kenneth MacDonald providing the lead in this story of a stolen painting and its attempted recovery.

In some respects, Morante presented a problem similar to Clyde Cook. Even more so than Cook, Milburn lacked a comic appearance. In some comedies, he wore a pencil-thin moustache; in others, he appeared clean shaven. Dressed in everyday clothes and possessing no strong pantomime in his repertoire, Milburn typified the average American, almost indistinguishable in a crowd. Unlike other situation comics (who might also fit this same description), Morante projected a neutral personality—nothing to get excited about one way or the other.

The fascinating part of his story lies in the fact that a market existed for this type of comedy in the neighborhood and rural theaters, which operated on a minimal film rental budget. Dozens of obscure comedians plied their trade more or less successfully on these undiscriminating screens, content to make a living just as dozens of obscure producers populated Poverty Row. Rarely did any of these comics attain sufficient stature in popularity or their work to rank among the Clown Princes and Court Jesters, but Milburn Morante deserves the accolade, if but for longevity and perseverance alone.

Charlie Murray

"He was a tremendous performer, on as well as off the screen. He had an endless storehouse of jokes and he never seemed to repeat one of them. I swear he couldn't pass anyone without telling at least two jokes. He loved to perform for people and they loved it." This glowing description of Charlie Murray was painted recently by Dixie Chene and quite accurately portrays the tremendous native sense of humor and entertainment that characterized the Laurel, Indiana, comic. Regarded by his co-workers as a delightful character, both on and off the set, Charlie loved to perform whenever he had an audience of at least one. As Dixie Chene continued, "I remember at the old Keystone studio when it would rain and we couldn't work. Charlie would put up sail cloth to catch the water, grab Harry McCoy and set him down to the piano; and to Harry's music, Charlie would dance on a stool or the smallest table he could find—never faltering. I can still vividly remember those threatening full bags of water above our heads and Charlie dancing underneath them."

Coming from a family of eight, Charlie had entered show business at a tender age and by the time he was thirteen, was already the veteran of a lengthy apprenticeship with the John Robinson Circus, working as clown, rider and leaper. Leaving the sawdust world three years later while recovering from an injury, young Murray followed a variety of paths; he worked medicine shows, repertory companies and even did a single act. Three more years of struggling proved to be sufficient for Charlie and he returned to his parents' home in Centreville, Indiana.

Back in Centreville, Murray became acquainted with Ollie Mack and before long, the two had formed a partnership and an act. This association developed into one of Charlie's deepest friendships and one of America's most successful stage comedy teams—one

Charlie Murray in character makeup at the Sennett studio, circa 1918.

Each Sennett comic developed his own special character and during his early Keystone days, Murray was synonomous with his role of Hogan. His imperious attitude toward Bobby Dunn was in keeping with *Hogan's Aristocratic Dream.*

which lasted for over two decades. Murray and Mack first appeared in *Our Irish Neighbors,* which opened in Mt. Clements, Michigan; and with a single exception *(An English Daisy),* they built up a long record of financial successes, and even appeared continuously for three years in *Finnegan's Ball.* In addition to performing in starring roles, this versatile pair also wrote their own plays—*A Night on Broadway* and *The Sunny Side of Broadway.*

But by 1910, Murray and Mack realized that they had enjoyed all of the best that a partnership could provide, and when new fields beckoned each went his own way. Turning his attention to the infant "flickers," Charlie joined Biograph in 1911, where he made his first appearance in *A Disappointed Mama.* Biograph did well by Charlie Murray and his work under the direction of Dell Henderson was rewarded by the establishment of his separate comedy unit. But when Henderson left Biograph to rejoin his old friend Mack Sennett at the new Keystone studio, Charlie went along for the ride. Murray's days with Keystone placed him before a growing and admiring public; the near-anonymity of the Biograph actors was replaced by the adulation that greeted most of the leading Keystone players. By the close of the World War I era, Charlie Murray had become one of the favorite comedians in motion pictures.

Charlie possessed a marvelously mobile face but he matched an expressive countenance with a masterful screen presence which no new upstart comic could ever upstage. Although a master at mugging, Charlie sufficiently tempered his comic emotions enough to show his awareness of the differences between stage and screen. Some comics whose success had been achieved on the boards (like Raymond Hitchcock and Hale Hamilton) had great difficulty in adapting their stage comedy to the more intimate motion picture camera. Admittedly, Charlie indulged in a healthy degree of comic vulgarity, but somehow he got away with it. In *Hogan's Wild Oats*, Murray emitted grandiose sneezes on a babe-in-arms, to the great distress of its mother, but the combination of his total lack of concern and her opposite degree of maternal distress completed the simple requirements for laughter.

Often teamed with Polly Moran, whose talents were probably never again so well displayed, Charlie's own low but funny humor permitted her to swing a broom wildly and without apology at her worthless husband. The primitive quality of photography and editing of the early Keystones (in comparison to the style and polish of the twenties) matched the fast and rough humor of both Charlie and Polly. But with the coming of the twenties and the ensuing onslaught of feature comedies, Charlie threw his burlesque character into a higher gear, while Polly's buxom comicalities changed only slightly, and at that never enough for her to achieve either high regard among fans or any kind of lasting fame.

Charlie's continually developing sense of humor often manifested itself in various jokes. One night in 1919, "Smiling Billy" Parsons threw a party for Billie Rhodes and invited a number of celebrities as well as National Film officials. It was a very formal dinner affair and soon the group had congregated in the dining room to be served the evening's delicacies. Of the waiters hired to augment the normal staff, one seemed to be unduly stoop-backed and awkward—a slovenly posture in place of the usual regal bearing of the Hollywood hired servant. Since this man was costing him money, Parsons grew increasingly impatient, and by the time the first round of dishes had been placed on the table, he spoke curtly to the inept waiter. The man stopped, held his position, then slowly

As Charlie's career at Sennett came to a close in the mid-twenties, *Flickering Youth* appeared in the person of meek little Harry Langdon to replace him on screen.

Charlie was most often the victim of ugly women without really knowing why. In this case (*The Hollywood Kid*), it's Louise Carver who's running the house, and Mr. Murray too.

raised himself to expose the incredibly comic face of Charlie Murray.

After an extremely successful eight-year association with Mack Sennett, Charlie dropped movies long enough to once more hear the applause of a real theater audience, when he ventured back to vaudeville in 1921. Following a thirty-eight-week tour, he freelanced with C. C. Burr and Hodkinson for two years before joining First National. It was here that his comedy shifted gears, as performances in *McFadden's Flats, The Life of Riley, Lost at the Front* and *The Laughing Venus* reflected his new concern for a clearer delineation of character. In six or seven reels, this was an absolute necessity and the failure of comics like Larry Semon and Harry Langdon to realize the importance of a better-defined screen character for the longer pictures was a prime reason for the abrupt ending of their celebrated careers.

Charlie's best-remembered screen appearances were in his pictures with George Sidney—the Cohen and Kelly series made for

Charlie Murray is probably best remembered today for the very popular feature comedies in which he teamed with George Sidney. *The Life of Riley* was followed by a lengthy series of Cohn and Kelly comedies before Charlie returned to the comedy short subject in the thirties.

Universal. Whether this is viewed sadly or not by those who recall his work with Sennett, one cannot deny that a new generation of kids in the twenties and thirties claimed this lovable comic for itself, and Charlie's screen popularity continued high. Off and on for six years, Murray and Sidney feuded their way through countless feature comedies. But as the friendly enemies began to wade through increasingly decrepit material and disinterested direction, the series finally came to a close and Charlie returned to the short comedy format.

Over the years, the movie-going public had found a place for Charlie Murray in its heart and he reciprocated in like manner, conceiving of the world as a place in which its inhabitants should work harder to keep life enjoyable. His devotion to home, family and work was aptly illustrated by the remark he once made to an interviewer who asked for a list of his "diversions." For once, Charlie dropped the comic façade and his answer came back quickly: "staying home nights."

Mabel Normand

Sometimes referred to as the female Chaplin of the movies, Mabel Normand was unquestionably the top-ranking comedienne of the early screen. No other comedienne was able to approach Mabel's versatility or popularity with audiences during her active years. And to her fellow players, she was the most adored woman in pictures. The adoration lives today. "She was everything you have ever heard about her," says Keystone actress and friend of Mabel's, Dixie Chene, "a kind, wonderful, generous woman." Another former Keystone leading lady, Minta Durfee, praises her with an intensity that has not lessened in over fifty years: "Mabel was the most beautiful woman God ever created!" "Mabel Normand was unlike any girl I have ever known," contends former stage and screen star Daphne Pollard, "no one was ever so full of life as Mabel. She was a creature totally of impulse and no lovelier a girl ever existed." Sadly, Mabel Normand's life was brief, her career short and her story studded with tragedy.

She came from humble beginnings, the daughter of a touring pianist who never quite rose above the nickel and dime vaudeville acts. After only a slight acquaintance with formal schooling, Mabel found a job at thirteen to help support the family. While working in the pattern department of a women's magazine, Mabel was introduced to Carl Kleinschmidt, a noted illustrator, who saw a future for her in modeling.

By 1908, Mabel was posing regularly for Charles Dana Gibson and James Montgomery Flagg, two of the nation's leading popularizers of the American female. At the suggestion of a friend, Mabel sought work in the movies and was given a few roles at Vitagraph. With a little experience in performing before the camera, she joined Biograph, where she met Mack Sennett. The two became fast friends and although they eventually planned to marry, the wedding never took place.

Considered to be the silent screen's finest comedienne, Mabel Normand's personal life read like a tragic scenario. This gag shot was made in 1915 at Keystone.

Mabel often played the flirting wife. Here she carries on with Harry Gribbon in Keystone's *Mabel, Fatty and the Law.*

Mabel recognized the comic potential of Charles Chaplin and their work together was marked by a mutual respect. Here Charlie's indignation is about to be followed by a slapstick riot.

Mabel with Mack Sennett and F. Richard Jones (her favorite director) on the set of *The Extra Girl*.

When Sennett left Biograph in 1912 to head the new Keystone Film Company, Mabel and Ford Sterling went with him. Sennett's conception of screen comedy was an immediate hit with audiences and his comedienne became famous almost overnight as "Keystone Mabel." Despite her diminutive size, "Keystone Mabel" slid easily into the rough and tumble atmosphere of the new Keystone studio. She not only endured the most rigorous requirements of the catch-as-catch-can methods of production, but as her associates attested, she could curse on occasion as effectively as a longshoreman in his favorite saloon. But in a period when the Keystone wardrobe department required little more space than a small closet, Mabel brought her fashionable feathers and plumes, and expensive beaded gowns to the simple, rustic surroundings of the Keystone lot. Despite better offers from other producers, she was to stay with Sennett through thick and thin for several years, until personal disappointments and her unfulfilled ambition sent Mabel searching for roles more challenging than Keystone could offer.

Too short in length and too fast in action to allow full use of Mabel's abilities, the Keystones involved only slapstick for the most part but now and then a role came along that called for something more than just a pratfall or pie in the face. Mabel knew that her talent was greater than the limited demands of slapstick, and although a very popular comedienne in the Keystone Comedies, she wanted to do features. She finally persuaded Sennett and his backers, Kessel and Bauman, to establish the Mabel Normand Feature Film Company in 1916. Entitled *Mickey,* the resulting film took two directors and nearly eight months to complete.

When Sennett screened a print of *Mickey* for Kessel and Bauman, the two were extremely upset with what they saw. It was not a Keystone by any stretch of the imagination, nor did the six-reel feature compare to Sennett's earlier slapstick feature hit, *Tillie's Punctured Romance.* Slapstick had been replaced by Mabel's warm and moving performance as the daughter of a Western prospector who went to New York, inherited a fortune and was pursued by a smooth villain who finally lost out in the closing reel as Mabel emerged tri-

As *The Extra Girl,* Mabel measures Teddy's nose for Max Davidson.

Mabel's favorite publicity still from *Mickey*.

umphant. Although not released until 1918, *Mickey* proved Mabel's claims and became a huge moneymaker.

After completing *Mickey*, Mabel went to Goldwyn on a five-year contract. As a friend explained the situation many years later, "Mabel loved everything and everybody—at Sennett's, it was his money and the romance; at other studio, it was the opportunity to show how good an actress she really was." Permanently estranged now from Sennett, bored and restless with life, Mabel began a style of living calculated to keep her occupied. In Mabel Normand's personality, the explosive combination of sensitivity and impulsiveness seemed perfectly wedded, but resulted in a financial recklessness and a disturbingly unending search for something to cling to. While she gave increasingly expensive gifts to almost total strangers, she was becoming more deeply lost, with no well-defined direction in sight. Caught up in a social whirl, she gave madcap parties and attended others, showing up late for work the next morning and sometimes disappearing for days at a time. Stories of her wild living were supplemented with rumors and hints of scandal but nothing definite appeared to confirm the gossip until 1922.

The Arbuckle case had hardly disappeared from the papers when William Desmond Taylor was murdered. A well-known and talented director, Taylor had been on very good terms with both Mabel and Mary Miles Minter. It was Mabel's misfortune to have been the last person with Taylor the evening he died and her attempts to recover certain letters she had written the director gave the press a field day. Although deeply involved with Taylor personally, Mabel was proven innocent of any connection with his death, but the outrageous publicity seriously damaged her career.

Instead of giving in, Mabel stood firm and continued with her work. It looked as if she was winning the fight when she was inadvertently involved in the murder of millionaire Cortland S. Dines. Her chauffeur, found standing over Dines' body with Mabel's pistol in his hand, was subsequently revealed to be an escaped convict. Her innocence was never questioned, but the ensuing publicity following so soon after the Taylor case dealt a shattering blow to Mabel's career.

During these tragic years, Mabel had continued to make interesting films, both for Goldwyn and Sennett. *Molly-O, Suzanna* and *The Extra Girl* remain as proof that Mabel was more than just another Sennett comic. Her dramatic ability was brought to bear in the emotionally moving scenes of these features and becomes even more powerful when the viewer realizes the great personal stress under which she must have worked during these years. Without enormous talent, it is difficult to conceive of anyone functioning so well in such trying circumstances.

But Mabel's career was almost over. The effect of the adverse publicity and her fast pace of living had begun to show. Appearing tired and ill in front of the all-seeing camera's eye, she supposedly turned to drugs to keep going. Sagging popularity combined with

Carl Stockdale instructs *Molly 'O'* in the fine art of silhouette portraiture.

her reluctance to continue making features, and producers became unwilling to risk their capital on further pictures until she regained her health and appearance.

Overnight, Mabel was back where she had started—in two-reel slapstick comedies. Only Hal Roach was willing to put her to work. Roach had hit upon a formula for extracting whatever star value might be left in the former greats and Mabel appeared in several of these comedies. Reminiscent of her earlier features, Mabel's work in some of these was quite good and showed occasional flashes of the talent that had been so wasted. As Paddy, the dance-hall girl in *The Nickel Hopper,* Mabel was presented with a part requiring both comic and dramatic ability and she brought it off well.

But Mabel Normand's name alone was no longer sufficient to guarantee success at the box office and her supporting casts were composed of virtual unknowns. The Hal Roach Comedies reached a different theater and patron from those of her starring features, and these were the twilight years of the silent film. Except for the ending, the scenario of her life had played almost as the script of these comedies.

Marrying Lew Cody in a desperate attempt to regain a normal life, Mabel discovered that she had tuberculosis after entering the hospital in 1927 for pneumonia. By September 1929, the little comedienne was in the Pottenger Sanitarium for treatment and never set foot on another movie lot. After six months of illness, Mabel Normand succumbed February 23, 1930, at the age of thirty-six. Sadly, close friends of Mack Sennett have remarked that when Mabel died Mack Sennett died with her. As bitterness gripped Sennett's spirit, only long years were able to transform his noticeable cynicism into a quiet resignation by the time of his death.

There is no pat reply to the question of why artists so often waste their talents. In Mabel Normand's case, not even her close friends really understood what force drove her to a point where the will to live flickered only dimly. Perhaps in her case, Mabel welcomed a release from the brief but trying script that had seldom turned out as she and Mack Sennett had written it back in 1912. Surely the most popular comedienne of the silent screen, her death ironically coincided with the demise of the silent comedy.

Our Gang

Although often credited as the father of kid comedies, the concept did not actually begin with Hal Roach; the Bébé series with René Dany began in France in 1910, to be followed two years later by the Bout-de-Zan series with René Poyen. Mack Sennett experimented with the idea in 1913 but abandoned it when "Little Billy" (Paul Jacobs) and his director Robert Thornby shifted their allegiance to the Sterling Film Company in early 1914. Little Billy" lasted about one year and was followed by the Fox Kiddies during World War I. Most likely, all of these series had their origins in the adventure stories of pulp-paper fiction.

Our Gang probably would never have existed had it not been for Ernie Morrison. As "Sunshine Sammy," he contributed youthful chaos and havoc to the Roach Comedies long before the coming of Our Gang. He was the plague incarnate for the struggling, bespectacled Harold Lloyd and the distressingly inept Snub Pollard. Directors Fred Newmeyer, Alf Goulding and Roach himself had long realized the comedy potential of children and so Sunshine Sammy was spun off into his own series in 1921-22. His box-office success crystallized the idea of an official "gang" of active, adventuresome young kids which began with *One Terrible Day* in September 1922.

Our Gang was a representative group of physical types and temperaments among neighborhood gangs. The beautiful young girl, sweetheart of all the boys, was first Mary Kornman and later curly, golden-haired Jean Darling, who looked something like a miniature version of Mae Murray. The fat boy was good-natured Joe Cobb, who stayed with the gang almost until he was practically a teenager. The pretty boys were wholesome-looking Johnny Downs and Jackie Davis. The freckle-faced, forever mischievous

An informal portrait of Our Gang, 1929. Jackie Condon, Bobby "Wheezer" Hutchins (held by Dorothy Vernon), Jean Darling, Joe Cobb, Mickey Daniels and Allan "Farina" Hoskins.

Baby sitting with little Bobbie Burns brings mixed emotions from Pete, Mary Ann Jackson, Jean Darling, "Farina," Harry Spear, Joe Cobb and "Wheezer."

boys were Mickey Daniels, one of Roach's most talented gang members and a much sought-after child actor, and Harry Spear, who appeared in all his impishness near the end of the silent period.

Allen Clay ("Farina") Hoskins followed the bare footsteps of Sunshine Sammy as the Gang's loyal Negro friend, and along with Joe Cobb and Mickey Daniels he stayed many years with the Gang, reappearing as a teenager in the early thirties. Clever, dexterous and unswervingly determined to succeed, the intense young tinkerer was little Jackie Condon and at the end of the silent era came two extremely talented youngsters—cute, pixie-looking little Mary Ann Jackson, brought over from the Sennett studio's *Smith Family* series and Bobby ("Wheezer") Hutchins, whose baby face always looked to be on the verge of tears. Last, but far from least, was Pete, the lovable dog with that incredible round ring encircling its right eye.

Our Gang was either one of the best-loved or most-hated series

Guest stars frequently made appearances in Our Gang Comedies. Dorothy Vernon is supervising Mickey Daniels's work, but as soon as she turns her back Mickey will disappear and join the Gang in another adventure.

After surveying the situation, the sad-faced Langdon realized it was going to be impossible to escape Our Gang. Left to right—Bobby "Wheezer" Hutchins, Mary Ann Jackson, Harry Spear, Jean Darling, Chubby Chaney, Joe Cobb and Allan "Farina" Hoskins.

of silent comedies. Fans were either charmed by the antics of children or repulsed, somewhat like the split affections of modern readers toward the *Peanuts* cartoon strip. But the *Peanuts* characters are perceptive and clever adults in children's clothes—a material extension of cartoonist Charles Schultz's philosophy—whereas the children in Our Gang comedies were typical children in a typical adult world, striving to be adult. Thus, the Our Gang kids were inevitably wrapping themselves in their mothers' dresses and fathers' old coats in an effort to act more grown up.

Forever on the threshhold of new adventures, the Gang was never bored and the imaginative, fanciful and simplified attitudes of children were faithfully retained. Grandmothers were warm and kind in a way that only a child could imagine, while the forever disgruntled school master was similarly, the villain of villains—the disciplinarian and dictator as typified by the mind of a school child. These characters were exaggerations, but exaggerations honest to the child's conception of his adult world.

When Harry Langdon announced that he was going to be married in 1930, Our Gang just couldn't resist a small celebration in his honor.

The policeman was one adult they wanted to avoid. Order and discipline were discarded on all possible counts. Although Our Gang was found busily creating an adult world on a small scale by constructing wooden cars pulled by dogs, gathering together materials for a one-ring circus or carnival, or garbing themselves in their parents' clothes, they were just as often clinging desperately to their own secure world. The Gang held onto a freedom impossible in the world outside the realm of childhood. Adults may desire to "play hookey" from the monotony of everyday work, but the Gang *did* play hookey and created a healthy amount of havoc before they were caught and forced back into the responsible world of the adult.

The mortality rate of Our Gang actors was expectedly high and distressing to a child actor. One day millions of moviegoers were laughing and paying to see you and the next day you were an unwanted adolescent. By the mid-thirties, the entire core of the Gang had changed with the different faces of George ("Spanky") McFarland, the new chubby little leader of the Gang; Carl ("Alfalfa")

Freckle-faced Mickey Daniels was one of Roach's most talented Gang members and a much-sought-after child actor.

Mary Kornman and Johnnie Downs act out one of the adult situations which characterized the Our Gang Comedies.

Switzer, who brought an uncontrollable cowlick along with his freckles and screeching voice; Darla Hood, the new childhood beauty; Tommy Bond, the villainous neighborhood bully; Matthew ("Stymie") Beard, that wily little Negro boy whose cunning was only surpassed by his laziness; and the two tiny pals, Billy ("Buckwheat") Thomas and Eugene ("Porky") Lee. "We really had a pretty good time making those comedies," Spanky McFarland recently admitted, "but there certainly was not much security in it. On an average, most kids were in the films for only five or six months." Spanky was an exception; he appeared as a regular member for a total of thirteen years (1931-44).

The series continued to make money for Hal Roach throughout the thirties, but he eventually added Our Gang to his list of rejects—which included Charley Chase, and Laurel and Hardy. All rights to the use of the name Our Gang were thrown in with the child actors themselves when Roach turned the series over to Metro-

Goldwyn-Mayer in 1938. Our Gang was disbanded in 1944 when the "club doors" closed for the final time. But its twenty-two-year history gave Our Gang the distinction of being the longest, uninterrupted comedy series in the history of motion pictures and one of the few to overlap both the silent and sound periods.

Although a collective success, the members of Our Gang were unable to carry on their success as individuals. Very few achieved any fame. But thanks to periodic revivals on television as "The Little Rascals," Our Gang is as well known to the younger generation of today as they were to those of previous eras, and they continue to bring amusement and laughter wherever their comedies are shown.

George Ovey

The years of the silent screen have often been called the Golden Age of Comedy, and golden they were. Movies were America's fifth largest industry and the demand for films seemed insatiable. With innumerable small production companies supplementing the efforts of the major studios, opportunities for comedians were almost unlimited and the demand for their services made it possible for nearly any comic to have a try at the screen and its potential rewards.

Movie studios were the logical goal for comedians on the vaudeville, burlesque and musical comedy circuits. In return for hard work and some degree of creative imagination, the movies offered high salaries, widespread adulation and relief from the monotonous routine of one-night stands in shabby theaters. Little wonder that so many like George Ovey took advantage of this escape from the stage.

Ovey's career began at an early age as the stage-struck urchin, selling "peanuts, popcorn, candy and chewing gum" scampered up and down the stairways of a theater gallery in Kansas City. Within four years, he was treasurer of the house and one night, when a travelling company arrived without a comedian, George volunteered to substitute and so received his first taste of life behind the footlights. When the stage company left Kansas City, Ovey went along with it. In the next decade, his best booking found him as end man with the Beach and Bowers Minstrels. Little George Ovey's theatrical career had never really left the ground.

But a chance meeting with David Horsley changed his fortunes. Horsley, an early producer and founder of Nestor, decided to expand his Made in America (MinA) Films by adding another comedy unit to back up Harry La Pearl and Murdock McQuarrie. Maintaining a low overhead was a fact of life for Horsley, and ac-

LADIES MUST DANCE
featuring
GEORGE OVEY
with
LILLIAN BIRON
AND THE GAYETY GIRLS

Although it was a starring series, The Gayety Comedies of 1919–20 marked the beginning of the path to obscurity for little George Ovey. He has obviously made a good impression on Lillian Biron in *Ladies Must Dance,* the eighth of The Gayetys.

cordingly he hired the least expensive talent available. Ovey fitted into this category perfectly, and seeing motion pictures as his big opportunity, joined MinA in June 1915. By August, Horsley had left MinA to form Cub Comedies, taking Ovey with him as Cub's star comedian.

For the next two and one-half years, George Ovey, dressed in baggy checkered trousers, striped shirts and a soup-bowl hat, appeared weekly on the nation's theater screens as "Jerry." Directed by Milton H. Fahrney and supported by Goldie Colwell, Janet Sully, Louis Fitzroy and others, the Jerry series was a Mutual release that brought Ovey some of the recognition that had eluded him for so long. Basically carbon copies of each other, his comedies used a stock formula in which the elements could be rearranged and interchanged at will.

The serious played as great a part in Ovey's screen roles as did comedy. Each film opened and closed dramatically, with comic interludes in between. Escaping from the police in *A Deal in In-*

It's George Ovey as *Henessey of the Mounted,* one of his Pacific Folly Comedies of 1921. Arby Arly has nothing to worry about? (Courtesy Don Malkames)

dians (1915), Jerry fell into the hands of the Indians, who decreed his death. Saved by the chief's daughter, Jerry was adopted by the tribe, but the chief sold him to a professor who needed a red man for a lecture tour. His benefactress followed the two into town, where she created such a disturbance that the police were called to quell the riot. Recognized by the officers, Jerry was returned to jail as the comedy ended.

As they were all single reels, Ovey's comedies never allowed time for the development of complicated plots; but even so, his skill was in creating an edge-of-the-seat situation and then playing it for as many laughs as possible. In *Jerry and the Outlaws* (1917), our hero eluded his sweetheart's guards (who had been stationed outside the house by her irate father—no self-respecting father in any comedy ever wanted anything to do with the hero) and they headed into the country for a ride.

Kidnapped by ruffians, the two were held captive in a deserted house while the ransom note was delivered. A decided nuisance,

Jerry was locked in the attic to keep him out of trouble. Turning his small size into an advantage, he wriggled to safety through a hole in the roof, and in a very tense moment freed his girl and captured the kidnappers.

Playing mainly smaller and second-run houses, the Jerry comedies acquired a substantial following of fans who enjoyed their laughs liberally mixed with chills and thrills. Cub Comedies were discontinued in 1918 and Ovey made a few Rainbows for Universal before joining Gayety Comedies in 1919 as star of the newly formed independent. This led to a series of Folly Comedies in 1921-22 for the even more obscure Pacific Film Company. His failure to enter the ranks of the big-time comedians rested in a continued one-dimensional characterization, for although the name had been· dropped, Ovey was still playing Jerry in 1922.

"Save the girl and bring the villain back alive" was the theme of *Hennessey of the Mounted*, a Folly Comedy in which Ovey was cast opposite himself as both hero and heavy. Watching this film today, the similarity with Cub Comedies made six years earlier was striking. Where other comics began with a single dimension, they were able to go on to flesh out the skeleton; Ovey just didn't seem able to go beyond the basic element. The Pacific Folly Com-

After his Pacific series ended, Ovey was seen mainly in comic supporting roles in features and serials like Universal's *Strings of Steel*.

George Ovey, whose greatest fame came with David Horsley's Cub
Comedies of 1915–17.

edies were his final starring roles; throughout the rest of the twenties, he provided the comedy relief for numerous features and
serials, in parts which were once again a logical extension of Jerry.

But there is no doubt of his popularity in the 1915-18 period;
George Ovey was a firm fixture in theaters across the country as
children filled the theaters on Saturday afternoons to watch their
little hero extricate himself from danger with a smile on his face.

Smiling Billy Parsons

Operating a profitable motion picture production company during 1915-20 was a task sufficient to demand one's complete attention; working as a successful starring screen comic at the same time was also a full-time job. Although Mack Sennett had managed to combine both pursuits in 1912-13, his company was small at the time and its product mainly split-reel comedies. But the National Film Corporation of America was a going concern in July 1915, one ready for expansion beyond its production of three full reels weekly. At the same time, its astute president and guiding genius was featured in the weekly comedy releases of MinA films. There was only one "Smiling Billy" Parsons in the business—a remarkable man who wore two completely different hats at the same time and made a success of both endeavors.

A former M.D. and ex-insurance salesman (a most unusual background for a screen comic), the thirty-nine-year-old Bill Parsons went into business for himself with National in the spring of 1915, acquiring the old Oz Film Studio (an organization formed to exploit the literary works of L. Frank Baum) at Gower and Santa Monica Boulevard in Hollywood. By July, he had two production units at work; one featuring himself and Rena Rogers, the other starring Russ Powell and Constance Johnson. Connie Talmadge left Vitagraph to replace Miss Rogers when she moved to L-KO. As an independent producer, National had no distribution facilities of its own and Parsons contracted to deliver his comedies for General Film release under the MinA name. David Horsley had originated MinA, but after a disagreement with General Film executives, gave up the brand and moved to Mutual, reconstituting what had been MinA under the label of Cub Comedies. This left Parsons's National comedies as the sole MinA product until the brand was discontinued in 1916.

"Smiling Billy," screen comedian and president of National Film Corporation, circa 1918.

By that time, National had grown to four units releasing weekly and "Smiling Billy" put on his president's cap to temporarily become the full-time president, devoting all of his efforts to National's growth. His attempt to translate Edgar Rice Burroughs's literary works into popular screen properties was marked by the phenomenal success of *Tarzan of the Apes* and assured National's secure financial position by 1918. At this point, "Smiling Billy" Parsons took three giant steps almost simultaneously: he married the popular Christie comedienne Billie Rhodes, stepped back in front of the camera with his new bride in a series of double reel Capitol Comedies, and purchased the William H. Clifford studio, embarking on an ambitious expansion program.

Isadore Bernstein had been brought into National as a full partner and his organizational skills were quickly put to work. Joe Brandt was hired to supervise the new serial program, a capacity he had filled admirably at Universal until company politics had turned him out. Flo and Carter de Haven were hired to do a comedy

Primarily a situation comic, "Smiling Billy" lived up to his nickname, regardless of the circumstances his script writers conceived.

Shown here while operating National Film and its six production units, William Parsons also directed and starred in his own series of Capitol Comedies.

series and the "Hall Room Boys" were brought to life in the persons of Gus Flannigan and Neely Edwards, a popular vaudeville team. Billie Rhodes was given her own comedy series and Henry B. Walthall's dramas rounded out the release schedule.

In addition to his other duties, Bill insisted on directing his own

Bill Parsons found time from a busy schedule to host occasional parties. This interesting candid shot found the president of National Film entertaining (left to right) Isadore Bernstein, Mary McIvor, William Desmond, Billie Rhodes, Flo and Carter de Haven, Harry Cohn and William Seiter. The amusing face behind Carter de Haven belongs to Charlie Murray, whose hobby was crashing parties disguised as a waiter.

films and Parsons's Capitol Comedies were released by Sam Goldwyn, giving them an exposure and degree of respectability otherwise unattainable by an independent. For over two years, "Smiling Billy" cavorted on screen in his popular situation comedies while actively involved with the leadership of an ever-growing business. Bill's screen humor revolved around the amorous adventures of a fat man, and with comedies like *He Did and He Didn't* and *Oh Bill, Behave!*, Parsons managed to attract an ever-increasing audience. Handling his weight inconspiciously, Bill discarded any gags that would have exploited his physique purely for laughs.

National's stature was also growing. The highly successful *Tarzan of the Apes* and release of the Capitol Comedies by Goldwyn Pictures had brought Bill into close contact with Sam Goldwyn, who increasingly relied on the shrewd comic's promotional abilities. Parsons was a master at the art of throwing parties; this was a part of the business as much a fixture to the movie world of the twenties as conducting business on the golf links was to the executive of the fifties. Goldwyn learned to send recalcitrant producers and exhibitors to Bill, who could sell pictures without ever showing them to a potential customer. By the time a reluctant exhibitor had been through an evening of ear-bending by his eloquent host, he was quite likely to discover that not only had he bought what he wanted, but everything else Parsons had offered him.

The dynamic producer had set his sights on producing *The Four Horsemen of the Apocalypse* and was negotiating for the rights at the time of his death in 1919. Although the National Film Corporation continued to exist for a time, its power died with the force and genius of its founder. Parsons's estate (valued at $250,-000) contained a $50,000 block of National stock but by the time his will finally cleared probate, the stock had dwindled in value to a mere $5,000. A few weeks later, National stock wasn't worth the paper it had been printed on—the corporation was defunct.

In spite of the fact that Bill Parsons didn't live long enough to make a real impact on screen comedy, his was a talent marveled at within the industry. Of course, audiences were unaware of the many-sided resourcefulness of this portly comic. Unfortunately, none of his MinA or Capitol Comedies seem to have survived the devastation of time but even though only a dim memory today, the remarkable "Smiling Billy" remains one of the Clown Princes and Court Jesters.

Snub Pollard

Harry "Snub" Pollard was living proof that a comedian could rise above his apparent lot in life. Lacking ability, material or both, many supporting comics were destined to remain just that, and as a result the depth of obscurity into which they fell is even outside the scope of this work. But Snub was fortunate —he had some of the necessary talent and the good luck to work under several directors whose understanding of comedy construction was well enough developed to showcase Pollard's strengths and gloss over his weaknesses.

Snub Pollard came to the movies in 1915, direct from a short-lived engagement with a touring Australian stage company. Hal Roach hired Snub to support Harold Lloyd in the Rolin Phunphilms, and for the next four years Pollard and Lloyd appeared together weekly in light-hearted single reels. When Hal Roach expanded production by promoting Lloyd to double-reel comedies, Snub was given top billing and carried on the single-reel series by himself. His first solo film, *Start Something*, was released in October 1919 and the series ended 109 reels later in August 1922 with *The Stone Age*.

A wide-eyed soulful look and an oversized drooping moustache combined with the gift of imagination and a keen sense of comedy to make Snub Pollard second only to Lloyd in popularity on the Roach lot. Hal Roach had many other comics working during these three years, but none proved to be as dependable as Snub and Lloyd. As Pollard lacked the bag of tricks used by many comedians, he relied instead on characterization, a difficult feat to accomplish in a fifteen-minute comedy. Fortunately, Snub had some of the best comedy writers and directors in the business to help channel his talents in the right direction.

Light and frothy, the Rolin Comedies had no serious message

Snub Pollard as he appeared in the early twenties.

Helen Mehrmann has great plans for our hero.

The jealous husband—Eddie Baker. The innocent wife—Marie Mosquini. And the victim of circumstances? None other than Snub, in *Punch the Clock.*

for the audiences. When not playing the henpecked husband, Snub was often seen as the middle-class bon vivant whose courage usually failed him in moments of crisis, but in a gallant gesture nevertheless carried through to the disastrous end. In *Looking for Trouble,* Snub decided to impress his girlfriend by going three rounds with a champion boxer and winning $500. His decision was based on a mistaken identification of the champ, but when the truth dawned it was too late. For two rounds, Pollard played the coward and the lady friend deserted his corner, but a lucky blow in the third gave Snub the win. Courage returned in the form of the $500 and our hero strolled off arm in arm with the champ's girl.

Although not dependent upon mechanical gags for laughs, some of Snub's best work was done in this format. *It's A Gift* (1923) represents the little comedian at his finest. Establishing Pollard in the opening scene as the inventor of a fireproof and nonexplosive substitute for gasoline, the camera cut to Snub asleep in his bed.

Over his head hung a number of cords. As the alarm clock signalled the start of another day, a feather tickled his foot. Awakening, Snub pulled cord after cord—shutting off the alarm, lighting the gas burner, cooking, and delivering his breakfast in bed. Done with rapidity and precision, the effect is to startle the audience. A brief respite followed in which Snub opened his mail and found a request for a demonstration of his gas substitute.

The action resumed as more cords came into play. One pulled the bedcovers off and back into place as curtains. Another provided his clothes in what must surely be the fastest dressing time recorded on-screen. His bed became an already-roaring fireplace with the final cord. Opening his garage, Snub rolled out a little bullet-shaped car and hopping in, calmly held out a large magnet. As another car passed by, Pollard aimed the magnet and his little car took off in hot pursuit. Various forms of catastrophe occured en route as Snub's attention was distracted. Meeting a pretty girl, he changed directions to follow her but stopped to save a drowning man with

George Rowe holds Snub's coffee as Eddie Baker prepares for the knockout.

Snub and his "magnet car" from *It's A Gift*. (Courtesy Blackhawk Films)

Snub isn't aware of it, but pandemonium is about to break loose once our inventor doctors the test cars with his gasoline substitute in *The Big Idea*. (Courtesy F. X. Bader)

Marie Mosquini, Jimmy Finlayson and "Snub" Pollard are in trouble.
The old man's teeth are missing. From *Sold at Auction,* one of Pollard's
two-reel comedies of 1923.

another of his inventions. Giving his waterproof shoes to a policeman, who promptly disappeared beneath the water, our inventor
hastily left the scene. Arriving for the demonstration, Snub gave
directions for the use of his gas substitute and calmly stood by as
the cars went wild, eventually meeting head-on in a mammoth
crash. At this point, he hopped back into his little car and disappeared behind a passing auto.

Drink Hearty, another of the early Pollard comedies, dealt with
the Prohibition theme and was a virtual comic ballet with Snub as
the bootlegger who operated a speakeasy in a barn. Pollard's calm,
nonchalant acceptance of the unusual as he continually headed into
each comic predicament was heightened when, at the exact moment
of each comic crisis, his eyes widened, his body stiffened, and his
nonchalance was transformed into a panic-stricken struggle for
survival. This very nonchalance was funny in itself, but the resulting panic he inevitably experienced rested in a basic ineptness and
was even funnier.

Having journeyed to the city to live with his aunt in *The Yokel*, Snub was supposed to marry his cousin. But after having seen *Cleopatra* in the flesh, our hero decided that city life wasn't all it was supposed to be. One of the Pollard Comedies distributed in 1927–1928 by Weiss Brothers Artclass, *The Yokel* was also one cf Snub's final starring roles. (Courtesy F. X. Bader)

Marvin Lobeck and Snub get the *Once Over* from the long arm of the law, who suspects our boys of being vagrants in this Pollard-Artclass Comedy of 1928. (Courtesy F. X. Bader)

In the summer of 1922, Hal Roach rewarded Snub Pollard by elevating him to full stardom in his own series of two-reelers. Snub's pace of working was much slower now—as he made only one film a month instead of one each week—and the additional time gave him an opportunity to experiment. As a result, some of his finest work was done in this series. *The Courtship of Miles Sandwich* burlesqued the Pilgrims with a combination of period dress and modern gadgets. *The Old Sea Dog* found Snub as captain of his own ferryboat, operating between docks forty feet apart, and with more troubles than any three sea-going skippers could possibly have had.

But the Snub Pollard Comedies did not light any roaring fires at the box-office, and after the thirteen in the series were finished, Snub went back to single reels. Roach didn't feel he could afford the luxury of the more expensive films without a healthy boost in receipts, which never came. By 1923, the majority of comedians on the screen were making two-reelers and exhibitors had a rather wide choice. Many of the theaters that had used the one-reel Pollard comedies didn't feel they could afford the higher priced two-reelers.

But Snub was chafing under the restrictions imposed by the cutback to single reels and made the same mistake so many other comics had. He left the Hal Roach lot in early 1926 to form his own company. The Snub Pollard Comedies were directed by Jim Davis and distributed by Weiss Brothers Artclass, an independent whose clientele numbered among the cheapest and least-discriminating theaters.

Davis was unable to present Snub's talent in the best light and the little comedian's starring days ended with the collapse of his own company. He certainly deserved a better end, but sophisticated situation comedy had replaced his style of slapstick and the new comedy vogue now relegated his once-popular comic to supporting roles and bit parts in sound films. But in his day Snub Pollard had made it close to the top—closer than many came.

Billy Quirk

American screen comedy and Billy Quirk's movie career began almost at the same time. Billy's not-too-successful stage career began in the gaslight era of the Gay Nineties and came to a conclusion in 1907 when he decided to try his luck in the "flickers." Applying at the Biograph studio in New York City, the Jersey City actor was hired as an extra. This near-guarantee of a steady salary motivated many of the stage actors who entered films in the early days. They preferred regular paydays to the seasonal or otherwise sporadic stage earnings.

By 1909, Quirk had played a variety of roles in Biograph pictures and was placed in a light comedy series. Billy quickly won a following among nickelodeon fans who knew him only as "Muggsy," the character he portrayed on screen. Biograph was one of the last of the pioneer companies to provide a cast listing of players, but fans recognized their favorites from the advertising outside nickelodeons and each Biograph player had his or her own coterie of loyal fans.

Billy's search for screen fame led him to the Solax Company in December 1911. Founded by Herbert and Alice Blaché, Solax had opened its doors in Fort Lee, New Jersey, in 1910 and was regarded as a leading independent producer of good drama. Quirk's popularity at Biograph combined with a Solax need for light comedies to add variety to its release schedule and Billy made the move from anonymity to his own starring series. At Solax, Billy continued to alternate between comedy and drama. In fact, his first appearance was a dramatic role in *Parson Sue*. The genial and irrepressible Quirk quickly became the best-known Solax player, overshadowing Darwin Karr (a fine dramatic actor of the period), Blanche Cornwall and Fanny Simpson.

Billy's Solax films are difficult to pass judgment on—only one

Billy's greatest fame came at Biograph, where he worked with future greats like Mack Sennett and Mary Pickford. (Courtesy Blackhawk Films)

or two seem to have survived the ravages of time. Although trade reviewers of 1912-13 are somewhat suspect sources (they tended to review almost everything favorably), their uniform enthusiasm for Billy's comedies can be taken as an indication that his films of this period were not only popular, but considered to be good by the standards of the day.

Unfortunately, such was not to be the case with his next group of films, if the same reviewers are to be believed. Billy left Solax a year later, responding to the enticements of Carl Laemmle's Universal Film Company. Laemmle was a pirate worthy of the name and the industry. After other companies had developed actors and actresses into screen personalities, Laemmle then "raided" their player roster for his own company. Again, none of Billy's Gem Comedies appear to have survived, but the critics who praised his work at Solax panned the Gems, complaining that they lacked stories worthy of his talents, a handicap even the best of comics found difficult to surmount. We can only surmise that Billy, supported by

Billie Baier, gave it the old college try before leaving Gem for Vitagraph in 1914.

It was at Vitagraph that Billy spent the most time and made the most comedies—many of which have been preserved—but it was also at Vitagraph that he started down the long road to obscurity. Billy was primarily a situation comic whose portrayal of a brash young man would be the route to stardom for Bobby Vernon, then just gaining experience as a screen juvenile. Usually seen as the rather cowardly young lad whose wish to marry Constance Talmadge was thwarted by her father, Billy's scripts called for an elaborate scheme to prove himself worthy. The scheme often collapsed enroute, but Billy always got the girl.

Billy's Vitagraph comedies were produced and directed by Lee Beggs, a portly veteran from the days at Solax, whose career faded along with Billy's. Taken as a whole, his material lacked that spark of ingenuity necessary for a situation comedian. As a result, Quirk's

Quirk's Vitagraph comedies like *The Egyptian Mummy* were overshadowed by the Vitagraph series made by John Bunny and the Drews. (Courtesy Blackhawk Films)

comedies were highly repetitious—see one and you had seen them all. Next to good material, the greatest asset for a comedian like Billy was a strong personality that projected favorably to the audiences.

As might be expected, there were other situation comedians whose material and personalities were stronger than Billy Quirk's and Vitagraph had two of the best—John Bunny and Sidney Drew. This was a major reason for Billy's diminishing popularity during 1915-16. Exhibitors who used the Vitagraph program found that their patrons preferred Bunny or Drew comedies to those of Billy Quirk and thus the demand for his films fell off sharply.

Billy was also a victim of changing tastes in comedy. The better and more popular situation comedians were able to resist the swing toward slapstick, which had received a strong boost from Keystone in 1913-14. But Billy lacked the good material and his one-dimensional portrayals held only a chuckle or two for fans accustomed to roaring with laughter at the antics of slapstick comics. Within a few years, the pendulum would swing back to situation comedy, but by the time it did, Billy Quirk was a forgotten man and overlooked totally by a new generation of moviegoers.

Quite active in various screen players organizations, Billy stayed in the industry and worked at whatever came his way. In October 1919, he signed a contract with the Eastern Film Company, a small independent located in Providence, Rhode Island—an indication of how far he had slipped professionally. But professional problems became intwined with personal difficulties, and the climax came in 1920, when the forgotten little comic attempted suicide.

In early February, Billy suffered a breakdown and entered Harlem Hospital in New York City. By Monday, February 9, the doctors feared he would not recover but the crisis arrived the following day when a delirious Billy Quirk threw himself from a third floor window. His fall was broken by a snowbank below, and Quirk gradually recovered.

Interestingly enough, many of his Vitagraph comedies utilized just this theme: after being rejected by his love's father, Billy would attempt a suicide, which always failed miserably. He then bounced back to win out in the end. But real life had no such happy endings. Recovered from his suicide attempt, Billy signed with Reelcraft for a series of independent comedies. But he was only a shadow of his former self, and faded quickly into obscurity.

To be sure, Quirk was not a major comic of the silent screen, yet he was one of the first to achieve fame—as fleeting as it was. His talent was sufficient to win him notice in the early days of the movies, at a time when movie-hungry nickelodeon fans had a limited choice of films to watch, but it was not enough to let him compete successfully with the ever-expanding group of comics who took the public's fancy by World War I. Fame is sweet, but also fickle.

Billie Reeves

That miracle the movie was quite generous to some personalities, catapulting them to a fame that neither the stage nor their talent could match. But other equally fine stage personalities were shattered by the experience of motion pictures. Billie Reeves was one such, and is remembered primarily today as a side-light of the early Chaplin craze. Both were graduates of the same professional school, Fred Karno's touring stage companies. Reeves had created the "drunk" role in *Mumming Birds,* which brought Chaplin to the attention of Keystone. But there the resemblance ended.

While touring the United States in one of Karno's companies, Billie's talent had caught the eye of Flo Ziegfeld and he subsequently appeared with prominent roles in the Follies of 1908, 1909 and 1910. Eventually, movies beckoned to Reeves as they had to Chaplin in 1913, but Billie had the misfortune of attracting the attention of one Sigmund Lubin.

Regardless of the many contemporary descriptions picturing Lubin as a clown, the little ex-eyeglass repairman was shrewd enough to turn an investment of practically nothing into a ten million dollar fortune during his twenty years in the industry. By 1915 the Lubin Manufacturing Company was operating six studios across the country. Technical superiority was Lubin's strong point; stories and casts were subordinate and remained primitive almost to the end. Lubin had no real stars, nor did he want any. Stars cost money and operating as close to the belt as possible, he was content with a steady income from filling a demand with whatever the market would consume.

But by 1915, Sig Lubin realized that unless he changed his ways, his days in the business were numbered. Up to then, Lubin Comedies had hardly deserved the use of such a descriptive term. The little man admitted this early in 1915 when he released a statement

Billie Reeves brought his successful stage act to the screen in 1915.

to the trade to the effect that new releases would have a purpose instead of being just aimless contortions. To this end, Lubin looked about for a new comic of some stature—who would not cost too much. Settling on Billie Reeves, he offered him a six-month contract in March 1915. Tired of knocking about the stage, Billie looked quickly at the promise of a featured series and signed.

Remodeling his Jacksonville studio quite extensively, Lubin put Reeves under the direction of Arthur D. Hotaling, who cranked out comedies like a doughnut machine (he boasted of over 700 to his credit in 1918). The little tightwad gave every appearance of being serious about spending money. But one tender point remained unresolved and ultimately resulted in disaster for Reeves. Lubin gently suggested that since Reeves and Chaplin had played the same role on the stage, perhaps Billie could "duplicate" Charlie's success. After all, a little imitation need not be called stealing—Billie Ritchie was already doing it. Reeves was understandably upset about this, for he had signed the contract with the idea of genuine, not imitation stardom. By no means a forceful personality, Lubin gave in, but Reeves was not forgiven for his independence. Lubin soon lost interest in making Reeves a star.

Supported by Mae Hotely (Hotaling's wife) and Carrie Reynolds, Billie made a total of twenty-six single-reel comedies. Hotaling had been directing Lubin comedies for some years without real comedians to work with and when he was assigned to direct the Reeves comedies, he wisely decided to give the little Englishman a free rein. The scripts of the first thirteen films were especially tailored for his music hall style of roughhouse comedy by a genius of the early art of photoplay writing, Epes Winthrop Sargent, and many of this series are undiscovered gems of comedy. Only recently have they come to light, to be enjoyed by comedy fans.

In sketches such as *A Day on the Force*, Billie's freewheeling comedic talents were given the green light and the result was spontaneous hilarity. In this particular case, Bill carefully noted each and every infraction of law and order as he followed a policeman along his beat. When the policeman removed his hat and jacket to rest on a park bench, Billie swiped his uniform and retraced the beat, attempting to kiss the nursemaid, extort fruit from a peddler, etc. The difference in his approach and its results provided laughs at a rapid pace.

But when his contract was renewed, Hotaling and Sargent were taken out of the unit and replaced by Earl K. Metcalfe (a former

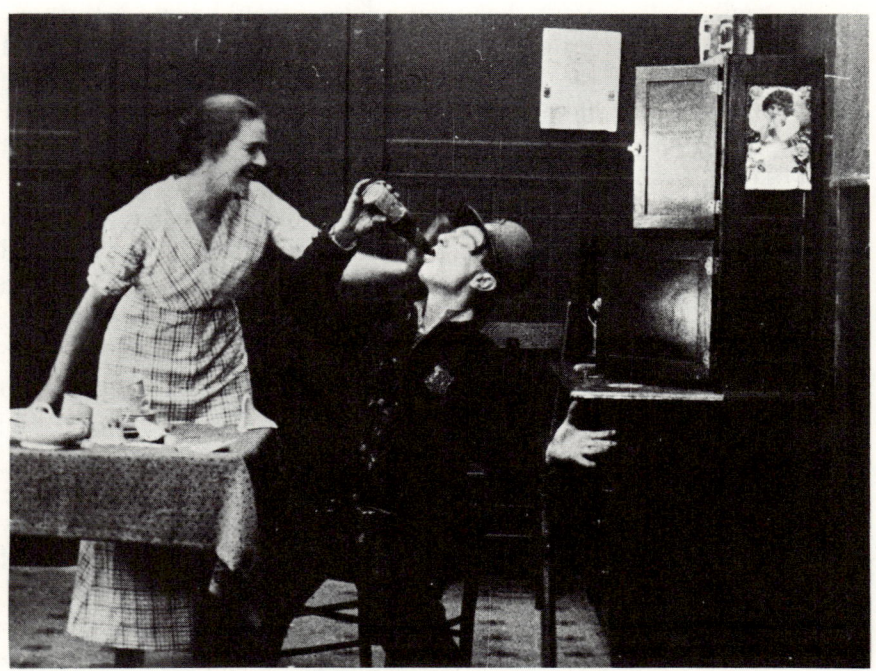

Billie's first few comedies were based on his stage routines and proved to be gems of visual comedy. This scene is from *A Day on the Force*. (Courtesy John J. Comfort)

actor promoted to director for this occasion) and Mark Swan. Swan had written scores of scripts for Edison, which should be enough said for any fans of early screen comedy. For those unfamiliar with Swan and Edison, it's sufficient to say that the Edison comedies were not inventive, amusing or funny.

Metcalfe was never more than a hack director and his decision to revamp Billie's image put him off on the wrong foot immediately, for the new series tried to imitate the success of Sidney Drew and other situation comedians. As a result, knockabout Billie fell quickly. He didn't have the lighthearted touch for it and he knew the characterization was all wrong. Disheartened with his movie career, Billie Reeves read the handwriting on the wall and, after personally appealing to Sigmund Lubin to no avail, left to return to the vaudeville stage for good.

The Billie Reeves Comedies were interesting for reasons other than the fact that many were *good!* Although rather bland in appearance, medium and long shots of Billie bear an uncanny resemblance to the deadpan Buster Keaton, who was still undiscovered by the movies at this time. But Billie was either not gifted with the many nuances of expression, which artists like Chaplin could deliver with a mere twitch of the nose or a lifted eyebrow, or else he chose not to employ such pantomime in his screen work. Disregarding the comedy makeup others felt compelled to wear for laughs, he often appeared without a hat and never used a moustache. His long hair, parted in the middle and combed down around his ears, gave Billy a rather shaggy appearance, especially when he was excited.

In some of the poses he struck for the Lubin cameras, there was another broad hint of Buster Keaton. Reeves began his famous boxing match with an absolute deadpan, betraying absolutely no concern or emotion whatever. For the most part, he used a look of sheer amazement or one of complete and smug confidence, relying upon acrobatics and his seemingly rubber body to carry the comedy.

Not to be outdone by other practitioners of the art, Billie did his female impersonation in *A Ready-Made Maid*. (Courtesy John J. Comfort)

"I've suspected you for some time, my dear!"

"And now I'm going to fix your lover!" Billie's films took on a semi-serious aspect as they moved away from slapstick to situation comedies like *His Wife's New Lid*, with Carrie Reynolds. (Courtesy Blackhawk Films)

But the restrictions of plot, cast and an unimaginative director in his second series, combined with release by a company rapidly downsliding, reduced this potentially successful comic to just another face in the lineup of comedians struggling for survival in a medium for which they were badly equipped to compete. For Billie's comedy forte was not of the sophisticated drawing room; his specialty was the roughhouse slapstick of the music hall. Artistically and temperamentally incapable of refining his style as Chaplin had done, Billie was dead under Metcalfe's direction.

Serving mainly as fillers for the less demanding theaters of 1915, Lubin films were hardly a showcase for an aspiring comic. Reeves undoubtedly had offers from other producers as his contract expired, but the Lubin fiasco had soured him on movies. As his stay with Lubin drew to a close, the stage looked more and more inviting and Billie took his leave with a large sigh of relief.

As more and more of the Billie Reeves comedies come to light these days, it's possible to see that the little Englishman had definite potential. He never would have been another Chaplin, but work with almost any other company would have given Billie the opportunity to develop an identity beyond a dimming memory tucked away in the hearts of those fans who recall the golden years of comedy.

Billie Rhodes

There were many ways to get into the entertainment world during the early 1900s and Billie Rhodes's path came right from a Hollywood script, circa 1935. As a very young girl, Billie charmed, fibbed and lied to get herself into show business without her father's knowledge. For her first audition, she sang one number and during the next song, the lyrics floated swiftly away from her memory. "I just told the cafe manager that I could also talk to my audiences; and so I recited something I knew, pretending to have purposely interrupted my song. He liked it so much that I didn't let on I had forgotten the words of my second song—and so I was hired."

When the manager asked if she had her own wardrobe, Billie quickly replied that she did and began to wonder which store would consider selling a $30 dress on credit to some foolish, starry-eyed young girl. But she did manage to get the dress as well as the job. After learning of his daughter's new career, Billie's father objected not to the fact that she would be singing in cafes and on the stage; but that she was working at all—in his estimation, respectable girls just didn't work outside the home or church. But he was easily won over by Billie's enthusiasm and the young San Franciscan was soon cast in the soubrette part in *Babes in Toyland* on the Orpheum circuit.

While nurturing her growing popularity on the stage and supper club circuit, Billie was approached by George Melford, a top director and talent scout for Kalem films. Struck by her good looks and convinced of her potential acting ability, Melford talked Billie into doing a few pictures with Carlyle Blackwell in 1911-12. As she would do so often in the future, Miss Rhodes returned to the stage after making several Kalem pictures and it remained for Al

Billie was discovered by George Melford while performing on the supper club circuit. He invited her to make her first films for Kalem.

CHRISTIE COMEDIES

Harry Ham, Billie Rhodes & Ethel Lynne

"How do you suppose this would look on me?" mused Billie to Jane Waller in *A Gay Deceiver*.

Christie to launch Billie on her comedy career. Melford had recommended that Al consider the young actress and Christie dropped by backstage after one of her performances, indicating his desire to cast her in his Nestor comedies. And so 1915 found Billie on the Christie lot at Sunset and Gower, one of the pioneering homes of screen comedy.

"We usually made one comedy a week. Although we had scripts, I really don't remember ever looking at one. The director briefed us on the action and we started filming. At Christie, I doubt that the actors were ever given the whole story before they began. It didn't make much difference, since the director knew what he was doing and what he wanted. Most of us took direction during the filming of a scene, without the usual briefing beforehand."

As Christie preferred to work with all the new arrivals and up-and-coming comics to set them on the right road (or at least the road he wanted them to follow), Al directed Billie's first film and then turned her over to Horace Davey. Thus Billie Rhodes could claim the rare distinction of being presented as a comedy star in her debut with Nestor. When Christie left Nestor to found his own independent company, Billie was also chosen to star in the first Al

E. Christie Comedy, *A Seminary Scandal,* an indication both of his high regard for her talent and of the public's acceptance.

During the two years that followed, the Christie studio found the going rough financially and Billie was among those comics given half-salary. (Some were simply laid off). In this interim period, she returned to the stage and when Christie ironed out the financial problems (with help from William Horsley), Billie rejoined Christie. Al had contracted with Mutual to produce the Strand Comedies and Billie once again was cast in his initial offering, *Her Hero.*

The charming personality of Billie Rhodes came across nicely on the screen and complimented the stories Christie chose for her. Moving gracefully, without the self-conscious awareness of good looks that characterized some screen comediennes, the winsome qualities of her face and personality were brought out more in her later feature-length comedy dramas, but her short comedies showed a young girl whose flights toward elopement did not come as a

Anthony Nagy prepares to film a scene after Al Christie finishes explaining how it should be played by Ethel Lynne, Billie Rhodes and Betty Compson.

result of city slickers sweeping her off her feet, but rather from her adventurous and somewhat mischievous inclinations.

Like Mabel Normand, she ardently avoided the burlesque types common among screen comediennes—from the super-sultry vamp to the scatter-brained farm girl—leaving roles like these for Polly Moran, Louise Fazenda and Alice Howell. Billie refused to do any roles that she did not consider tastefully conceived and this very integrity contributed to her eclipse as a star. She was to forfeit second-class screen roles for first-class engagements in night clubs, leaving her motion picture fame behind.

While working for Christie, Billie was contacted by William Parsons, who had chosen her from among the Christie comediennes to do two pilot comedies for his National Film Corporation. While awaiting a verdict from National's New York distributor, Billie continued working for Christie, although under increasing tension. When she finally left to join "Smiling Billy" Parsons in a lengthy

George French invokes help from above as Harry Hamm reveals his intentions toward Billie in *A Seminary Scandal,* Christie's first independent production after leaving the Universal fold.

Billie teamed with Joe Rock in her last series of short subjects. She would soon return to the stage, forsaking her Hollywood career.

series of Capitol Comedies released by Goldwyn, Billie and Christie were not on the friendliest of terms. Christie felt that Parsons had robbed him and in some respects, he was correct. Off-screen, Billie became Mrs. William Parsons.

By 1922, Billie's career had started to fade. She had done a fine series of serio-comic features directed by Louis Chaudet, but all were released independently and failed to reach the better theaters. A series of comedies for Joe Rock was followed by more independent features, such as *Night Life in Hollywood* and *Aladdin; or the Wonderful Lamp*. And at this point, Billie shifted her career back to the stage, spending the rest of the twenties singing in Chicago night clubs.

Fortunate in having other avenues open to her talents, Billie Rhodes was never consumed by the intense drive to be a star and readjusted quite easily to the demise of her screen career. Living today in semiretirement in North Hollywood, Billie still muses about

Billie Rhodes at home. After her marriage to "Smiling Billy" Parsons, president of the National Film Corporation, Billie joined her husband briefly in his Capitol Comedies released by Goldwyn.

"the good old days," surprised to discover that people still remember the vivacious young girl who for a short time was a leading comedy star.

Billie Ritchie

An old adage holds that "imitation is the sincerest form of flattery." If true, it can be said that Chaplin, Sennett and the entire Keystone troupe certainly had just cause for rejoicing. Perhaps they didn't regard the Lehrman-Knockout Comedies as flattering, but there's no doubt that they were imitations.

When Henry ("Pathé") Lehrman left the Sterling Film Company in October 1914, he went into Carl Laemmle's office, closed the door and exited a few hours later with the greatest coup of his career. Lehrman had convinced Laemmle, one of the shrewdest powers in the industry, to participate in forming L-KO. Even more amazing was the fact that Lehrman accomplished this in spite of just having been fired from Sterling, one of Laemmle's Universal affiliates.

Studio space was arranged at the corner of Gower and Sunset in downtown Hollywood and Lehrman hired three ex-Keystone directors to staff his four production units. Taking a cue from the establishment of Sterling, Lehrman raided other companies for whatever players he could find and filled out the roster by hiring unknowns with no screen experience. But his prize possession was Billie Ritchie, a 140-pound bundle of electricity and a graduate of the same English music hall comedy troupe that had sent Chaplin, Laurel, Reeves and others to the screen.

Born in 1877 in Glasgow, little is known of Ritchie's early years, although he later claimed his stage career began when he was but ten years old with a role in *Ten Night in a Barroom*. It is known that Ritchie went from vaudeville and musical comedy to one of Karno's touring companies and arrived in the United States for a Broadway run, playing the same drunk role in *A Night in an English Music Hall* that brought later notice to Reeves and Chaplin. After touring the Orpheum circuit, Ritchie left Karno and went over to

Billie Ritchie.

Different cameras were used to capture this scene from one of Billie's comedies, and provided stock footage which was used in dozens of L-KO Comedies during 1915–16.

Gus Hill's musical revue, *Around the Clock*, where he developed the character of "Bill Smith, the Man from Nowhere," a role he recreated in numerous L-KO Comedies.

L-KO went into production in July 1914 and three months later released its first comedy, *Love and Surgery*. No one in the business had expected an excess of originality from Lehrman, but few were prepared for what they saw when the initial L-KO Comedies were released. The Sterling Comedies had been blatant forgeries, but at least they had contained a genuine Keystone comedian. L-KO Comedies were an almost exact steal of the Keystone farce style by virtual unknowns.

Snappy and fast-moving, the L-KO Comedies were long on physical action and short on plot. Led by a caricature of Ford Sterling, the Keystone Kops were imitated down to the last jacket button. While vulgarity played a large role in some of the Keystones, L-KO used it constantly.

From the music hall stage, Ritchie brought his tramp character to the screen and the resemblance to Chaplin brought audiences up straight in their seats. Although Billy West was the only man ever to imitate Chaplin and bring it off, Ritchie inevitably invited comparison. He claimed to have used the tramp character in 1887 while performing with his three sisters in vaudeville, with Fred H. Graham while playing "Baron Near Broke" in *Cinderella* and in the role of a street musician in *Early Birds* while with the Karno Company.

In 1915, after a year on the screen, he unequivocally claimed to be the originator of the tramp character, complete with makeup, and of the comedy style with which it was associated. Chaplin, wisely restrained by his legal counsel in an effort to avoid a doubtful court battle, never reacted publicly to this one-sided feud, but his associates maintained that he said plenty in private.

L-KO Comedies were a success and found their place in theaters across the country. *Partners in Crime*, the second L-KO to be released, was typical of their content. In this single reel, Ritchie played a bum who, broke but attracted to a cute girl, decided to go partners with Fatty Voss and earn a little money by stealing. As might be expected, the second-story man (Ritchie) popped into a bedroom looking for jewels, while his partner stood watch outside. Audiences roared when a pretty young girl, scantily clad for that day, popped out of the bed. A chase occupied the remainder of the reel, bringing the comedy to a close. Not very strong fare but today it holds up as well, if not better, than many of the Keystones of the period.

L-KO relied on standard plots as vehicles for Ritchie's exaggerated slapstick. To teach his spouse a lesson, Billie hired Dan Russell to stage a fake robbery in *A Meeting for a Cheating*. Of course, wifey discovered the scheme, and to further complicate matters a real thief walked in just before Russell arrived. Everyone took to the rooftops for the inevitable reel-ending chase.

Although Hank Mann left Keystone to join L-KO in May 1915, Billie Ritchie continued to be the mainstay of the company, supported by Frank "Fatty" Voss, Louise Orth and Gertrude Selby. Ritchie's popularity can best be explained by recalling an interview he once gave in which he stated that of all the people in the audiences, the highbrows occupied a comparatively small portion and someone had to amuse the rest of the crowd. For the period in which he worked, this had validity.

Ritchie continued to grind out comedy after comedy, but in the meantime, Lehrman had become more obnoxious to Carl Laemmle daily. As part of the original agreement, Abe Stern (a relative of Laemmle) had been made studio manager and he gradually consolidated a stronghold on the company, firing or forcing out the original directors. The last to go, Henry Lehrman finally

Billy Ritchie in comic garb.

Billy Ritchie

departed in 1916. After Lehrman's departure, Stern took over complete control. Production suffered as a result and L-KO went on to acquire the reputation that finally led the exasperated Abe Stern to chastise his critics with the now-classic line, "L-KO Comedies are not to be laughed at!"

Under contract to his director and not to L-KO, Billie left to join Lehrman at Fox, where comedy units were being established for the first time and the Sunshine Comedies starring Ritchie began in 1917. As Fox had money to spend, more time and care was spent on these two-reelers, but Lehrman lost interest in actual production (those who knew him claim he was simply lazy) and became quite careless in his staging, leaving much of the work to assistant directors while taking screen credit. Billie worked well under Lehrman's direction but seemed to flounder somewhat when "Pathé" was not present.

Unfortunately, Ritchie's career came to an end in 1919. The victim of an ill-staged stunt, he was sidelined with internal injuries but came back to work before he was fully recovered. As a result of the accident and subsequent layoff, Billie's sense of timing had suffered, and while shooting scenes for an animal comedy, he was attacked and quite badly bitten by the ostriches. Although forced to retire temporarily from the screen, Ritchie did a few small comic bits in features during 1920-21 but never regained his old form and died as a result of his injuries on July 6, 1921.

Billie Ritchie's screen career is a difficult one to evaluate and certainly depends upon whether you lean toward the exaggerated vulgarity of slapstick or favor a more subdued form of comedy. But credit for the initial strength of the L-KO comedy program must be given to Ritchie and Lehrman. During the five years he was active on the screen, Billie Ritchie's films were many and successful. Remembered today primarily as an imitator, it is sad that the few of his films that are still in existence today are in the hands of film collectors and not generally available for screening.

As the majority of the L-KO and Fox Sunshines seem to have disappeared, it is doubtful that very many will soon find their way into the hands of either serious students of screen comedy or the general public. Over the years, historians have passed off the L-KO Comedies as not being worthy of consideration and at the same time have credited Lehrman as a creative comedy director. Not until more are rediscovered can this unusual judgment be challenged.

Al St. John

The crazy, rambuctious shenanigans of Al St. John's screen character were nothing more than reflected exaggerations of the real St. John. Full of life and a lover of pranks and practical jokes, Al was the perennial country rube who saw the world as a place to enjoy. Had St. John found himself in a school house, he could not have remained there long before disappearing into the woods with fishing pole in hand. His enthusiasm and energy, both great screen assets, were controllable only when channeled into activity, usually some form of mischief.

Thumbing his nose at school at an early age, Al St. John decided that the hallowed halls of higher learning held nothing for him, especially when compared to the world of show business. While most children used their bicycles to peddle to school or run errands, young St. John explored every possible stunt he could perform on a simple bicycle and soon was good enough to perform as a trick bicycle rider at a local theater on weekends.

Walter St. John did not agree with his son's chosen way of life and when his wife's younger brother, Roscoe Arbuckle, ventured into the "disreputable" theater and then movies, the elder St. John was not about to have Al follow in his young uncle's footsteps. Roscoe smoothed matters over by promising not to find work at Keystone for Al, but the determined boy finally talked his Aunt Minta into helping him.

Minta promised to give Al the opportunity to see Mack Sennett personally and one day when Sennett offered to take Minta and Mabel Normand to lunch, she knew this was the right moment; Roscoe was away on location and would never know. Calling Al at the drugstore where he worked as a soda jerk, she outlined the plan of action.

Somewhat later, as Mack and the girls were standing outside a

Al St. John, the perennial Keystone country hick.

Al has done it again—he's *A Winning Loser*. Rose Pomeroy will teach him his lesson one way or another and then it's Vera Reynolds's turn.

small fenced-in area near the studio, a boy appeared riding up and down a hill on his bicycle—He stood on his head, went through the handlebars, rode it backwards—every imaginable trick he knew. The amazed Sennett jabbed Mabel excitedly, practically shouting in her ear, "Look at that kid, just look at him!"

"You look at him," Minta replied, suddenly realizing the furor Roscoe would create should Sennett actually hire her nephew.

Coming up the hill, Al passed the astonished group and threw out a casual, "Hi, Aunt Minta." Sennett was even more excited. When he asked Minta if she knew the boy, she explained the relationship to Mack. Sennett motioned for the youngster to come back and offered him a job at $3.00 a day. Al accepted immediately and started work the next morning.

When Roscoe Arbuckle returned and discovered his nephew at work inside the studio gates, he was speechless. To Roscoe's outraged burst of orders, Al simply replied, "I work here." Seeing visions of Walter St. John breathing fire and brimstone at both of them, Arbuckle firmly replied, "That's what you think!" But if there was another in the world as stubborn and immovable as Walter St. John and Roscoe Arbuckle, it was Mack Sennett—and Al St. John stayed on at the Keystone studio.

During St. John's early years with Keystone, his foolhardy personality became a most valuable asset on the wild and wacky Keystone lot. Sharing the trick driving with Dave Lewis, Al doctored the cars himself to make them operate in exactly the way he wanted. Al's favorite stunt was removing the brakes from the right-hand wheel and soaping the street, a practice permitting some hair-raising spins for the driver and any riders courageous enough to hang on. Al became so proficient that he once challenged the great Barney Oldfield. The racing master came across the finish line first but Al had passed Oldfield on every corner. If the race track had ended with curves instead of a straight stretch, Al St. John might well have beaten the great Oldfield at his own game. Al was not

When Al joined his uncle, Roscoe Arbuckle, in the Comique Comedies, he was given larger supporting roles. In this frame enlargement from *The Butcher Boy,* he shared acting honors with a newcomer, Buster Keaton (r). (Courtesy Jerome M. Kraemer)

Vera Reynolds and Al St. John appeared together in many of the Keystone-Triangle Comedies. An accomplished bicycle artist, Al saw himself as *A Self-Made Hero*.

Who's *The Happy Pest?* It's Al St. John catching an eyeful in a **Fox** comedy of 1921.

only an excellent stunt driver but an excellent all-around athlete capable of performing the extremely high dives and more difficult comic stunts required of the Keystone stars.

By 1915, Roscoe Arbuckle finally acquiesced to his nephew's determined ambition and began to use him in his own comedies. Arbuckle gave Al the chance to pull himself from bit parts into more substantial roles. In the earlier comedies, Al had usually been cast as a small-time thug who carried out the dirty work upon which the rather contrived Keystones depended. But St. John was not content to remain a plot device for the rest of his career and sought an identifiable character like Mack Swain's "Ambrose" or Chester Conklin's "Walrus." He settled on the country hick, sporting a tight-fitting skull cap, plaid shirt with string tie, floppy shoes, a couple of blackened teeth and checkered pants so large they had to be held up by a healthy pair of suspenders.

Al St. John's comic rube was a good contrast to Arbuckle's screen character. To Roscoe's agile but struggling nature, swept up in a determination to succeed, and usually coming up the winner with his unforgettably effervescent smile, Al was most often

As *The Hayseed,* our hero was in his element. Over the years, his
costume had been refined, along with his characterization of the rube.

Al is about to become *All Sealed Up* with Aileen Cook. He would soon return to short comedies and then create an entirely new career as the grizzled sidekick of numerous singing cowboys in the thirties and forties.

his fun-loving friend—the one who balanced Arbuckle's firm determination with a mischievous love of uncomplicated pleasure. Al St. John was gaining momentum in the world of screen comedy.

When Arbuckle left Sennett in late 1916 to work on his own, Roscoe offered Al supporting roles and his rube character continued to flourish and grow under Arbuckle's guidance. When Roscoe went into features, Al St. John parted company with his uncle and made a few comedies on his own for Paramount before joining Fox. Although he managed to cling to his rube portrayal during the early twenties, Al's energetic, fast-moving and well-constructed comedies were of a dying breed. The twenties had brought a changing face to the world of movie comedy.

When St. John joined Educational in 1924 to work in the Tuxedo and Mermaid Comedies, he abandoned the character he had worked so hard to perfect, becoming the clean-cut, wholesome young

In the mid-twenties, Al abandoned his country character for that of the sophisticated city boy. His work in sound films was not at all satisfying to him, even though he worked with such lovelies as Aileen Cook.

man who sported white shirts and bow ties, coats, even two-toned
or white shoes with spats. He was still an energetic youth, but more
level-headed than the playful spirit of his earlier character.

By the late twenties, Educational started to loan out St. John to
other studios for small roles in features films but disillusionment with
sound features quickly brought him back to the two-reel comedy.
Reunited with his uncle in the Vitaphone shorts that signalled Arbuckle's return to the screen, Al quit the two-reel comedy field altogether when Roscoe died in 1933, feeling that much of the spirit
of this comedy form had died with the silent screen and one of its
most gifted artists, the inimitable "Fatty" Arbuckle.

During the remainder of his career, Al St. John launched himself
into the western film. As "Fuzzy Q. Jones" or simply "Fuzzy" St.
John, one of the silent screen's talented comedians was transformed
into a grizzly old side-kick to several of Hollywood's most popular
western stars. But in 1950, Al objected to the poor quality of the
"Lash" La Rue westerns in which he had been cast and quit motion pictures for good. Until his death in January 1963, Al St. John
made highly successful personal appearance tours throughout the
United States and England, turning over much of his earnings to
muscular dystrophy research.

The motion picture camera captured many great comic moments
of his country rube character but Al St. John has been remembered
over the years chiefly for his bewhiskered western roles of the
twenties and thirties. Only recently have some of his Educational
comedies such as *The Iron Mule, Curses* and *Stupid But Brave* come
to light to be studied and enjoyed by a new generation of comedy
fans.

Larry Semon

During the early twenties, few comedians were more popular than white-faced Larry Semon. Enthusiastically received by audiences around the world, his comedies rivaled those of Chaplin, Keaton and Lloyd in popularity. Although mere mention of his name today invariably brings forth praise from those old enough to remember, the artistry of Larry Semon seems to have dimmed through the years, until he is no longer numbered among the giants.

The son of a professional magician, Larry was born in West Point, Mississippi, and schooled in Savannah. After graduation, young Semon was drawn to New York City, where he put a considerable talent to work as a cartoonist for the *New York Sun* and other newspapers. Amateur dramatics occupied his evenings and led directly to Vitagraph, where Larry was hired to direct the Frank Daniels comedies. When these were discontinued, Larry remained to write scripts and direct Hughie Mack, the rotund comic who tried to fill John Bunny's shoes after the grand old Vitagraph comedian had passed away.

The Mack comedies were reasonably successful; but Semon was longing to star himself, and Albert E. Smith soon gave the young writer-director an opportunity to show what he could do. The Drews were no longer with Vitagraph and reissues of the popular Bunny comedies helped to fill out the release schedule. Vitagraph clearly needed a fresh new comic and in July 1917, Larry stepped before the camera to begin an extraordinary career with a single reel comedy, *Boasts and Boldness.*

Quite a departure from the usual Vitagraph domestic comedy of Bunny and the Drews, the Larry Semon Comedies were filled with wild and fantastic gags thrown off at an unbelievable rate throughout each film. Larry took a very short time to establish and develop a plot, spending most of the film in a chase or even several

Out of costume, Larry Semon lectures "Snuggles," Dorothy Dwan's toy poodle.

chases. Two of the greatest stuntmen in the movie industry, Bill Hauber and Richard Talmadge, worked constantly in the incredibly fast-paced Semon comedies and Larry regarded Hauber's stunt work of such excellent quality that he often gave him billing in the opening cast credits. Hauber not only saved Semon from countless sprains, bruises and broken bones, but also from wasted money and time in production. Many times entire chase sequences of the Semon films were shot while the star of the picture was in New York or on vacation, since all of the action shots could be filmed with Hauber (or Talmadge) and the closeups held until Larry's return to the studio.

Although giving his director full authority on set, Larry Semon possessed an excellent story and gag mind and would sit for hours in story conferences with the director and gagmen to work out the stories and the profuse number of gags. Gags meant everything to Semon, even overshadowing the comic himself in Larry's estimation, and their conception and successful execution became a near-obsession. "He might take a whole day to shoot one scene," recalled

Larry and his wife, Dorothy Dwan, enjoy deep-sea fishing while on vacation from work at the Pathé studio in 1926.

"How did this happen?" asks Larry as he surveys the wreckage.

Semon's finest director, Norman Taurog, "and if he were displeased with the day's work, the whole thing would be set up the next day. Larry was an absolute perfectionist." Oliver Hardy, who worked with Semon in the early twenties, once remarked that with the exception of Stan Laurel, he never knew anyone who put more work into the successful construction of a gag than Larry Semon.

By 1918, Semon had graduated to the two-reel comedy. Within a year, he was considered to be on the threshold of greatness and one of four comics seriously threatening Chaplin's hold on the public. Charlie's output had dwindled to just one or two new films, while Semon, Arbuckle, Keaton and Lloyd were making six or more appearances each year. Unquestionably, one of the prime reasons for Larry Semon's success was his exceptionally talented group of

Because of films like *The Perfect Clown,* Larry's popularity declined with a sickening thud in the mid-twenties and his premature death in 1928 removed this Clown Prince and Court Jester from the scene before the complete acceptance of sound by the industry. No one can tell how Semon would have fared in talkies, but his silent subjects are beginning to enjoy a revival today. (Courtesy Jerome M. Kraemer)

As Larry reached the end of his screen career, years of worry and hard work had left their mark on this fading comic. His characteristic make-up was abandoned for features such as *The Perfect Clown*. (Courtesy Jerome M. Kraemer)

associates—veteran story writer C. Graham Baker and brilliant gag-men Lex Neal and Marty Martin, superb action photographer Len Smith, and comedy chase director Norman Taurog. In addition there was that unforgettable cast of supporting players—super-villainous "heavy" Oliver Hardy, beautiful leading lady Lucille Carlisle and later Dorothy Dwan, top Negro comic Spencer Bell, and the unfortunate fat figure of Frank ("Fatty") Alexander—who seemed to receive more physical punishments and extraneous goo in mud puddles, flour bins and other areas of assorted unpleasantness than any other supporting player in silent comedy.

Based upon a cartoon figure he had drawn as a youth, Larry's character had now evolved into a permanent image of the overgrown dumbbell—white clown makeup, bowler hat, tennis shoes and high pants that came about chest high, held up by suspenders that looked like overgrown rompers. Wearing a simple grin, his screen character accepted the completely ridiculous situations encountered as being perfectly natural, questioning nothing on his merry way.

Short comedies like *No Wedding Bells* made Larry one of the most popular of the Clown Princes and Court Jesters.

The success of Larry's films was great enough to allow him the luxury of making fewer pictures and still keeping his hold on the public. By 1922, he was earning $3750 a week straight salary, $1500 a week living expenses and a percentage of the pictures; but success was taking its toll. Semon had always been a bit difficult to work with, but he was becoming increasingly temperamental. Scenes would be reshot if other comedians received more laughs in the theaters than Larry himself. In addition, Semon was nurturing a personal longing to make his own feature-length version of L. Frank Baum's famous story, *The Wizard of Oz*. This obsession became a central point of conflict between Larry and Vitagraph executives, and finally led to a split of the production company with director Taurog giving up almost two years of contract. In addition, Semon worried about production costs, profit and loss, his popularity and a thousand other problems.

The year 1922 marked a turning point in Semon's career. Larry had continued to be lavish with Vitagraph's money, and time after time he exceeded his budgetary limits. In a period when a good two-reel comedy would cost $18,000 to $20,000 to produce, Semon would sometimes spend up to $150,000 on a two-reeler and if he were so inclined, he might take off an afternoon to play baseball. Vitagraph resented this extravagance, for they felt that they had made Larry a successful comic. After completing *The Sawmill*, Vitagraph president Albert E. Smith took his star comedian aside and suggested he produce his own pictures, which Vitagraph would continue to release. Larry balked at this, and a long period of bickering ended in Smith's refusal to renew his contract. Semon's Vitagraph comedies had returned a handsome profit, but the increasing production costs had not brought a proportionate increase in gross income. The narrowing profit margin soon reached a point where Smith felt he would rather lose Larry's services than to continue to deal with the headaches the comedian was creating. Larry was forced out on his own.

From 1924 to 1928, Larry made short comedies and features which were released through Chadwick, Educational and Pathé, but it was a downhill path. "Larry was a clown, not a comedian," Norman Taurog once explained. "He couldn't play characters, or wear the everyday clothes of Harold Lloyd. He was identified with one outfit—that funny nose, big mouth, painted-on make-up and

Henpecked? Not Larry! He's just attached to *The Girl in the Limousine*.

Larry Semon.

pants up to his chest—and he was a physical comic, a gag comic only. That's why we spent a fortune on his chases. But a person couldn't take those wild gags and that fast stuff for five reels. That was Larry's failing, for he should never have left the two-and three-reel picture." Soon, critics attacked Semon, trade journals panned his work, and public adoration turned into declining box-office receipts—all that he had worried about was now coming to pass. The pace of worrying increased and his films showed it. Time-worn clichés crept into his work and personal difficulties compounded his increasing problems.

The end came in 1928. Once worth well over a quarter of a million dollars, Semon was now in debt for almost a half million. Declaring personal bankruptcy in March, he left Hollywood and pictures behind him and returned to New York City and vaudeville in an effort to recoup his fortune and revive a flagging career. A nervous breakdown, complicated by pneumonia and tuberculosis, ended his career forever. Death came to the sad-faced little clown on October 8.

Larry Semon's reputation with film historians has greatly diminished over the years. A major reason for this tarnish is the unavailability of his Vitagraph comedies, which seem to have almost disappeared. A few scattered prints do remain in private collections, but Vitagraph was notorious for the destruction of negatives and prints that had served their purpose. The bulk of Semon's films available to the public today are from the Educational-Chadwick period and do not accurately reflect the talent of this once-popular clown prince.

The recent renewed interest in silent comedy has brought to light many films considered lost forever and there is little doubt that one of these days, a representative selection of Semon's best work will be uncovered. When that happens, much of the criticism so lightly handed down in the past will have to be reevaluated and Larry Semon's stature will surely rise again.

Ford Sterling

For almost two decades, Mack Sennett's Fun Factory remained the unchallenged focal point of screen comedy and many of the early comedians developed their style and reputations while working under Sennett's watchful eye. But surprisingly enough, only Chaplin (the one comedian whom Sennett could neither understand or appreciate) went on to greater fame, a record that may leave the reader wondering if the organization was actually greater than its talent. This is a defensible point of view, for without exception, each comic who left the fold assumed the responsibility for his own career. Chester Conklin, Charlie Murray and a few others prospered to a degree, but most struggled with a declining career. Ford Sterling was an excellent case in point.

Sterling's career began on a hot summer night when John Robinson's "big top" arrived in his home town. Although still a boy, Ford departed with Robinson's circus when it left LaCrosse, Wisconsin. His romance with the sawdust world took Sterling from odd jobs to featured performer, with a billing that read, "Keno, the Boy Clown." The wider path of show business led him from circus to stage to Broadway, eventually taking him, as with so many others, to Biograph's East 14th Street studio and the movies.

As a comic, he appeared in the Sennett comedies, working with Fred Mace and Mack to form the triumvirate of Biograph's best slapstick unit. Although quite primitive, the Biograph comedies of Sennett departed from the accepted comic format of the day, clearly revealing the influence of Sennett's burlesque background. Sterling's experience fitted into Mack's pattern very nicely, and when Keystone was formed he needed no great amount of persuasion to join Mace, Sennett and Normand in the new venture.

The Keystone Comedies found instant favor with audiences, and as one of the small nucleus that brought them into existence, Ford

Ford Sterling—one of the four original Keystone comics.

shared the public acclaim with his co-performers. When Fred Mace left the lot in early 1913 to make comedies on his own, Ford undertook the burden of lead comic for Keystone and even the budding career of Roscoe Arbuckle was unable to challenge his position at the time.

Sterling's comic portrayals descended from the stage heavies and burlesque humor of the day. His roles ranged from a dyed-in-the-wool villain (as in *A Mud Bath,* in which he drained the lake to even a score with Mack and Mabel) to the unsympathetic and cowardly Jewish stereotypes, Meyer and Cohen. The closest he came to a part of heroic proportions was Chief Teheezal of the Keystone police force, under whose guidance the caricatures of law and order became the best-known constabulary in the world, the Keystone Kops.

Sterling's popularity was so great that at times Sennett had three production companies working at once, with Ford hopping from

Mabel Normand and Nick Cogley (behind her) look on as Ford attempts to open the safe in *Hide and Seek,* an April 1913 split-reel release of the new Keystone Film Company. Note the exaggerated makeup and facial contortions.

Ford's best-known role was Chief Teheezal of the Keystone Kops. Here he is surrounded by Keystone's finest—George Jeske (who impersonated Ford in the later Sterling Comedies), Al St. John, Edgar Kennedy, Joe Deming, Hank Mann, Rube Miller and Fatty Arbuckle.

one set to another for closeups and the personal comic bits that no double could enact. A brilliant "mugger," Ford could arch and twitch his eyebrows, and so twist his mouth and eyes that they would seem to chase each other back and forth in restlessness. His comedy style was expressive, broad and quite heavy-handed. Finesse was not a part of his style and if the scene called for a pratfall, Sterling took a bone-shattering one. Working in the so-called Dutch makeup, his villains took absolute delight in wreaking whatever havoc they could, but even more joy in tipping off the audience beforehand as to what could be expected next. It was burlesque comedy (vintage 1890, *Curse the Villain* style) and audiences responded with sheer delight.

Although considered to be the top comic on the Keystone lot by late 1913, Sterling was restless. Sennett had consistently refused Ford's request for a salary beyond the $250 weekly he was receiving and Sterling started looking for a more profitable financial arrangement. As his position on the lot was now being threatened by the growing popularity of Arbuckle, Swain and Conklin, Ford was not

Harriet Hammond has put the hex on Ford in Sennett's *Don't Weaken;*
he can't hold out much longer.

particularly happy when Sennett introduced his latest addition, a
young Englishman named Chaplin. But no amount of threatening
or cajoling seemed to move Sennett, so Sterling turned to an offer
from Fred Balshofer.

While associated with the New York Motion Picture Corporation
(the parent of Keystone), Balshofer had made an arrangement with
Carl Laemmle in which the latter would release any pictures he
could make featuring either Sterling or Mabel Normand. Knowing
Ford's discontent (and that Sennett had none of his top comics under written contract), Balshofer was able to press this advantage,
and Sterling agreed to join the newly formed company, lending his
name to the venture in the process.

Henry Lehrman immediately left Keystone to direct Sterling,
and while he was at it, Balshofer brought off a wholesale grab of
players in the best Laemmle tradition—enough to staff his initial
needs. At first the arrangement worked fine as Lehrman and Sterling
got along well together for a few months. Ford continued his Keystone characterizations under the guise of "Snookee" and Emma
Clifton did a fair imitation of Mabel Normand. Although a talented

Chief Teheezal has a few questions for the fair Minta Durfee, who would do well not to open the door any further in *Our Daredevil Chief*.

Ford had Minta Durfee in his clutches in *Dirty Work in a Laundry*. Sterling was very popular as Keystone's meanest villain.

comedy director, Lehrman had taken the easy way out and produced passable imitation Keystones. As the results were not long-lived, the Sterling Comedies did not irritate Sennett as did Lehrman's later L-KO Comedies, which were even more blatant imitations.

Ford's success soon went to his head and between ever-increasing arguments with Lehrman on-set, he began to assume the role of star and playboy after hours. Fortunately for Balshofer, he had also acquired the services of Robert Thronby and Paul Jacobs, the director and star of a proposed series of Keystone Kid Comedies. The "Little Billy" comedies had been popular at Keystone and continued so under the Sterling brand. Ford's temperament and his continuing absences from work led Balshofer to cast George Jeske (later a well-known comedy director in his own right) in his roles. With the same makeup that Sterling used, Jeske proved to be an identical double and thus the Sterling brand was able to last somewhat over a year without the services of Sterling.

After being discharged by the company bearing his name, Ford eventually came to his senses and Sennett took him back in 1915. His return to the Keystone screen was made with little effort and Sterling was soon back in harness again, pulling his share of the load in the new Keystone-Triangle releases. But that irresistible urge continued, his temperament returned and in the spring of 1917, Ford Sterling again left Keystone, this time to join the new Fox comedy unit. Although he would once more return to the Sennett lot in 1918, Sterling's days of glory were over. An independent series directed by Reggie Morris for Special Pictures Corporation in 1920 interrupted his tenure on the Sennett lot and after a final break with the King of Comedy in 1921, Ford labored throughout the rest of the silent era doing supporting and bit roles in features. He had changed his burlesque Dutch comedy character for the sophisticated humor of coats and tails, an unfamiliar and ill-suited territory for a grand villain of comic melodrama.

Ford tried a comeback in two-reel sound comedies for Al Christie but failed to click, and until his death in 1939, he remained one of the forgotten comics of the early screen. His career was remarkably analogous to that of Paul Panzer, the villain of *The Perils of Pauline*. Unable to adapt himself successfully to the lighter comedy of the twenties, the screen passed Sterling and his heavy-handed comic style by. With a reputation of being hard to work with, Ford was unable to offer much competition to the new wave of comics who came to the screen following World War I. As the years passed,

Debonair Ford Sterling found it hard to choose between Marvel Rea and Alice Maison. He also found it hard going when he substituted the hat-and-tails comedy for his burlesque mannerisms.

Ford appeared with Louise Brooks in *The American Venus,* Frank Tuttle's 1926 Paramount picture.

everyone remembered Ford Sterling of Keystone fame, but few gave him either the opportunity to work or the kind of roles that a melodramatic comic villain needed to remain on top. As a result, Ford's reputation today rests chiefly on the laurels gained as one of the charter members of Keystone, probably the most creative and popular aggregation of comedians ever gathered under one roof.

Slim Summerville

The silent screen had an ample number of character comedians—those instantly recognized faces for which few fans could provide a name but whose appearances on screen were always welcomed with hearty laughter. Although few of these comics were memorable in any sense of the word, there are some who immediately come to mind when silent screen comedy is recalled. Slim Summerville is one who richly deserves such tribute.

George J. Somerville came to the screen when versatility was the magic word that opened studio gates, and by the time he was twenty-one Slim had played every imaginable role at Keystone. Mack Sennett claimed Slim as an original member of that legendary but ever-changing clan, the Keystone Cops, but he also played bartenders, bell-hops, firemen, detectives, dog catchers and pugilists. Quickly becoming one of the best of the featured players on the Keystone lot, Slim was usually found in supporting roles with Charlie Murray, Syd Chaplin, Chester Conklin and Louise Fazenda.

Ever on the lookout for different comedy combinations that might click with the public, Sennett attempted to create a new comedy duo by teaming tall Slim with diminutive Bobby Dunn. As a team, they never achieved great popularity with the fans, partly because their flow of films was somewhat erratic. But Summerville and Dunn became inseparable pals and a good amount of frivolity and carefree escapades followed this pair off-screen as well as on.

Despite the tight, ill-fitting clothes and sauntering gait that characterized Slim's screen appearances, there was an unquestionable sincerity and honesty about Summerville, and it came through to audiences. Slim often found himself cast in a rural setting; whether or not the myth of wholesome country vs. corrupt city is indeed fallacious, twentieth-century sophistication had not yet branded the myth untenable and Summerville epitomized the

Slim Summerville's versatility as a comedian and director kept him busy for over three decades as one of the most sought-after supporting actors in the movies.

supposed country virtues. Not a hick or rube in the boisterous tradition of the rural humor found in early screen comedies, Slim came across to audiences as a sincere, hard-working—perhaps even a little slow-witted—individual who had easily won the affection of the entire population of his small hometown.

On screen, his desires were simple and basic; although he might have a difficult struggle winning the shy, pigtailed Louise Fazenda, at least the whole town was rooting for him. If he faced battle with a city slicker, eventual triumph came through perserverance and unswerving integrity—not deception or dishonesty. Fitting nicely into the Will Rogers mold of rural wit and wholesome country values, uncorrupted by the vices of the city, Slim was chosen by Rogers as his support in *Life Begins at Forty*—a tribute in itself to the Summerville image.

Although Sennett dropped a great number of comedians when the Keystone-Triangle studio underwent a change of banners in 1917 to reappear as the Sennett-Paramount organization, Slim was not one of them. While appearing with Polly Moran and Ben Turpin in the early Sennett-Paramount comedies, as well as in numerous others with Louise Fazenda, the tall, lanky comedian grew

Slim was teamed briefly with little Bobby Dunn. Here they square off in *The Winning Punch*.

A likeable fellow whose honesty was 24-carat, Slim usually won in the end, but his work was cut out for him with Teddy and Glen Cavender in *A Dog Catcher's Love.*

restless and was ready to try new territory. And so Slim joined the exodus of Sennett comedians to the new Fox comedy lot in 1918, where he met with considerable success.

During the early twenties, many well-known comedians of the World War I period found themselves slipping into premature obscurity. Fortunately Slim was able to shift to the other side of the camera, and he saved his career by directing many Fox Sunshine comedies during this unsettled period of changing comedy styles. Summerville continued as a successful comedy director through the mid-twenties for Film Booking Office (F.B.O.) and then made some of the Universal Blue Birds, which starred Charles Puffy and Arthur Lake. But realizing the value of his capabilities as a character actor, Universal decided to switch Slim back to acting in 1927 and started him off with a series of supporting roles in feature-length dramas.

By the latter twenties, character parts in feature films had become a full-time business and many studios stood in line eagerly to

Slim as he appeared at the height of his career with Mack Sennett's Keystone-Triangle troupe in 1917.

When Sennett left Triangle to make his own comedies for Paramount, Slim was one of the few comics he kept under contract. Here is our hero as he appeared in the first Sennett-Paramount comedy, *Roping Her Romeo.*

acquire Slim Summerville's services—among them United Artists, Pathé, Warner Brothers, Fox and Tiffany. With the coming of sound, he conquered the new medium with a successful appearance in Lewis Milestone's masterpiece, *All Quiet on the Western Front.* As Slim had so easily weathered the difficult transition from silent to sound films, Universal cast him in a series of two-reel talking comedies in 1930, directed by some of the silent era's finest comedy directors—Alf Goulding, Harry Edwards and Stephen Roberts. But with the rise of the cartoon and double feature program, the Slim Summerville Comedies eventually joined a great number of other two-reel comedies in the cemetery. Their end came in 1932 and Slim turned once again to character roles in Universal and later Twentieth-Century-Fox features.

Throughout his lengthy film career, Slim Summerville had never faltered in presenting his stringbean figure as a character who, despite many costumes and roles, retained an unswerving honesty and simplicity in all his characterizations—from bit parts in the Keystone Comedies of 1913 to supporting roles in features of the mid-forties. His untimely death in 1946 at the age of fifty-two removed one of the American film's most beloved character actors from an industry he had served so well.

Mack Swain

Many clowns of the silent screen discovered that their fame was irrevocably bound together with the character and/or makeup that they used on screen, and with the success or failure of this portrayal went their fortune. Capitalizing on a memorable or unforgettable make-up limited the opportunity to demonstrate acting ability and some comics became so closely identified in this manner that they found themselves overshadowed by the greater acceptance of an identity that never existed. Breaking out of this mold required a courage seldom summoned; most went to the end of the line without ever trying to divorce themselves from the unreality. But Mack Swain was forced to take this step, and in so doing he created an entirely new career on the screen.

Swain had joined Keystone in October 1913 after a lengthy stage career and in the four years he spent there, created and perfected the character of "Ambrose." This was far more than just a name used by the movie-going public to identify the man; "Ambrose" conjured up the entire appearance and slapstick acting of Mack Swain. The huge moustache, deeply darkened eyes and long thin wisp of hair down the middle of his forehead constituted the make-up that once led James Agee to describe him as "looking like a hairy mushroom, rolling his eyes in a manner patented by French romantics and gasping in some dubious ecstasy."

Mack's Keystone years were among the busiest of his life. He appeared in a majority of the Fun Factory comedies and starred in quite a few with Chester Conklin of "Walrus" fame. "Ambrose" and "Walrus" were almost as popular with fans as The Fat Boy and Keystone Mabel. When Triangle was formed, Swain found his status at the studio challenged by the influx of stage comics whom Sennett hired, but none made a permanent impression on audiences and they left almost as fast as they came, restoring Mack to his former high position.

Mack Swain as "Ambrose," the characterization and makeup that almost overwhelmed this fine comic's career.

Ambrose's Fury turned to meekness when Alice Davenport pointed the finger and said, "Get to work or get out!"

When Triangle's highly paid stage stars began to falter at the box office, the dependable Mack Swain found his stock rising again. Hank Mann, Dora Rogers, Mack and Vivian Edwards supported "Shoeless Joe" Jackson in *A Modern Enoch Arden*.

Adept at the exaggerated emotion involved with the varying forms of Keystone farce comedy, Mack Swain was perhaps at his best as the blustering banker who leered lecherously at other women behind his wife's back. Going to great lengths to effect liaisons with pretty young girls or other men's wives, Mack was always caught in the end but could turn a bluster into a bawl without batting an eyelash.

Mack was lured to L-KO in 1917 by the promise of more money than Sennett was willing to pay and spent about a year working under the direction of Jack Blystone. The Mack Swain Photo Comedy Company was established on the L-KO lot to produce two-reelers. Blystone took the easy way out—he capitalized on "Ambrose" to such an extent that it is virtually impossible today to distinguish Mack's L-KO Comedies from his Keystones.

Still seeking the big career boost, Swain and L-KO parted in 1918 and Mack replaced Stanton Heck in support of Billy West in his Bulls Eye Comedies. However the influenza epidemic of 1918-

May Emory had better watch her step; *Vampire Ambrose* has designs.

By the time *The Pullman Bride* was filmed in 1917, Mack and Chester
Conklin had long been known to fans as "Ambrose" and "Walrus."

Mack left Sennett in 1917 to make a series of L-KO Comedies and then joined the independent Frohman Amusement Corporation where Poppy Comedies such as *Heroic Ambrose* finally destroyed the value of his screen character by their very shallowness. (Courtesy Blackhawk Films)

19 soon cancelled this project. Frohman Amusement Corporation then contracted with Mack for a series of one-reel Poppy Comedies, where once again "Ambrose" overshadowed his creator. Solely exploitation items, the Poppy Comedies relied heavily on "Ambrose" and little else. *Heroic Ambrose* opened with several examples of various diving techniques by a group of bathing beauties and slowly worked into a short and slender plot revolving around "Ambrose's" winning of Lottie Cruze's hand in marriage by rescuing her and her boyfriend after their boat capsized.

Frohman ran into financial difficulties in 1919-20 and Mack moved into the Jean Perry Comedies. Herald Productions took over the responsibility of finishing this series of double-reel comedies. Instead of rising from its high point at Keystone, Mack's career had descended steadily. In desperation, he moved to Fox in 1920 in an effort to stave off complete anonymity. At about this same time, a personal quarrel with a vindictive producer resulted in his complete disappearance from the screen—a tribute to the authority and power that could be exercised within the industry.

Mack was rescued from limbo by his friend Charlie Chaplin, whose stature by this time was great enough to defy almost anyone in the business. Swain responded to this career-saving move by abandoning "Ambrose" and giving the best performances of his career. *The Pilgrim*, which followed *The Idle Class, and Pay Day*, turned out to be a marvelous spoof on small-town puritanism. As a whole, Mack's portrayal of the hypocritical deacon was brilliant—especially so in the sequence in which Swain and Chaplin strutted down the street in a prayerful manner, just after Charlie had stolen a bottle of home brew from the back pocket of Mack's trousers and then fell upon a thoughtless child's discarded banana peel.

Swain's greatest role is generally conceded to be the part of Big Jim McKay in Chaplin's *The Gold Rush*. Started in February 1924,

Alberta Vaughn had better watch out—Jack Cooper and Mack are up to no good and Andy Clyde knows it. The public had become so accustomed to the "Ambrose" makeup that Swain was not recognized by many fans without it.

it took a full fourteen months to complete this feature comedy. The scenes of Charlie and Mack eating an old shoe to avoid starvation remain as one of the most famous sequences in all screen comedy,

Mack's career received a new lease on life as a result of his role in Chaplin's 1925 feature, *The Gold Rush* and he worked steadily until his death in 1935. This interesting scene with Dorothy Granger came from *Lighthouse Love,* a 1932 Sennett comedy.

and as Chaplin had prophesied, Swain's work in the film brought offers from many leading producers.

During the latter twenties, Swain was in demand. He worked for M-G-M, First National, Paramount, Universal, Christie, Chadwick and others. Having abandoned "Ambrose" in 1921, Mack's second screen career now blossomed in feature films and lasted until 1935, when Swain suffered a fatal internal hemorrhage while visiting Gig Harbor, Washington. In today's times, when broad humor and comic simplifications are a refreshing relief from the pseudo-sophistication of modern screen comedy, Mack Swain is remembered primarily as the "Ambrose" of Keystone characterization that almost led the real Mack Swain into a needlessly premature obscurity.

Fay Tincher

When Al Christie decided to expand his own comedy company in 1919, it was no accident that he chose Fay Tincher as the one comedienne capable of carrying two full reels of comedy. Christie had other comediennes in his talented stock company at the time, but none possessed the many assets of Miss Tincher. Young and beautiful, a successful movie comedienne with a large following of fans, Fay's vivacious screen personality had some of the elusive qualities of Mabel Normand. The solid background that years of stage training had given her provided the foundation for her firm grasp of comedy and drama, which is so evident in her screen work.

Success had really been an easy achievement for this resourceful Topeka, Kansas, girl who entered the insecure and fickle world of show business after graduation from the Ziegfeld Musical College in Chicago. Her appearances on the New York stage included performances with Joe Weber in *Dream City, The Magic Knight, Twiddle Twaddle* and other Broadway plays. But Fay's greatest fame came not from the footlights; it wafted on a thin beam of light emanating in the dimly lit movie theaters of the silent era.

In 1914, Fay Tincher decided that there were other worlds to conquer and left her now-substantial career in the theater for the uncertainty of motion pictures. Fay's screen career began in New York City—one of the pre-Hollywood movie capitals—and in her earliest films for Reliance and Majestic she continued to exercise her acting abilities in both dramatic and comic fare. Over a year before D. W. Griffith's name exploded across the entertainment world with his *The Birth of a Nation*, the famed director had recognized the dramatic skills of the young Miss Tincher, and cast her in the role of the vamp in one of his earliest and best-known feature-length pictures, *The Battle of the Sexes*. But by the close of 1914, Fay had

The youthful radiance of Fay Tincher captivated viewers of the mid-twenties.

Al Christie had a joke he just couldn't hold any longer and Fay reacted in this production shot from the early twenties.

found her metier in the world of film—comedy leads. Having worked earlier in the year in Majestic's "Billy" series, Fay soon settled herself into the area of film comedy, and after the release of her initial Mutual Komic Comedy in 1914, she concentrated her efforts in the short-comedy realm.

The Komic brand had been created especially for Miss Tincher, who essayed the role of Ethel, the gum-chewing stenographer. Under the direction of Edward Dillon and supported by Tod Browning, Max Davidson and others, Fay's bold striped dress and wide-brimmed hats became a trademark at Komic. But beneath the glossy exterior trim, a most competent actress was at work, and within a few short months her character of Ethel was so well-received by fans that Komic capitalized on her creation and consciously attached the name "Ethel" to nearly every comedy in the series—*Ethel's Doggone Luck, Ethel's New Dress, Ethel's Deadly Alarm Clock*, etc.

During the following year, Fay joined company with "Shorty"

Hamilton and stage star De Wolfe Hopper when the Triangle Film Corporation created a featured comedy series for each of these three stars. Made at the Fine Arts studio, the Fay Tincher Triangle Comedies were offered to exhibitors as extra comedy bonuses along with Triangle's most famous comedy product, Mack Sennett's Keystone Comedies. Following the completion of these comedies, Fay went to Fox and then back to Triangle before accepting Al Christie's offer to inaugurate his venture into two-reel comedies.

Preparing to challenge the recent efforts of Mack Sennett, Charlie Chaplin and other major studios to move into the two-reel (and longer) comedy format, Christie chose the petite-appearing but rugged Miss Tincher for his star comic lead in a comedy series set in a western locale. In *Rowdy Ann, Dangerous Nan McGrew, Wild and Western* and *Go West, Young Woman,* the diminutive Fay Tincher was enveloped by ten-gallon hats, six-shooters and holsters,

Told she must go to an exclusive finishing school, *Rowdy Ann* vows to return West. What Fay Tincher did to the school brought laughter in theaters across the country, and proved Christie correct when he hired her to carry his name into the realm of double reel comedies.

huge shaggy chaps, and cowboy boots; but she managed to emerge from under this mountain of western paraphernalia as a sympathetic comedy heroine, and a good number of the best laughs revolved around the improbable figure of this tiny and charming comedienne who overcame her wild and woolly opponents by dint of sheer determination. Her work at Christie in these comedies ranked among the best on the screen at the time; both fans and critics alike had nothing but praise for the versatile Fay Tincher.

But the box-office success of these and other Christie Comedies allowed Al Christie to greatly expand his stable of comics in the early twenties and soon Fay found herself nearly lost in the shuffling of comediennes and actresses as they came and left the Christie lot. A fame that she had worked so long to achieve slowly began to slip away between Christie's casting and his indecision, and so Fay Tincher and Al Christie parted company.

Although it was not to last long, Fay's greatest fame was yet to come—a fame that was to be followed closely by that incredible

Fay was hired by Christie to spearhead his entry into the two-reel comedy domain in 1919. This improbable little comic heroine brought loads of cash into Christie's coffers.

obscurity which blanketed the thriving career of innumerable silent screen stars as they approached the microphones of the new talkies. But while it did last, the fame (which came suddenly in the unlikely guise of the female lead in a celluloid version of the Sid Smith's Sunday newspaper cartoon strip *Andy Gump*) was delicious and fully savored by Miss Tincher. "The Gump" series cast Joe Murphy (and later Slim Summerville) in the role of Andy Gump, with Fay as his wife Min and little Jackie Morgan as their son Chester. Although Joe Murphy portrayed Smith's cartoon character with a nearly identical facial copy—from shiny bald head on top to a chinless chin on bottom (with the protruding ears, beady little eyes, monstrous nose and bushy whiskers stuck somewhere in between), Fay played a relatively straight character. Dropping the comedy paraphernalia of her Komic and Christie days, she had adopted the more domestic everyday costume and manners demanded by movie-goers of the twenties.

Shooting the series during the fall and winter months, with an average of two two-reelers a month for the season's package of

Imagine being tracked down by Fay and her luscious deputies! There are worse ways to go!

Fay's greatest fame arrived in the form of the "Andy Gump" series for Universal. While Joe Murphy created the role of Andy, he was eventually replaced by Slim Summerville (shown here).

Thoroughly stereotyped as Min Gump, Fay's active career ended as the Gump series was brought to a close in 1929. The emergence of the talking comedy compounded the situation and Fay simply disappeared from the screen.

twelve, this team turned out Andy Gump Comedies for five years. The incredible pace was maintained from the fall of 1923 to the late winter of 1928, with a list of directors that eventually looked like a Who's Who of Hollywood comedy. As one of the series' directors, Norman Taurog, once exclaimed, "My God, they were successful! They just went on and on with seemingly no end ever to come." But end it did, and during her five years in the series, Fay Tincher and Min Gump had understandably become inextricably entwined; at the close of production, Fay was so stereotyped that she was rendered virtually inactive. The additional factor of sound pictures only complicated the situation, and while Fay Tincher was an exacting actress with previous stage experience and training, *and* a versatile screen comedienne, she disappeared, along with so many others, almost overnight from the screen she had conquered over a decade before. While the pecuniary orientation of the producers could be understood and excused during this transition period, the fickleness of the public, in whose adulation many of the Clown Princes and Court Jesters has basked so long, cannot be. The disappearance of so many favorites from the screen, with no explanation to their fans, should have brought roars of protest, as is the case today when certain popular television series are summarily removed by network executives. But it did not, and therein lies one of the great unexplained mysteries of stardom.

Ben Turpin

You might not recall his name, but the face was unforgettable. Throughout the twenties, thousands laughed weekly as the little man strutted on-screen and the cameras dollied in for a closeup. But few fans realized as they wiped their eyes dry that a lengthy struggle had preceded Ben Turpin's rise to stardom. His picture career had begun around 1907, shortly after Essanay opened its doors for business. Ben, a veteran of many years in burlesque, became their first comedian, and true to the custom of the day spent his time off-camera sweeping floors. It would be another decade before fame touched Ben's career.

But in that decade, he acquired the raw material that Mack Sennett would melt into permanent prosperity—the crossed eyes, dominating camera presence and split-second timing. Turpin labored in near-total obscurity until Charlie Chaplin cast him in his first Essanay comedies—*His New Job, A Night Out* and *The Champion.* However, an uneasy association soon developed between Turpin and Chaplin. As Chaplin's veteran cameraman and early Essanay photographer Rollie Totheroh later explained, "Ben wanted 'equal time' with Charlie and salary to match. When Charlie saw Ben getting as much of the show and publicity as himself, he let Ben go after having brought him out to California from Chicago."

Although Turpin later acknowledged his debt to Chaplin, Charlie adamantly refused to allow Ben the opportunity to gain greater stardom and success from a team arrangement at Essanay in the manner of Lyons and Moran at Universal. Turpin may have learned much about comedy from Chaplin, but Charlie brought an abrupt halt to their work together. While the films which resulted from this "partnership" brought Ben a contract with Vogue and featured roles, Turpin's days with Essanay and Vogue are generally forgotten now, overshadowed by those years when he was the most popular and dependable drawing card on the Sennett lot.

Ben Turpin in a scene from an extremely rare Turpin Essanay comedy, *Mr. Flip* (1909). This short film was composed of vignettes in the life of an incurable flirt. (Courtesy Don Malkames)

Turpin's road to fame and fortune began in 1917 when he joined Mack Sennett's zany crew of funmakers. Sennett quickly took advantage of Ben's peculiar appearance and ordered frequent and lengthy closeups of Turpin's face—an asset that Essanay and Vogue had totally overlooked. Sennett sharpened Ben's pacing and cast the little Frenchman in those roles best suited for his talents—low burlesque charades with a solid lining of satire.

Ben's ludicrous appearance lent itself beautifully to almost any role the little scarecrow played, from politician Gerald Montague in *A Blonde's Revenge* to Sheriff Cyclone Bill in *Yukon Jake*. His deft portrayal of this western hero contained a small touch of straight-shooting Bill Hart, a dash of Royal Canadian Mountie, and a large portion of pure coward—totally destroying the conventional western stereotyped hero. But it was in his travesties on well-known films that Turpin really scored. *Romeo and Juliet, Three Foolish Weeks* and *The Shriek of Araby* were parodies without equal in their absurd satire and outrageous burlesque.

As *The Shriek of Araby*, Ben parodied Rudolph Valentino's fantastic success in *The Sheik*.

Ben looks on as Rube Miller checks out Lillian Hamilton's shoe size in one of the early Vogue Comedies.

"I'll finish him off right now!" shouts Ben as Vivian Edwards tries to restrain him from applying the coup-de-grace to Alfred Gronell in *An Innocent Villain*.

As the dashing Rodney St. Clair, Turpin sliced Eric Von Stroheim down to size with just a stare at the audience. From black leather boots to dangling monocle, Ben was an exact copy of the lecherous heavy that had brought fame to Von Stroheim. He seemed to be saying, "I'm just putting you on" and each eye twinkled separately. Fans could buy that with a hearty chuckle but when Ben got down to serious love-making with Natalie Kingston or Madeline Hurlock, it was just too much.

Inevitably, the reel closed with Ben face-to-face with the cuckolded husband and inevitably, his opponent was twice his size and many times nastier. But Turpin's cool display of courage and ridiculous swordmanship, aided and abetted by his rolling eyes and twittering moustache, always triumphed in the end.

Standing straight as a baton, with his scrawny little chest pushed out and his sparrow-like head thrown back, Ben's adam's apple gyrated in cadence with his crossed eyes, creating a sight that was difficult to forget. Lying on a tigerskin rug, with passion flaming

Ben Turpin a baker? Phyllis Haver had her doubts in *Love and Doughnuts.*

Madeline Hurlock has nothing to fear from Kewpie Morgan as long as *The Daredevil* holds his ground.

in his revolving eyes, Ben made the shallow sultriness of all screen vamps a farce. The mere thought of this strabismic caricature of manhood gradually breaking down the cold reserve of luscious Madeline Hurlock never failed to inspire thousands of homely would-be lovers the world over.

Ben thought and acted comedy, both on and off the screen. He enjoyed having visitors on the sets and went out of his way to entertain them. "I'm Ben Turpin, and I make a hell of a lot of money around here—in fact, I get paid first and what's left over goes to the others" was inevitably followed by a backward somersault, known in the trade as a "108." Ben's compulsion to perform this stunt scared Sennett to death. Fearing that his most valuable property would seriously injure himself needlessly, Sennett was forced to tack a notice around the studio to the effect that any person working on the lot would be fined $100 "if anyone bribes, asks or demands a '108' from Ben Turpin."

Highly superstitious, Ben dreaded a return to the poverty he

Eric Von Stroheim? Not a chance! It's Ben as the dashing Rodney St. Clair.

had known years before when he earned $20 weekly at Essanay as janitor, shipping clerk and comedian. As a result of this, and his lack of formal education, Turpin was very susceptible to suggestion. This made him a perfect patsy for the practical jokers around the studio who enjoyed making him the butt of their pranks. They especially delighted in taking Ben's cigar or old derby and nailing them securely to the floor while he was away. When he returned to the set, Turpin would reach down to pick up whatever belonged to him, and in the process rip it to shreds.

The studio wits also loved to get together and think up new "old-wives' tales" to tell Ben about his crossed eyes. He fell for every story. One invented "truth" was the "fact" that too much sun caused the uncrossing of crossed eyes; after this story was "confirmed" by enough people, Ben would nonchantly head for the nearest shade tree at every possible opportunity during filming breaks.

But old Ben had the last laugh. The early years of struggling

Where is My Wandering Boy Tonight? Courting Madeline Hurlock, that's where, and it makes Dot Farley just sick at the discovery.

When Louise Carver lets go, our *Harem Knight* is going to take a cold dip in a wet pool, as Marvin Lobach and Dave Morris look on.

led him to invest his money. While others played the market, Turpin bought real estate, tended to his property carefully and managed it wisely. As a result, he was able to retire from the screen shortly after his career reached its peak, without the professional degradation and personal necessity of appearing in independent potboilers to earn his living. For reasons unknown, he did star in ten comedies made by Weiss Brothers Artclass during 1928-29. One of these, *The Eyes Have It,* reveals Turpin as a tired trouper who surprisingly managed to hold the film together in spite of the story, supporting cast and director.

Jealous of his success, some fellow comedians regarded Ben Turpin as a crude and uneducated freak who possessed no real talent other than a pair of crossed eyes. But laughter was the proof of the pudding for comedians and Ben Turpin gave the screen some of its funniest parodies and low comedy, in films that have stood the test of time.

Bobby Vernon

Populated by a fantastic assortment of clowns, buffoons and other ill-dressed absurdities, the world of silent screen comedy held little room for the comedian who embodied the "boy-next-door" image associated with Bobby Vernon. But the gentle and self-effacing Vernon was also a determined, optimistic talent whose destiny could hold only success. Lacking the boisterous practical joking of an Al St. John, Bobby's quiet teasing nature contained a healthy reserve of spirit and energy but without the unrestrained exuberance of a Larry Semon.

Born Sylvion de Jardin, the youthful comic was quite successful on the stage, appearing mainly in San Francisco and Los Angeles. While playing an engagement on the same bill with Kolb and Dill (a famed Dutch comedy dialect humor team of the period), Bobby's talent caught the eye of Max Dill. Dill marked Vernon as his replacement should an accident ever upset the team, and according to Bobby's mother, Dorothy, "Dill did have a bad accident when he broke his leg and Bobby replaced him in the show for a short while. Despite skepticism on the part of many people, Bobby was very successful with Kolb."

This is even more meaningful when you consider that Bobby Vernon was but a teenager at the time. Only sixteen when Max Asher brought him to the movies, Bobby's screen character was based primarily upon his own personality and in his desire to retain both his individualism and youthful qualities, he refused to submit to the burlesque tradition of disguising his age by using a ridiculous costume and makeup. Working first in Universal's Joker Comedies and then Sennett's Keystone-Triangle Comedies, Vernon was only sporadically buried underneath the outrageous costumes of farce or rube comedy. Along with the Jokers in which Bobby played a

Bobby Vernon, one of the few silent screen comics who was successful with the "boy-next-door" image, as he appeared at the height of his fame with Christie.

As a young hoofer on the West coast vaudeville circuits, Bobby replaced Max Dill (of Kolb and Dill) while the famed Dutch comic recovered from a broken leg.

cannibal king or bedraggled hobo, there were also many pictures like *Love and Electricity* (1914), in which the amorous attentions of the struggling working-class boy for a beautiful young lady (Louise Fazenda) presaged the boy-girl comedy that Bobby's humor later typified. While he occasionally played a foppish character for Keystone, right around the corner were the romantic comedies of Bobby Vernon and Gloria Swanson, which managed to survive the irrepressible slapstick humor of Mack Sennett, and set Bobby onto the path of the more subdued comedy he was soon to follow at Al Christie's studio.

Joining the Christie forces in 1917 after the producer had already broken away from Universal to release his comedies independently, Vernon possessed a potential in comedy romances that Christie recognized and developed by teaming Bobby with the young lovelies on the Christie lot—Ethel Lynn, Vera Steadman,

Bobby Vernon initially gained fame in Keystone-Triangle Comedies with Gloria Swanson (standing) but Vera Steadman (holding his arm) would prove to be an invaluable feminine lead a few years later in his Christie Comedies.

Viora Daniel, Dorothy Devore, Clare Seymour, Dorothy Dane and Josephine Hill. The titles of Bobby's early Christie Comedies illustrate Christie's awareness of the box-office value of romantic comedies—*Married By Proxy, Does Your Sweetheart Flirt? Love and a Gold Brick, Marrying Molly* and *Fair, But False.*

Charming Vera Steadman was perhaps Bobby's prize leading lady, and she was a prize worth winning. At a time when so many female comic leads were nonentities or of the "dumb cluck" variety, Vera Steadman was a more determined and exacting young lady whose tolerance, understanding and sense of humor outweighed her exasperation with her struggling young suitor. Although Bobby had worked with Vera in earlier days at Keystone, it was several years later at Christie before he was able to take advantage of her gifted talents as a leading lady in his own comedies.

Bobby was not strictly bound to romantic comedy in the twenties. In *Second Childhood* (1922), the comedy revolved around the hairbrained scheme of his business partner (Earl Rodney) to save

Bobby Vernon was not above a touch of the ridiculous in his work at Christie.

Using his family name, Sylvion de Jardin, Bobby was introduced to movie fans by Max Asher in the Universal Joker Comedies of 1913.

their floundering institution. As the leading figure in the scheme, Bobby was forced against his will to impersonate a child, "Little Oscar," complete with sailor suit, shorts, suspenders and a Jackie Coogan-type haircut. If a script required the actor to be attired in children's clothes, or even a woman's dress (as in *Married By Proxy*), Bobby responded without complaint. Bobby Vernon's prime concern was his desire to create laughter, and for over fifteen years he succeeded brilliantly in this quest.

As the big kid sister who unintentionally betrayed every one of "Little Oscar's" secrets in *Second Childhood* (and one of Chris-

While at the Sennett studio during 1916–17, Bobby occasionally played foppish characters, as in this scene with Ford Sterling and May Emory from *The Hunt*.

Bobby's forte, the romantic comedy, began in 1916 with a series co-
starring Gloria Swanson, who would soon join Cecil B. DeMille and
rise to stardom as one of the twenties' most glamorous screen actresses.

"Second Childhood" found Bobby masquerading as "Little Oscar" in an attempt to save his floundering business. Seen here with him is his mother, character actress Dorothy Vernon.

"The Barnyard Cavalier" featured Bobby in a swashbuckling Fairbanks-type role, a rare departure into the realm of farce comedy.

The thirties found a balding Bobby Vernon coasting into middle age as Robert Vernon, comedy supervisor for Paramount Pictures, coaching a young crooner named Harry Crosby.

tie's best stock players of the twenties), Babe London today numbers her work with Bobby Vernon as the most enjoyable of a long career. "Those comedies were actually fun to make. Our stories were fully written out, with all the gags and situations, but we still moved at a leisurely pace. If Bobby or the director thought he could get more out of a scene, we'd all sit around, knock around different ideas and put a few of them to the test." Spontaneity was an essential factor in the production of Bobby Vernon Comedies; yet this comedian had some of the finest directors and gag men in the business—directors Harold and William Beaudine, Earl Rodney, Walter Graham and William Watson, and writers Hal and Frank Roland Conklin and Sig Herzig.

Bobby Vernon worked for over a decade with Christie—an association of mutual profit and loyalty. Yet, interestingly enough, as Dorothy Vernon has pointed out, "Bobby never had a written contract. He always told Al, "I've always been treated well here and although I've been getting a lot of offers from other companies, I'll keep to my word and stay here as long as you want me." Christie wanted Bobby just as long as he could afford him but with the headaches incurred by the arrival of talkies, as well as personal financial reverses created by the Depression, Al Christie was finally forced to close his studio. Mack Sennett and later Hal Roach soon followed suit—the days of the great two-reel comedy short had come to an end.

In the thirties, Bobby Vernon became Robert Vernon, comedy supervisor for Paramount Pictures. Despite the thinning hair on the top of his head and the addition of a dapper-looking moustache, the youthful smile and boyish face never disappeared. But on June 28, 1939, Bobby Vernon's career came to a premature close with his tragic death at the age of only forty-two. The screen had lost one of its finest comedy talents.

Billy West

When he is remembered at all by film historians, Billy West is recalled simply as an imitator. Thus he has traveled down the pages of time in the shadow of Charlie Chaplin. But West was much more than an imitator; he was another dimension of Chaplin's Tramp.

Born Roy Weissberg, Billy was brought to the United States from Russia at an early age. The family settled in Chicago and his father became a peddler, selling wares from door to door in search of the American Dream. He never found it, but young Billy was more fortunate. He discovered and fell in love with the theatre. As with most immigrant boys of that era, Billy left school to go to work and soon had his own act as a chalk cartoonist on the vaudeville stage. It was here that he met the Chaplin image.

While playing Aaron Jones's vaudeville palace in Chicago, Billy met Ralph Kettering (Jones's publicity agent) who suggested a Chaplin performance in a local parade. It caught the fancy of an audience that believed it had actually seen Charlie in person. As a result of the favorable reception (or deception), Billy polished the performance, which included a girl and a policeman, and played the United Theater Circuit with his new act. "Is He Charlie Chaplin?"

Levinson and Symonds, a Chicago law firm, caught the act and decided that Billy was their man. They formed the Smile and Laff Film Company and hired Billy at $350 weekly. This was a $1000 pay cut for the little comic, but he was convinced that movies could do more for his career than the vaudeville stage ever would. More capital was needed for this venture, so a third partner named Jaffe was brought into the fold. The company's name became the Joy Film Company. They made one picture, sold it to the Unicorn Film Service and went out of business arguing about how to split

Discussing the sequence to be filmed, Billy confers with Oliver Hardy and Ethelyn Gibson, as cast and crew stand by.

the profits. Unicorn acquired Billy's contract and made three more films through its subsidiary, the Belmont Film Company, before it too collapsed.

Through one of those intricate deals common to the early days of motion pictures, Billy's contract with Unicorn became the property of the Caws Comedy Company, which went into business as the King Bee Film Company. Arvid Gillstrom, a former Keystone director, supervised the Billy West King Bee Comedies and Billy wrote many of the scripts himself. And so began Billy West's climb to fame.

Billy's King Bee Comedies were made in 1917-18. At this time, Chaplin was at Lone Star making his famous series of Mutual-Chaplins. Charlie had entered films in 1914, making thirty-five in a year with Keystone and then doing a series for Essanay in 1915-16 before West started his motion picture career. Thus, Billy had a relatively large number of Chaplin films that he could have modeled his scripts after, but it's to his credit that the Billy West Comedies bore no relation to Chaplin's previous films.

Chaplin's screen character started out as a cynical and greedy little tramp, but by 1917 it had evolved into a more sympathetic personality, although a vicious and mean streak occasionally reasserted itself. He was not above stealing fruit from a peddler or kicking a policeman and pinching a girl. Very little of this ever appeared in Billy's films.

As mentioned earlier, Billy's tramp was another dimension of Charlie's. Where Chaplin's little fellow exhibited a tendency toward cynicism, tempered with a degree of hopeful optimism (which was always badly bent by the fadeout), Billy's tramp was the cheerful optimist who was treated pretty decently by fate. Most of his problems came about as the result of his own carefree ineptitude.

As in the case of Chaplin's screen character, Billy's characterization was shallow in his early films, which relied rather heavily on slapstick for laughs. In *Cupid's Rival* (his fourth King Bee), it was

Billy takes a break between scenes while Babe Hardy and the rest of his unit ham it up for this publicity shot, taken in front of the realistically detailed but false buildings on the King Bee lot.

Dropping his Chaplin imitation in the early twenties, Billy adopted a "man-of-the-world" costume and character.

difficult to determine the star, for Billy was stiff and unnatural. In addition, his foil or comic heavy, Oliver Hardy, was on screen much of the time, nearly stealing the show.

But as time went by and King Bee rolled along, Billy developed and refined his on-screen personality, relegating slapstick to the conclusion of a situation that he had carefully built step by step. Oliver Hardy's blustering "heavy" also developed into a more delightful character, but a most pleasing aspect of the later King Bees was the presence of many lovely ladies: Ethelyn Gibson, Leatrice Joy, Helen Spencer, Ethel Burton, Florence McLaughlin, Myrtle Lind, Ellen Burford, Rosemary Theby and others. Ethelyn Gibson and Leatrice Joy most often supported Billy, for they were able to improvise and react to whatever antic the little comedian might try next.

Billy's later King Bees also strengthened the reputation he had carefully built up. They were all double-reel comedies with a rec-

One guess at what happens next, as our runaway from the funny farm takes up barbering.

Score one point for Billy West, who didn't even muss his hairdo. While Chaplin's hair was naturally wavy, Billy slept many nights with his hair in curlers to achieve this necessary effect.

This rare scene from *His Waiting Career,* Billy West's third film, shows the comedian in his early development of the Chaplin imitation he perfected so well.

ognizable story composed of several comic vignettes. One such was *His Day Out,* which opened with Billy's escape from a mental institution. Free at last, he enjoyed a momentary dalliance with Leatrice Joy, much to Oliver Hardy's annoyance. Disposing of Hardy, Billy and his new girl left the park for her father's barber shop. Father (Bud Ross), who himself had an amorous streak, turned the shop over to Billy, and left to pursue his latest love.

Billy proceeded to work over five customers, much to the amusement of his new girlfriend. For example, after shaving a customer who then refused to pay, Billy strapped the fellow back in the chair and, reversing the vacuum cleaner he had used to clean up the beard, promptly reapplied the chin whiskers in their original condition. This was not the malicious humor of Chaplin's Keystones nor the sad humor of his Essanays; for you modern readers, it was Billy De Wolfe in baggy pants and pantomime. Almost all of Billy's King Bees are available for viewing today and a surprising quantity of his later Bulls Eye and other comedies have survived. We're fortunate to have practically an entire series from beginning to end in which the development of a screen character can be seen.

Our ambitious hero strikes a sad pose as sly Leo White toasts Ethel Burton in *The Hero*. Note the interesting nudes decorating the wall behind Billy.

Fed up with Oliver Hardy's nonsense, Billy gives him the business as Rosemary Theby looks on.

After giving up the Chaplin imitation, Billy never regained the popularity he had known in 1918-19 but he made some fine comedies in the twenties. Still living in the Hollywood he entered more than fifty years ago, a modest Billy West today dismisses his later comedies as examples of the twenties' obsession with mechanical gags. "They weren't very good; they were made when the essentials of every short comedy were commonly known as 'fire, water and wires' and every comedian had hooks on the back of his neck." But a rescreening of the West comedies made in the twenties divulge a star's overly-harsh self-criticism. *Don't Be Foolish* is a minor classic of carefully thought-out sequences and sight gags, smoothly blended together and moving to a climax at a rapid pace. Billy West was one of those few screen comics who believed that standing around doing nothing was just padding and *Don't Be Foolish* is certainly an example of moving screen comedy.

As pointed out earlier, historians have treated Billy rather shabbily. One suspects that either they haven't bothered to study his films, or else they've become so awed by Chaplin that Billy's use of Charlie's costume and mannerisms smacks of profaning the Great God Pan. Either way, they have proven themselves to be short-sighted, for even though Billy freely admits that he imitated Chaplin, his films prove to be a delightful romp in a completely different direction.

Epilogue

And so we have come to the end of a long journey—
after rolling back the years for the reader in a way which we hope
has made it a pleasant and all-too-short experience. As we pointed
out at the beginning, the choice of comedians and comediennes
included within the preceding pages did not necessarily exhaust
the possibilities inherent in a work of this nature.

While researching and discussing our efforts with retired comics
and fans of the period, it soon became obvious to the authors that
many less important, although equally fascinating, comics were
not to be represented between these covers—Big Boy, Jimmy
Adams, Eddie Baker, Al Alt, Eddie Barry, Billy Dooley, Arthur
Stone, Monte Collins, Erle Montgomery, Joe Rock, Arthur House-
man, George Rowe, Bert Roach—the list seems endless.

Up to this point, we had always accepted the importance of the
comedy short subject to the industry, but the very lengthy list of
those who are not found in this book and the work they did served
to illuminate and underscore the *enormous* importance of this
entertainment form. Only serials and their practitioners have received less credit than the men and women who worked in short
comedies, and yet the results of their efforts constituted one of the
mainstays of an industry whose growth revolutionized the American
concept of entertainment and, to a lesser degree, the American
way of life.

Obviously, this book has not exhausted the subject of comedy
and those who created it in the golden years of the screen, but it
is our hope that we have shed new light on the topic, and in the
process restored some of the lustre to the now-faded reputations
of those who made life a little lighter and brighter for millions of
movie fans.